POWER
PLAYERS

POWER PLAYERS

FOOTBALL IN PROPAGANDA, WAR AND REVOLUTION

Ronny Blaschke

First published by Pitch Publishing, 2022

Pitch Publishing
9 Donnington Park,
85 Birdham Road,
Chichester,
West Sussex,
PO20 7AJ
www.pitchpublishing.co.uk
info@pitchpublishing.co.uk

ISBN 978 1 80150 358 7

Typesetting and origination by Pitch Publishing
Printed and bound in India by Replika Press Pvt. Ltd.

Contents

Introduction

THE FUTURE of football is called Lusail. On the northern edge of the Qatari capital Doha, the 2022 World Cup Final is to take place, in front of more than 80,000 spectators in the Lusail Iconic Stadium. Moats and columns, solar panels and facades reminiscent of traditional Arab boats: the stadium will be the attraction of a new city district. After the World Cup, the arena will be downsized to make room for shops, schools and a clinic. Qatar is working with Chinese companies on the construction. A milestone for diplomacy and trade between the two countries. And a symbol for the football industry.

For almost a century and a half, Europe has claimed sovereignty over football. This was only really appropriate in the first decades, but by the beginning of the 20th century at the latest, the game had spread to almost all continents. Football shaped everyday culture in Argentina, Egypt and Iran – and thus also became interesting for those in political power.

For a long time, fans of English, German or Spanish clubs were not interested in developments outside their leagues; that only changed at the beginning of the 21st century. More and more major competitions were awarded to South Africa, Brazil and Russia instead of Western Europe and North America. It is likely that the World Cup will be held in China for the first time in the 2030s. Moreover, investors from Russia, China and the Gulf States have secured shares in European clubs – and expanded the political influence of their governments.

Sports officials like to explain that the global attention of sport can open up societies. Several studies argue against this. For example, in the past 30 years, more than two million people have been displaced for the organisation of Olympic Games. Structures have sprung up in almost all World Cup and Olympic venues: airports and roads, residential areas and local transport. But in most regions, a minority benefits: politicians, officials and construction companies. The country that has suffered most from this is Brazil. Before the 2014 World Cup, the security apparatus was ramped up and police violence increased, especially in the favelas. Many of the stadiums and sports facilities for the 2016 summer Olympic Games in Rio are hardly being used properly. At the same time, education and health care are suffering from financial shortages.

Sporting events and human rights: one thinks of money-grabbing autocrats, of forced labourers on construction sites, of social groups drifting apart. But even beyond the host countries of major events, everything in the billion-dollar industry of football is connected to everything else. Our well-tempered stadium attendance in Western Europe is linked to the exploitation of Asian jersey seamstresses. Fans are outraged when Spanish clubs play their Super Cup in Saudi Arabia. But they are less aware that sponsors and marketers of their favourite clubs have long been intertwined with Chinese, Russian or Arab corporations. Fans demanded a boycott of the World Cups in Russia or Qatar, but then again many belonged to the TV audience of millions. And they were surprised that industrialised nations like Germany suddenly depend on natural gas from Qatar, after the Russian invasion of Ukraine.

It is just as true for the globalised economy as it is for football: No matter how critical you may be as a consumer, you are part of a system in which people are harmed. This book focuses on football as a political and economic instrument of power in the 21st century. *Power Players* takes aim at the control centres of the future, especially China and the Persian Gulf states. These are the countries that are arguably the best at organising political influence through football.

Footballers who risk their careers for political criticism are rare

But this stage of development in Eurasia was preceded by a century in which football became increasingly intertwined with politics, economics and religion. This book presents the spectrum of interests, dependencies and constraints. For example, in unstable times, regions have strived for autonomy, especially in Spain, where Catalans and Basques use their stadiums as a backdrop for separatism. In the Balkans, football accompanies the ethnic and religious search for identity. For many fans in Serbia and Croatia, nationalism is part of folklore. Argentina probably has the most vibrant civil society – but football hardly plays a role in the commemoration of the military dictatorship that also hosted the 1978 World Cup.

'Football in Propaganda, War and Revolution.' The subtitle links big, heavy terms that are often used in the wrong context, even in football. Not in this case: the book traces how fans and players revolted against autocrats. During the Arab Spring in Egypt in 2011, the Gezi protests in Istanbul in 2013 and in Ukraine in 2022, ultras and hooligans allied in street fighting against autocratic regimes. Many died or are now being monitored by secret services. The motivations and structures of these protest movements are described separately in this book. Comparisons between different societies and eras will be avoided.

Footballers who risk their careers for political criticism are rare. If they don't want to be critics of the regime or are not allowed to be because of contracts, do they have to serve propaganda? They could remain silent, but some also make an autocracy seem acceptable. German international Julian Draxler signed an open letter of thanks to the Russian people after winning the 2017 Confederations Cup, not even letting his concerns shine through between the lines. Lukas Podolski appeared in a tourism video for Turkey. Mesut Özil invited President Erdoğan to his wedding. Ronaldinho posed with Chechen autocrat Ramzan Kadyrov and helped the far-right Jair Bolsonaro into the presidency of Brazil. These players did so from a position of privilege. Many of their colleagues in Syria, Libya and Iraq had no choice. They had to pay their respects to the rulers, or else face expulsion, sometimes even torture and imprisonment.

This book is based on research in 15 countries on four continents, in Europe, Asia, Africa and Latin America, with a total of 180 interviews between 2017 and spring 2022. However, a World Cup summer in Russia or a two-week stay in Argentina is not enough to become an expert on developments there. The reports and analyses are based on researchers, fans, journalists or players who have spent years in the countries and regions concerned. *Power Players* is not a travelogue. Anecdotes describing the author in rusty taxis, on dusty football pitches, in smoky pubs or luxury offices of Qatari officials should have no place here. Instead, it is a sober, fact-oriented derivation of the causes and backgrounds. Information to form opinions. No culture, no matter how foreign it may seem to us, should be presented as exotic.

Reporting on football in China or Qatar usually focuses on the violation of human rights. That is also a central theme for this book, but it cannot be the only one. Whether Kosovo, Rwanda or Iran: everywhere, national teams are among the rare symbols with which competing ethnic groups equally identify. Whether Turkey, Bosnia or China: everywhere ultras support their clubs with colourful choreographies (visual demonstrations, often involving fans holding up pieces of card or paper, which together form a big image across an entire grandstand) and country-specific chants. Whether Croatia, Russia or Afghanistan: everywhere, activists are setting themselves apart from corrupt elites with creative projects.

It is also exciting to see whether other governments such as Azerbaijan, Kazakhstan or India will mingle with the 'Power Players' in football. How can civil societies in authoritarian-ruled states be strengthened without putting themselves in the foreground with superior thinking? The historical, political and religious circumstances are complex. This book is not meant to look at other states through Western European glasses. It is an attempt to put oneself in other perspectives. A contribution to overcoming clichés, alienation and fears.

Snipers Behind the Stands

In the multi-ethnic state of Yugoslavia, nationalism was officially forbidden, but it broke out in the football stands. Hooligans from Serbia and Croatia went to war as volunteers, and in Sarajevo, Bosnia, a stadium was right on the front line. Today, many fans play down the crimes. Whether with chants, choreographed images created by fans, or a drone above the pitch: football accompanies the ethnic and religious search for identity. And sometimes, as in Kosovo, it helps build a new nation.

THERE IS not much room to pose on the tank: the queue gets longer and longer. Children wait excitedly, fathers hold their mobile phone cameras ready. The tank looks freshly cleaned, the front is painted with stripes in red and white, and in between is the logo of Red Star Belgrade, Serbia's most famous club. It is late summer of 2019. Behind the tank, Belgrade stretches to the horizon, the almost 80m-high Church of Saint Sava juts out from the sea of houses. Children climb onto the tank, laughing, jumping and waving red scarves. Some fathers make sure that the Serbian Orthodox Church is also visible in the photos. Then they move on to the fan shop or the snack bar, there is not much time left before kick-off.

In the neighbouring country to the west, Croatia, the tank is viewed with less composure. This T55 is said to have been in service in Vukovar in the early 1990s. The city in eastern Croatia was an important location during the Yugoslav wars between Serbs and Croats. Vukovar was largely destroyed by Serb units, hundreds of people fell victim to executions. Red Star Belgrade nevertheless calls the tank an 'attraction'. Photos of the club were shared thousands of times on social media. The tank is to remain next to the stadium for a few years; the city administration and football associations see no problem with it 'as long as there is no shooting'.

In the Croatian capital, fans of Dinamo Zagreb do not want to put up with this. In August 2019, they position a tractor next to their stadium 'Maksimir' for a short time. That, too, is a symbol: during the war, many Serbs from Croatian villages had fled across the border on tractors. Families, circles of friends and whole communities broke up.

The Western Balkans had evolved over centuries into a patchwork of ethnicities, denominations and traditions. In the second half of the 20th century, socialist Yugoslavia was considered the most diverse state in Europe, with six republics and four religions, with four languages and two alphabets. But from the 1980s onwards, economic crises, tensions and nationalism led to a growing longing for 'ethnically pure' individual states. Around 140,000 people died in the wars of disintegration in the 1990s, and more than four million fled or were displaced.

Seven states emerged from Yugoslavia's legacy: Slovenia, Croatia, Bosnia and Herzegovina, Serbia, Montenegro, North Macedonia and Kosovo. There are still conflicts over territories, ideologies and national consciousness, also over religions and historical interpretations. The populations face each other in a complex relationship: the Serbs, predominantly Christian Orthodox; the Croats, the majority of whom are Catholic; the Muslim Bosniaks; and the ethnic Albanians in Kosovo. Football particularly illustrates the search for identity.

Through provocations between fans and players, through hostile banners and graffiti in the stadium, even through riots and the glorification of crimes. Football as part of the war – in the Balkans this is no exaggeration.

Hundreds of hooligans joined a paramilitary force

Anyone walking through the Serbian capital Belgrade quickly comes across markings made by football fans. Graffiti and stickers on house walls, bridges, street signs. Either in black and white by the supporters of the Partizan club. Or in red and white, the fans of *Crvena Zvezda*, Red Star. They are martial motifs showing hooded men ready to fight. There are also dates that recall club successes and historical events in Serbian history, many dating back centuries, others only three decades. Near the Red Star stadium, a plaque is dedicated to the victims of the Yugoslav wars, next to an Orthodox cross and the club logo.

It was mainly the politician Slobodan Milošević who fuelled Serbian nationalism in the late 1980s and drove the disintegration of Yugoslavia with his war rhetoric. At that time, more than a quarter of the eight million ethnic Serbs lived outside their own constituent republic: 1.4 million in Bosnia and Herzegovina, 580,000 in Croatia, 200,000 in Kosovo. Milošević and his followers wanted all Serbs to be united in one state. They grumbled about economic problems and emphasised the contrasts between the ethnic groups. This went down well with many Serbs. Their incomes were worth only half as much as in 1980. Unemployment grew, foreign debts increased, the exchange of goods between the republics declined. In spring 1990, nine out of ten Yugoslavs rated the relationship between the population groups as bad or very bad.

During that time, fan groups developed into an influential subculture, especially in Belgrade. 'In socialist Yugoslavia, nationalism was officially forbidden, but it burst out in the stadium,' says Krsto Lazarević, who worked as a correspondent in Belgrade and contributes to a podcast about the Balkans. From the 1980s onwards, members of the mafia gathered in the stands of Red Star, violent men who were involved in robberies, protection rackets and murders. Among them: Željko Ražnatović, known as Arkan, who had several convictions. With his companions Ražnatović was allowed to distribute Red Star merchandise, and he also took over the leadership of Delije, the most important fan association.

In a report for the German Friedrich Ebert Foundation, the publicist Krsto Lazarević analyses the political connections of the Serbian football fans. For example, Željko Ražnatović brought the nationalist supporters into line with Milošević in collusion with the secret service. Moreover, in October 1990 he founded the Serbian Volunteer Guard, a paramilitary force that hundreds of hooligans joined. Their nickname: 'Arkan's Tiger'. Ražnatović went to war for the dream of a Greater Serbian Empire, first against Croatian, then against Bosnian units. Murders, rapes, expulsions: Ražnatović and his fighters committed war crimes. 'He kidnapped patients from a hospital in Vukovar and had them killed,' reports Krsto Lazarević.

Red Star became a symbol of Serbianism. When the club won the 1991 European Champion Clubs' Cup in Bari, Italy, its fans barely waved Yugoslav flags. In the winning photo, eight players showed the Serbian salute, two outstretched fingers and a thumb. At home games in the following months, Red Star supporters also celebrated the war, some mercenaries displaying street signs from destroyed Vukovar in the stands.

The Dayton Agreement in the US state of Ohio put the 1995 war between Serbia, Croatia and Bosnia to rest. The International Criminal Tribunal for the former Yugoslavia, based in The Hague, was soon to indict 161 people for serious crimes, but there was also talk of 15,000 to 20,000 supporters in the police, military or administration.

Many perpetrators were able to escape prosecution. Željko Ražnatović rose to become a heroic figure. His marriage to the singer Svetlana Veličković, called Ceca, was broadcasted on Serbian television in 1995. A year later, Ražnatović bought the Belgrade club FK Obilić, named after a Serbian knight from the 14th century. Even with criminal dealings, Ražnatović led the club to the championship in 1998 in an already severely shrunken Yugoslavia. Because of an international arrest warrant, he avoided away matches in European competitions. In 2000, Ražnatović was shot dead in a Belgrade hotel lobby. Had he become too powerful for politicians, because of his knowledge? The exact background is still unclear today.

According to Krsto Lazarević, playing down war crimes is part of Serbian fan culture. An example is provided by former General Ratko Mladić, who was responsible for expulsions of non-Serbs from Bosnia-Herzegovina and for the Srebrenica massacre in July 1995, in which 8,200 Bosnian men and youths were murdered. Mladić was only arrested in 2011 and sentenced to life imprisonment for genocide in 2017. Many Serbs, however, see Mladić as a defender of their culture. After his conviction, ultras from Red Star Belgrade chanted his name. Fans of rivals Partizan thanked Mladić's mother. Players from a club in Novi Sad in northern Serbia wore white T-shirts with Mladić's portrait.

Brutal volunteers for dirty work

For centuries, the Western Balkans were under the influence of great powers: Austria-Hungary in the north, the Ottoman Empire in the south and the Russian Empire in the east. In the Red Star Belgrade Museum, religious motifs stand out alongside trophies, medals and triumphal images. There are paintings, figures and coats of arms of the Serbian Orthodox Church in Cyrillic script. After the suppression of the denominations in socialist Yugoslavia, Orthodoxy experienced a revival in the past decade and a half. It is not the only development that connects the country with Russia, says former Belgrade correspondent Krsto Lazarević: 'An attachment to Moscow is an important feature of Serbian nationalism.'

In the Red Star stadium, Gazprom's blue signage is omnipresent. Before the home match against Zenit Saint Petersburg in 2011, folklore groups in Serbian and Russian costumes performed and guest of honour Vladimir Putin was cheered. Volunteers from Serbia also signed up for the war for the eastern part of Ukraine from 2014. During their 2014 championship celebration, Red Star fans displayed a flag of the self-proclaimed 'Donetsk People's Republic', the eastern Ukrainian city had been occupied by pro-Russian separatists. At another match, they displayed a banner in Russian: 'Older brother, tell me if I'm imagining things or if our mother is finally waking up. Hail Russia, Ukraine and Serbia.' After the Russian invasion of Ukraine in early 2022, Red Star ultras chanted: 'Russia, Russia.'

Filip Vulović doesn't care for this kind of football, yet he has to deal with it. The student is one of the organisers of Belgrade Pride, a series of events organised by the LGBTIQ+ community with workshops, concerts and a street parade that takes place annually in September. On a Sunday morning, he gives a tour of the group's information centre, which is located near Belgrade's pedestrian zone. Between brochures, posters and activists' photos, timelines inform about the history of their movement. Vulović moves to the left to the beginning and points to the image of a man covered in blood. 'Belgrade was in a state of emergency,' he says. 'Hate and violence everywhere, that left deep wounds for us.'

Vulović is speaking of Belgrade Pride 2010. For weeks, hooligans, right-wing extremist politicians and representatives of the Orthodox Church had stirred up opposition to it. Patriarch Irinej, the head of the church, compared homosexuals to 'child molesters', priests called for protest. On the day of the procession, around 6,000 hooligans from all parts of the country poured into downtown Belgrade. They attacked LGBTIQ+ participants and police officers, 150 people were injured, the damage ran into millions. 'The city looked like a war zone, the police were completely overwhelmed and took many of our participants to a forest area,' says Vulović. 'I was going through puberty at the time and gradually found out that I liked men. That experience set us back a lot.' In the years that followed, the Serbian government banned the Pride parade, ostensibly to protect its participants.

Mirjana Jevtović sees it differently. For almost 20 years, the investigative journalist has been observing Belgrade's football fans for the TV magazine *Insajder*. 'For some politicians, hooligans do the dirty work in the streets,' she says. 'The riots at Pride 2010 made the government look very bad. There was a lot of criticism from the opposition.' Representatives of the opposition at the time are now in power in Serbia: Aleksandar Vučić of the so-called Progress Party became defence minister in 2012, prime minister in 2014 and president in 2017. Vučić often emphasised his former affiliation with Delije, the fans' association of Red Star. Since 2014, the Belgrade Pride parade has been allowed again: with thousands of police officers – and without incident.

Insajder is one of the few media in Serbia that independently reports on the crimes of the hooligans, on homicides, human trafficking, drug sales. This has consequences: fans of Partizan Belgrade stabbed an inflatable doll at a home match, which was supposed to represent editorial staff member Brankica Stanković, accompanied by the cry: 'You will end up like Ćuruvija.' The journalist Slavko Ćuruvija had been shot in front of his house in 1999. Brankica Stanković received police protection, but she continued to do research, for example on hooligans who rose to become entrepreneurs and security guards and who prevented protests against the government in the stands. 'Unfortunately, our research rarely has consequences,' says Mirjana Jevtović, and lists who comes and goes at Red Star Belgrade: policemen, lawyers, civil servants. The work of *Insajder* doesn't really produce changes in behaviour because civil servants and other important people are so influential at Red Star. Football is a symptom of corruption and the concentration of power under President Aleksandar Vučić. Since 2012, Serbia has been a candidate for membership of the European Union, but is a timely admission realistic? Mirjana Jevtović is sceptical, also because of the poor relations with neighbouring states.

A pillar for national identity in Croatia

Travelling from country to country in the Balkans, one quickly notices how deeply rooted the antipathy between the people still is in many places. This is not always openly expressed in conversations. And the symbolism is also subtle and enigmatic: in historical museums, in devotional objects or at memorial sites, for example in Zagreb. The footballing centre of the Croatian capital is the Maksimir, Dinamo's stadium. The outer facade of the west stand is decorated with a painting that can be seen from 100m away. On it is a general on horseback with a blue flag, next to it the club logo, with Catholic church towers in the background, then 50m further on is a commemorative plaque. The motif shows soldiers with rifles, surrounded by angry fans in the stadium, supplemented by an inscription: 'For all Dinamo fans, for whom the war began on 13 May 1990 in Maksimir and ended with the dedication of their lives on the altar of their homeland Croatia.'

The plaque was donated by the Bad Blue Boys, the most influential fan group at Dinamo, founded in 1986, named after the US movie *Bad Boys* starring Sean Penn. Like many other groups, the Bad Blue Boys carried their national consciousness into the stadium, encouraging the break-up of Yugoslavia, with banners, chants and violence. They supported the election campaign of former officer Franjo Tuđman. His anti-Yugoslav party, the Croatian Democratic Union, or HDZ, won the first free parliamentary election in Croatia in April 1990. A few days later, on 13 May, Dinamo Zagreb was to meet Red Star Belgrade in Maksimir. For the US broadcaster CNN, it was soon one of 'five football matches that changed the world'.

Hours before the game, hate chants and brawls broke out in the city. At the stadium, opposing groups of fans broke through fences, threw stones and destroyed seats. The driving force behind the Delije was Željko Ražnatović, known as Arkan. Supporters stormed the pitch, several players took refuge in the dressing rooms, but Zvonimir Boban stayed outside for a time, the then 21-year-old Dinamo player kicking a policeman who had previously beaten a Croatian fan. 'For many Croats, Boban's kick was a symbolic rebellion against Yugoslav institutions, which were often dominated by Serbs,' says Dario Brentin, who researches nationalism in football at the Centre for South-East European Studies at the University of Graz. 'In the formation of the Croatian nation, 13 May 1990 is considered a fundamental pillar. Regularly, actions commemorate this modern myth.'

Many Serbian media described the riots as a plot by the new Croatian government to further weaken the multi-ethnic state of Yugoslavia. Franjo Tuđman, Croatia's first democratically elected president, also argued in football for 'upright Croatianism' and against Serbia's 'aggressive aspirations to great power'. He said that 'after the war, a nation would be recognised primarily in sport'.

On 3 June 1990, the Yugoslav national team played a match against the Netherlands in Zagreb. The Croatian spectators whistled down the Yugoslavian anthem. Three months later, fans of the southern Croatian club Hajduk Split stormed the pitch at a home match against Partizan Belgrade and burned a Yugoslav flag.

As the second constituent republic after Slovenia, Croatia declared its independence from Yugoslavia in June 1991. The Yugoslav People's Army, which was dominated by Serbia, opposed this, with paramilitary support, and four years of war between Croats and Serbs followed. During this time, Franjo Tuđman's entourage formed the nostalgic attitude that Croatian culture had been better before socialist Yugoslavia. Between 1941 and 1945, the fascist movement had been in power in the 'Independent State of Croatia', with the acquiescence of the National Socialists. This 'Ustasha' government had strived for an ethnically homogeneous Greater Croatia. It banned Serbian associations, dissolved mixed marriages and suppressed the Serbian-Cyrillic alphabet from public life. Half a million Serbs, Jews and Roma fell victim to its policy of extermination.

After the Second World War, the Croatian independence movement in Yugoslavia was suppressed. From exile, it called for protests against the communist regime. Many nationalists in the 1990s linked their resistance against Belgrade to the 'steadfastness' of the Ustasha. Franjo Tuđman played down their murderous actions. Symbols that had long been banned came back into fashion, such as the red and white chequerboard pattern in the Croatian coat of arms, which is said to have its origins in the 15th century but was cultivated above all by the Ustasha. Street names were dedicated to the Croatian freedom movement.

Croatia withdrew its football clubs from the Yugoslav league and built its own national team. As a sign against the communist past, the authoritarian ruler Franjo Tuđman had the Zagreb club Dinamo renamed Croatia. At a speech to fans he said: 'Whoever sings for Dinamo is an agent from

Belgrade.' Only after his death would the name change be reversed. While Croatian armed forces were fighting Serbian troops in the early 1990s, sport established itself as a pillar for a national identity in Croatia, according to analysis by researcher Dario Brentin, naming leading figures of the time: NBA basketball player Dražen Petrović, tennis player Goran Ivanišević, handball player Ivano Balić.

After the pushback of the Yugoslav army and the Dayton Agreement in 1995, growing nationalism favoured the trivialisation of fascism. For example, Davor Šuker, then a striker for Real Madrid and later president of the Croatian Football Association till 2021, posed in 1996 in front of the grave of Ante Pavelić, once the leader of the Ustasha. In 1998, at the World Cup, the joy over the Croatian team's third place was mixed with hostility towards Serbia among many fans. Franjo Tuđman had himself been filmed and photographed with the players several times in France.

Ultras present coats of arms and flags of militias

And what is the social climate like more than 20 years later? A Saturday afternoon on the eastern outskirts of Zagreb. In the wood-panelled clubhouse of NK Čulinec, people are discussing top level football over soup and beer, while 'small' football takes place between family homes. The guests are the self-governing amateur club NK Zagreb 041, whose members got to know each other in the environment of the professional club NK Zagreb; in their ultra group 'White Angels' they positioned themselves against discrimination with banners, chants and concerts. They were met with hostility, were in conflict with the presidium – at some point they had enough and in 2014 they founded their own club.

One of the driving forces among the 150 members of Zagreb 041 is Filip. He stands behind the bench with his friends and encourages the players. Again and again he turns around and looks at the surrounding houses, bushes and cars. 'We stay in the group and pay attention when people we don't know show up,' Filip says. 'We have been attacked several times, since then my wife and child rarely come to the games.' Once, masked hooligans from the Bad Blue Boys attacked them with batons and pepper spray, another time they provoked them with a banner: 'Refugees Not Welcome'. Zagreb 041 has been campaigning for refugees for a long time.

Filip's family comes from Dalmatia, from the south of Croatia, so he also looks with interest from afar at Hajduk Split, the country's second big club. On his mobile phone, Filip shows videos of choreographies (visual displays created by fans holding up pieces of card to create a huge picture) and chants. Torcida, the largest fan group at Hajduk, often takes up historical events, mostly around 5 August, the 'Victory Day'. At the beginning of August 1995, Croatian units had recaptured occupied Serb territories. In August 2019, Torcida depicted the destruction of a Serbian tank in an elaborate choreography, accompanied by billows of smoke and rapturous applause in the stadium. Other groups also display coats of arms and flags of militias that had fought against Serbs.

In the anthology *Back at the Stadium Crime Scene*, German sociologist Holger Raschke uses numerous examples to explain how football in Croatia creates publicity for political content: in April 2011, Croatian General Ante Gotovina was sentenced to 24 years in prison for war crimes against Serbs at the International Criminal Court and a few days later, players wore T-shirts with Gotovina's likeness at a first division match between HNK Šibenik and NK Zadar. In 2012, Gotovina was acquitted on appeal, and the Torcida group celebrated this in Split with a large choreography. Then in 2013, after Croatia's accession to the EU, a minority law in Vukovar required the additional inscription of official signs in Serbian Cyrillic. The

Hajduk Split team ran onto the pitch with a banner: 'For a Croatian Vukovar'.

'In the Balkans, there is no differentiated remembrance of the Yugoslav wars,' says Zagreb columnist and blogger Juraj Vrdoljak, who has been reporting on social factors in sport for more than ten years. 'In Croatia, the memory of the Ustasha crimes is mostly denied.' Graffiti of swastikas and Ustasha symbols is emblazoned with football references on house walls, bridges and even school buildings, sometimes in combination with Catholic motifs such as the Vatican flag. 'The historical background for nationalism is not sufficiently addressed in society,' Vrdoljak finds. 'And prominent examples contribute to normalisation.'

After the Croatian team qualified for the 2014 World Cup, defender Josip Šimunić showed the Ustasha salute and shouted 'Za dom spremni' ('For the homeland') with the fans in Zagreb. Many media criticised Šimunić – several fan groups showed solidarity with him. Awareness of the problem was also limited in 2018: the Croatian team came second in the World Cup in Russia, and Marko Perković, founder of the right-wing rock band Thompson, was present on the open-top team bus at the welcome party in Zagreb. His band has been popular with many fans and players for years, but in some European countries they are banned from performing.

Clubs with communist symbolism founded all over the country

Croats and Serbs: the relationship of tension is centuries old and shaped different political systems, especially in the 20th century. Between the two world wars, Serbs assumed a privileged position in the new Kingdom of Yugoslavia, writes Marie-Janine Calic, an expert on south-east Europe at the Ludwig-Maximilians-University Munich, in her book *History of Yugoslavia*. Among the 656 ministers of the short-lived governments were 452 Serbs and 137 Croats. Yugoslavia's first national football team, on the other hand, was founded in Zagreb in 1919, and most of the players had Croatian roots. 'Football illustrated a political dispute of principle,' explains British historian Richard Mills. 'Some officials called for centralisation in Belgrade, others wanted more autonomy for the regions.' In 1929, the football federation was moved to Belgrade. As a result, Croatian players boycotted the Yugoslav national team, which is why the squad for the first World Cup in Uruguay in 1930 featured almost exclusively Serbs.

After the Second World War, the partisan fighter Josip Broz, known as Tito, established a communist one-party state, according to the Basic Law a 'community of equal peoples'. Every person was a citizen of Yugoslavia and one of its constituent republics. Tito had critics removed and banned intellectuals from their professions, but he did not act as brutally as Josef Stalin in the Soviet Union. In addition to cultural clubs, reading societies or music groups, football was supposed to spread Tito's motto: 'Brotherhood and unity'. Clubs with communist symbolism were founded all over the country: Red Star, Partizan and Proletar, also Slobodan (in English free), and Napredak, (progress). 'Many clubs with clear ethnic backgrounds were banned,' says Richard Mills, author of the book *The Politics of Football in Yugoslavia*. 'That's how the communists wanted to stop tensions between population groups early on.'

But there were exceptions like Hajduk Split, founded in 1911. The southern Croatian port city of Split had been occupied by Italian troops in 1941. Hajduk refused to play in the Italian league and joined the Yugoslav partisans as an army team in 1944. After the war, the communists wanted to transfer Hajduk to Belgrade as a showcase club, but the club refused. After Hajduk won the Yugoslav championship in

1950, students in Split formed the Torcida fan group. Before a match they disturbed the night's rest of the visiting team Red Star Belgrade with whistles. Some members were charged, and out of concern for Croatian nationalism, the regime pushed Torcida underground.

In the 1950s, the Yugoslav economy had one of the highest growth rates in the world, with industrial production increasing by 14 per cent annually until 1960. More than five million people moved to the cities for work, and a tourist industry developed on the coasts. The figurehead Tito allowed freedom of travel and strikes to a certain extent. 'In the factories, workers were given more influence, and football clubs also allowed their players more freedom of choice,' reports Richards Mills of the University of East Anglia in Norwich.

The multi-ethnic national team carried Yugoslav ideas out into the world. It won silver three times and gold once at the Olympics between 1948 and 1960, plus fourth place at the 1962 World Cup and lost in two European Championship finals in 1960 and 1968. The big clubs were welcome guests at international tournaments. In 1964, 73 per cent of the Yugoslav population described relations between the republics as good.

But the upswing ended in the 1970s. Unemployment, national debt and social inequality between the regions grew. In 1975, Slovenia was seven times richer than Kosovo. 'Socialist ideology lost concrete meaning,' writes Calic. More and more people turned away from the multi-ethnic state and cultivated ethnic traditions with traditional costumes, folk songs and monuments. According to Calic, the loss of old certainties led to a 'revival of religions'. And these developments were to accelerate rapidly after 4 May 1980: during the match between Hajduk Split and Red Star Belgrade, the stadium announcer proclaimed Tito's death.

In the following decade, ethnic tensions culminated in demonstrations, riots and violence, including around the football clubs. The Yugoslavian national team continued to be among the European leaders, winning bronze at the 1984 Olympics. Since its foundation in 1919, most of the national players had come from Serbia and Croatia, but at the 1990 World Cup in Italy, shortly before the wars of disintegration, Yugoslavia had one of the most ethnically diverse teams in its history. There were five players from Bosnia and Herzegovina, two from Montenegro, two from Macedonia and one from Slovenia, and Yugoslavia reached the quarter-finals, where they lost to Argentina.

In autumn 1990, the Yugoslavian national team was one of the best in the world. They won their first qualifying matches for the 1992 European Championships against Northern Ireland, Austria and Denmark. 'The best players have always met in sports schools, as youths,' says Dario Brentin, a social scientist who studies football in the Balkans. 'The players met regularly in the Yugoslav league, because they were not allowed to move abroad for a long time. So, friendships developed in which national origin and identity didn't really matter.' Players like Robert Prosinečki, Darko Pančev, Davor Šuker or Predrag Mijatović believed they belonged to a 'golden generation'. In 1987 they had won the World Youth Championship in Chile. And now, at the 1992 European Championship in Sweden, they wanted to complete their development with the perfect result, with the title.

The national coach was Ivica Osim, born and raised in Sarajevo, the political and cultural centre of Bosnia. The European scholar Ivan Korić quoted Osim in an essay for the journal *East-West. European Perspectives* with the following words: 'The Yugoslav journalists criticised me terribly. They always wanted to see the players from their constituent republic in the team. I got into trouble with the public and with the journalists because of that. But I followed my own line. It never mattered to me which republic someone came from.

Once I said to the journalists: "I don't care where the players come from. Only the best will play. And if I have to, I will also play with 11 Kosovo Albanians. They belong to us, too. And if they are the best, they will play." With that I had made it clear that I would not let myself be pressured. But Yugoslavia was practically destroyed even before the World Cup in Italy. It was a broken state.'

In October 1991, Osim travelled with the Yugoslavian squad to his home town Sarajevo for a friendly match, the occasion being the 70th birthday of his former club, FK Željezničar, (Locomotive in English). At that time, Slovenia and Croatia had already declared their independence. In Sarajevo, people still seemed to have hope: before the game, players released peace doves. In the stands, 20,000 spectators cheered their already diminished national team. Bosnia and Herzegovina was the only Yugoslav republic in which there was no clear majority for a single ethnic group within the population. And this was also evident in Sarajevo in 1991: of the 530,000 inhabitants, 49 per cent were Muslims, 30 per cent Serbs, seven per cent Croats. No community in the area was ethnically homogeneous, mixed marriages were a matter of course.

A fan tried to save a woman and was shot
However, after a referendum in March 1992, the Republic of Bosnia and Herzegovina also declared itself independent. The Bosnian Serbs did not want to accept this and they formed the Serbian Republic of Bosnia and Herzegovina, later Republika Srpska. In that charged atmosphere, FK Željezničar was to host the club Rad Belgrade in Sarajevo. On the same day, Serb forces from the remaining Yugoslav army occupied a police academy near the stadium. They fired indiscriminately at civilians, including at the stadium. Players and fans managed to get to safety.

Serbian soldiers drew a siege ring around Sarajevo, quickly occupying more than 70 per cent of Bosnia and Herzegovina. Ivica Osim, who had successfully led the Yugoslav national team through qualification for the 1992 European Championship in Sweden, had not heard from his family for some time. Even before Yugoslavia's exclusion from the tournament, he resigned as national coach. 'This is the only thing I can do for this city. To make you remember that I was born in Sarajevo,' Osim said at a press conference.

Without their popular coach, the shrunken Yugoslavian team continued their journey to Sweden. Their hotel in the coastal town of Ystad was close to a camp for Balkan refugees. The Swedish police feared protests against the team, so they moved their camp to Leksand in central Sweden. On 30 May 1992, 11 days before the start of the Euros, the United Nations passed Resolution 757, which dealt with sanctions against Yugoslavia in areas such as trade, diplomacy and culture. The following day, the Yugoslavian team was excluded from the European Championship. The team had to stay in Sweden for a few more days because of travel restrictions. They were also barred from qualifying for the 1994 World Cup and the 1996 European Championship.

Ivica Osim's thoughts had long since turned to his home town of Sarajevo. 'The Grbavica district around the Željezničar stadium became a war zone,' says Bosnian journalist Danijal Hadžović, who has been covering politics and football for ten years. 'The front line ran right through the neighbourhood.' Serbian snipers posted themselves on surrounding high-rises and shot people trying to get water and food. The majority Muslim Bosnians, also called Bosniaks, fired back from the other side. Jerky film footage shows parts of the stadium going up in flames. Soldiers entrenched themselves behind the clubhouse, the lawn resembling a crater. 'Those who left their homes risked their lives,' says Hadžović. 'There was no thought of a normal life with free time.'

Nevertheless, some youngsters in Sarajevo did not want to be deprived of their hobby, recalls coaching icon Osim in an interview with the Austrian magazine *Ballesterer*: 'The young children could at most play in a safe hall or in the house. But when they played outside, it often happened that they were shot at from above. There were many deaths. That was the cruellest thing you could imagine. Children were in school and went out to play, and then they were shot.' In total, around 100,000 people were killed in the Bosnian war between 1992 and 1995, and more than 11,000 during the almost four-year siege in Sarajevo.

Even today, the traces of the war are still present in the Grbavica district: walls of houses with bullet holes, shattered window panes, crumbling plaster. On the other hand, the stadium of FK Željezničar, a club founded by railway workers in 1921, is brand new. A plaque on the west stand commemorates the victims of the war. It was donated by the ultra group Maniacs. Many fans identify with commemorative campaigns, explained political scientist Alexander Mennicke in his bachelor's thesis. The ultras sing the praises of their battered neighbourhood at every home game and sometimes present fighting soldiers in choreographies. They gather on the anniversaries of the Srebrenica genocide and organise memorial tournaments for Dževad Džilda, a leader of the fans who tried to save a woman who had been shot in 1992, but was killed by a sniper.

There is no longer any question of an ethnically mixed society in Bosnia and Herzegovina, comments south-east Europe researcher Marie-Janine Calic. After the Dayton Agreement in 1995, the state remained within its pre-war borders, but was separated into two entities. The Federation of Bosnia and Herzegovina, ruled by Muslims and Croats, received 51 per cent of the territory and thus a symbolic majority. The Serb-dominated Republika Srpska was awarded 49 per cent. During the war, 2.2 million people fled or were displaced in Bosnia and Herzegovina. Today, the vast majority of municipalities have population majorities of over 90 per cent. Bosniaks, Serbs and Croats live separately. In Sarajevo, half of the population was Muslim in 1991; now it is more than 80 per cent.

Nevertheless, Dženan Đipa wants to emphasise what unites society, not what divides it. In the Football Association of Bosnia and Herzegovina, Đipa is responsible for social projects, for girls' tournaments, health care and the school league. He suggested a café on the edge of the Old Ottoman bazaar district in Sarajevo as a place for the interview; nearby are mosques, a Catholic cathedral, an Orthodox church and a synagogue. 'We are a small country,' Đipa says. 'If we want to be successful in business, culture or football, we have to work together.' But what he then tells us about the history of Bosnian football rather suggests that there are not many idealists like him.

The social division after the war also carried over to the game. Bosniaks, Serbs and Croats initially held their own championships, but at the beginning of this millennium, after long negotiations, they came together in a professional league. The establishment of a national team was overshadowed by discussions about ethnic backgrounds. Sergej Barbarez, for example, played successfully in the Bundesliga, among others for Borussia Dortmund and Hamburger SV, but he initially declined invitations to international matches from his home country Bosnia and Herzegovina. The reason: his Croatian-born mother was threatened by nationalists in his native town of Mostar. In 2007, 13 players boycotted the Bosnian national team; in their opinion, the football association placed more emphasis on the nationalities of the players than on their sporting talents.

The conflict line runs through the football of Mostar

As the geographical centre of the western Balkans, Bosnia and Herzegovina has been claimed by Bosniaks, Croats and Serbs for generations. These conflicts resulted in what is probably one of the most complicated political systems in the world. In order to meet all demands, the country is divided into 14 sub-regions, with 14 regional governments and 14 parliaments. The highest state presidency consists of a Bosniak, a Croat and a Serb representative, and the presidency changes every eight months. The cost of this apparatus is estimated at £6bn annually. However, the gross domestic product is less than £16bn and the unemployment rate is around 30 per cent.

According to UEFA rules, the Bosnia and Herzegovina Football Association may only have one president. Bosniaks, Croats and Serbs sit on its board with five representatives each. Will there be tensions? Dženan Đipa, a member of the association's staff, does not want to reveal any internal details. Only this much: the national team plays home games in Zenica or Sarajevo, cities with a Muslim majority. An appearance in Banja Luka, the capital of the Serbian-majority Republika Srpska, seems unrealistic for the time being. 'We should pay more attention to the youth, who have nothing to do with the war,' says Đipa, showing photos on his mobile phone of successful sports festivals. 'Football can promote cohesion; religion doesn't matter on the pitch.' Đipa travels across the country with his projects. It is not so much the children he has to talk gently to, but rather their parents. The mood between the cities can be very different.

Sometimes the conflict line runs right through a city, for example in Mostar in Herzegovina, a region in the south-west of the country, not far from the border with Croatia. Mostar illustrates the complexity of the Bosnian war: at first, Muslims and Croats fought there together against Serbs. Soon Croat nationalists wanted Herzegovina to join their 'Croat mother state' and the Croats turned against their allies. In hours of shelling, they also destroyed Mostar's landmark, the Stari Most, an arched bridge from the 16th century. After the war, the ethnic division of the city solidified: almost exclusively Catholic Croats live in the western half, Muslim Bosniaks in the eastern half.

The landmark, the Stari Most, was renovated and reopened in 2004, and since then tourism numbers have been growing steadily. 'For our guests, the segregation in the city is not really visible, there are no walls, everyone can move freely,' says Esmer Meškić, who grew up in the eastern part. During the war, his father belonged to a Bosniak unit. As a small child he was interned in a Croatian camp for a few weeks, with his mother and grandparents. After the war, he went to a class with only Muslim pupils. At 16, he joined the ultras of Velež Mostar. The workers' club, founded in 1922 and named after a hill, had been a symbol of the multi-ethnic urban society for decades and was honoured by Yugoslav President Tito; even today, the Red Star is part of the club's emblem. 'Before the war, Velež fans lived all over the city, but that is no longer the case,' says Esmer Meškić. 'As a young ultra, I thought carefully about when to go to the western half of the city. Some streets and bars I avoided.' Things are slowly getting better, he adds, but there is still no talk of a relaxed coexistence.

For almost 20 years, Velež Mostar had played its home games on the western side in the Bijeli Brijeg stadium, which translates as White Hill. But with the dissolution of Yugoslavia, Velež lost its home ground to HŠK Zrinjski Mostar in 1992. The club with Croatian roots had been founded in 1905 and banned by the communists in 1945 because of its national symbolism and links to the fascist Ustasha. After its re-foundation, Zrinjski won the championship in Bosnia and Herzegovina six times. However, many ultras would rather cheer for their club in an enlarged Croatian league. The streets around Bijeli Brijeg in the western part of Mostar are marked with their graffiti, including martial motifs, swastikas and symbols of the Ustasha. 'Fans of Zrinjski have celebrated the destruction of our historic bridge,' says Esmer Meškić. 'For us, this is a great provocation.'

But the hostilities can have even worse consequences, as Alexander Mennicke has worked out in his bachelor's thesis on national identity in Bosnian football. In it, the political scientist focuses on the small town of Široki Brijeg, located 20km west of Mostar and inhabited almost exclusively by Croats. 'People feel they belong to the Croatian nation and propagate the Croatian republic on Bosnian soil – Herceg-Bosna, a term that has appeared again and again since the beginning of the 20th century,' writes Mennicke. Referring to the local first division football team NK Široki Brijeg, he says, 'What makes it special is that only Catholics are allowed to play football at the club.' In one choreography, the ultras from Široki Brijeg recalled 'Operation Storm', in which Croatian units drove out Serbian troops in 1995. In another, they presented European Cup opponents Beşiktaş Istanbul with a crusader with the words: 'Bulwark of Christendom.'

Things often escalated when Široki Brijeg met clubs with predominantly Muslim supporters, as happened on 4 October 2009 at the home match against FK Sarajevo. Ultras threw stones and fought. In the chaos, a Croat allegedly grabbed a policeman's gun and shot Vedran Puljić, a fan of FK Sarajevo. The perpetrator was arrested, but managed to flee hours later and make his way to Zagreb, where he does not have to fear extradition. 'The wounded fans from Sarajevo came to us in Mostar,' says Meškić, a supporter of Velež Mostar. 'We offered them places to sleep and food, and that strengthened our ties.' To this day, the death of Vedran Puljić has not been properly solved.

Meškić recounts his memories in Mostar in a café near the renovated arched bridge; as tourism manager, he often leads groups through the alleys of the old town. He looks over to the Museum of War and Genocide, a place of remembrance with harrowing pictures and videos about the genocide in Srebrenica. 'Every country in the Balkans has its own historiography,' says Meskić. 'But we have to teach our children the objective truth. And that can be found at the International Criminal Court.' Many of his friends and acquaintances have moved to western Europe for better jobs, but he wants to stay. 'I cannot hate every Croat. Crimes are committed by individuals, not whole populations.'

In Kosovo football gives a bit of hope

On my research trip through the western Balkans, optimists always stand out, decision-makers with constructive, progressive ideas, and so it is in Pristina, the capital of Kosovo. 'We want normality without hate. We want to look forward,' says Eroll Salihu, secretary general of the Kosovo Football Federation since 2006. 'But it is made very difficult for us.'

Kosovo had played a special role in socialist Yugoslavia, with a population majority of ethnic Albanians and a Serbian minority. Dictator Tito refused Kosovo the status of a constituent republic, but granted it more autonomy in 1974. The majority Muslim Kosovo Albanians remained underrepresented in leadership positions. Mixed marriages between Albanian and Serbian Kosovars were rare. In the 1970s, Kosovo's per capita income was only 38 per cent of the Yugoslav average. In education, medicine and industry, there was a gap to republics such as Slovenia, Croatia and Serbia. Many Kosovars felt culturally connected to the western neighbouring state of Albania anyway.

'We did not want to be second-class citizens. In football we could show who we are,' says Salihu. In the office of the football association, a narrow corridor leads to Salihu's office; on the walls hang historical pictures, including a team photo of Pristina FC. Salihu was a talented youth player when the oppression of Kosovo Albanians increased in the early 1980s after Tito's death. The Serb-dominated police cracked down on Kosovars, and ethnic Albanians in the Yugoslav army fell victim to a series of murders. Gradually, protest sentiment grew among Kosovars. At a 1983 Pristina FC match in Belgrade, visiting fans chanted 'E-Ho! E-Ho!', a show of respect for Enver Hoxha, the dictator of Albania. The police intervened in the stadium and the Yugoslav leadership demanded an official apology.

Salihu goes into raptures when he thinks of Pristina's home games, between 1982 and 1988 in the first Yugoslav league, often in front of more than 30,000 spectators. 'Wins against the Belgrade clubs made us forget our worries for a while,' says Salihu. The Yugoslav parliament took back Kosovo's autonomy in 1990, Serbian President Slobodan Milošević had Albanians forced out of state offices. Their school system was severely restricted, many of their parties and associations were banned.

Numerous Albanians built up underground structures in education and health care. Salihu was in his mid-20s at the time and at the peak of his athletic performance. He was one of the first players to demand the secession of Kosovar clubs from the Yugoslavian game. In the new Kosovar league, Salihu scored the first goal, on 13 September 1991. But independence was closely watched by the Serbian police, Salihu repeatedly received threats and was interrogated. In his book *Kosovo Football: From Slavery to Freedom*, sports journalist Xhavit Kajtazi describes the parallel structures in Kosovar football in the 1990s, including secretly organised tournaments with smuggled balls from abroad. A photo in the book shows players having to wash in a river.

Soon afterwards, the UÇK, the 'Kosovo Liberation Army', appeared and attacked Serb targets. Hundreds of thousands of Kosovars left their homeland. Eroll Salihu moved to Germany, played for the regional league team Wilhelmshaven and obtained his coaching licence. He had to watch on the news as the tensions led to the Kosovo war in 1998, between the Serb-dominated Yugoslav army and the UÇK. The first ever NATO combat mission led to the withdrawal of Yugoslav troops in June 1999. More than 13,000 people died.

Within a few weeks of the war, 80 per cent of Kosovar refugees returned home. Salihu, whose house in Pristina had been destroyed, also wanted to help with the reconstruction. 'In the beginning it was very difficult to build structures in football,' he says. 'We were isolated internationally.' The Kosovar league lacked sponsors and spectators. The national team, which had already been founded in 1993, rarely found opponents for matches. And that was not to change any time soon, even after Kosovo's declaration of independence in 2008. To this day, 115 of the 193 UN member states recognise the Republic of Kosovo – but for the Serbian government, it remains a breakaway province of its own territory.

With a handful of staff, Salihu campaigned with FIFA and UEFA for the recognition of the Kosovo Football Association. From 2014 onwards, FIFA allowed the Kosovan national team to play official friendly matches, but without the national flag and anthem. The team celebrated its premiere with a home match against Haiti in Mitrovica, in the north of the country. Many Serbs saw this as a provocation, because the city is divided: the population living north of the Ibar river is almost exclusively Serbian. However, the stadium in Mitrovica was the only one in the country that met a minimum standard (incidentally, it is named after Adem Jashari, a co-founder of the UÇK). Classes were suspended for the match in the Albanian-dominated southern half of

Mitrovica. Some fans burned a Serbian flag. Even today, NATO soldiers are stationed in Mitrovica to prevent clashes between the ethnic groups.

Kosovo has been independent since 2008, but is still not a member of the United Nations. To properly establish itself in the international community, the government is seeking admission to global organisations. Kosovo is a member of the International Monetary Fund, the World Bank Group and the European Bank for Reconstruction and Development, but not of the cultural association UNESCO or the police network Interpol. The Kosovars celebrated their admission to the International Olympic Committee (IOC) in 2014 as a breakthrough. Their jubilation was great when judoka Majlinda Kelmendi won the first gold medal for the young state in Rio 2016. The excitement was even greater in May 2016 when their football federation became the 55th member of UEFA and the 210th member of FIFA. Salihu proudly displays the framed admission certificates in his office, his correspondence with the associations fills entire folders: 'There was no argument to keep us out for so long. But now we want to make the most of our chance.' He sits candle-straight in his chair.

For a long time, Salihu and his colleagues were on the road in European leagues, building up their national team. They visited players whose parents had left Kosovo during the war. Salihu recalls an international match between Switzerland and Albania in 2012, when nine of the 22 players had Kosovar roots, including, on the Swiss side, Xherdan Shaqiri, who played for Liverpool, and Granit Xhaka of Arsenal. Salihu wanted to prevent more players from opting to play for the teams of their second citizenship. Thus, the Kosovar circle of potential national players grew to 180 professionals. And the Kosovar national team quickly built up a good reputation: in the new UEFA Nations League, they won their group in League D, undefeated. They also impressed in the qualifiers for EURO 2020 against Bulgaria, the Czech Republic and England. On the long away trips, sometimes more than 1,500 Kosovars were present, despite the high hurdles for obtaining a visa within Europe.

For almost two years, the Kosovar team had to play home matches in Shkodra, in the north of Albania. In 2018, the renovation of the new home ground was completed in Pristina, a few minutes' walk from the pedestrian zone. It is a functional stadium surrounded by a massive theatre building and hip bars. The Kosovar Football Association sometimes receives 100,000 ticket requests per match, but can fulfil fewer than 14,000. The stadium is named after Fadil Vokrri, the long-time president of the football association who died in 2018. Vokrri had been the only ethnic Albanian to play for the Yugoslav national team. 'We had many good players,' says Eroll Salihu. 'But on the big Yugoslav stage we had no chance. A clear discrimination.' Vokrri is one of the few Kosovars who are highly recognised in Serbia because of his former time with Partizan Belgrade.

'Football manages to do in Kosovo what politics does not: it gives the youth a bit of hope,' says journalist Eraldin Fazliu of BIRN. The Balkan Investigative Reporting Network with its 400 employees is one of the few independent and critical media networks in the western Balkans. Fazliu says that the sporting upswing of the Kosovar team has plunged many compatriots into an identity dilemma. He himself had fled to Denmark with his family as a teenager. Fazliu loved football, but he could do little with the Yugoslavian national team: 'In my youth, Kosovo had no flag and no anthem. The country was in a sad state. But we longed for belonging. So many friends and I supported the Albanian national team. We can't just wipe away that time today.'

Ninety per cent of Kosovars are ethnic Albanians. For many of them, only one nation counts, the Albanian nation. In their view, this nation also extends to those states where

Albanian minorities live: in Serbia, Montenegro, Northern Macedonia and Greece. Many ultras of Kosovar clubs have long been loyal to the Albanian national team, but with the success of the Kosovar selection, the number of Albanian flags flown by fans in their stands has decreased. But there is also trouble: players like Milot Rashica, Herolind Shala and Alban Meha had already played a few games for Albania before they switched to the newly created Kosovo national team. In the Albanian media, they were also called traitors.

The best players grew up abroad

For a long time, Western Europe showed little interest in Albanian identity, but that changed on 14 October 2014 in the EURO 2016 qualifier between Serbia and Albania. Before the match, Serbian spectators threw stones at the Albanian team's bus, protests and whistles drowned out their national anthem. 'Kill the Albanians!' Serbian fans shouted as a drone flew over the pitch with a flag in the 42nd minute. On it: the outline of 'Greater Albania', as nationalists would like to see it, plus the images of the former leaders Ismail Qemali and Isa Boletini, who had won Albania's independence from the Ottoman Empire in 1912. On the pitch, Serbian defender Stefan Mitrović grabbed the flag and Albanian players charged at him. The game was abandoned.

The tensions in the days that followed are documented in a separate article on Wikipedia: a planned visit to Belgrade by Albanian Prime Minister Edi Rama was postponed, probably partly because his brother Olsi Rama was initially held responsible for the drone, which he later denied. In the Kosovar capital Pristina, hundreds of fans celebrated the match with a motorcade and fireworks. Flags of both countries were set alight in the border areas between Serbia and Kosovo. Even in the diaspora, for example in Vienna, men with Serbian and Albanian roots went at each other.

Many Serbs do not accept Kosovo as an independent state, but only as the historical heartland of their culture and traditions. As justification, they point to the Battle of Kosovo in 1389, where the Serbian army fought in vain against the Ottoman Empire near present-day Pristina. Fans from Belgrade often thematise the battle in their banners and slogans, writes British correspondent Jack Robinson in the online portal *Prishtina Insight*. Also, during the outbreaks of violence in 2008 after Kosovo's declaration of independence, hooligans even attacked the US embassy in Belgrade. More than six centuries after the Battle of Kosovo, about ten per cent of Kosovars are ethnic Serbs, mostly living in villages among themselves, for example near Pristina in the municipality of Gračanica, the site of an important Serbian Orthodox monastery.

Opposite the monastery, on a roundabout, there is a statue depicting Miloš Obilić. The Serbian knight is said to have killed the Ottoman Sultan Murad I during the Battle of Kosovo. In 2015, fans of Red Star Belgrade posed next to the statue. Like hundreds of times before in their stadium, they celebrated themselves as defenders of Christian Europe against 'Islamic invaders'. Several times, Red Star Belgrade played charity matches in Gračanica. On Kosovar territory, fans raised the Serbian flag and sang the Serbian anthem, reports Robinson. Some stopped in Pristina on their way home. They waved flags with the outline of 'Greater Serbia', wore T-shirts with the year 1389 and chanted: 'Kosovo is Serbia!'

'At some point the red line was crossed, we couldn't allow that anymore,' says secretary general Eroll Salihu. In 2018 and 2019, his federation banned Red Star Belgrade from playing guest matches in Serbian enclaves of Kosovo. He says: 'We want to accept Serbian players in our leagues, but they receive a lot of pressure.' Serbian employers in Gračanica are said to have threatened female footballers with dismissal if they played against Albanians. In doing so, they were following a course set in Belgrade: nationalists and hooligans threatened Serbian Kosovars with violence if they did not vote for the Serbian List, the main Serbian party in Kosovo, in elections. Many Serbs also complain of hostility and threats from Albanians. Some sections of fans still sing the praises of the UÇK liberation army.

These are not the only problems of the 1.8 million Kosovars, more than half of whom are under 25. A third of the population lives below the poverty line, youth unemployment is over 50 per cent, and Kosovo ranks 85th in Transparency International's corruption index. Since the war, the international community has invested more than £4bn, yet industry, health care and tax administration are only just beginning. Migration remains high, and so the country depends on payments from the 800,000 Kosovars abroad.

At every home game, leading politicians meet in the stands. Some post photos with national players on social media. 'This instrumentalisation of sport is sad,' says journalist Eraldin Fazliu. 'Our best players grew up abroad after the war. We should create structures so that such talents can also grow up in our country.' Fazliu is happy that football connects young people in his country. But he also knows that sport can deepen existing rifts. Ukraine, for example, does not recognise Kosovo and in 2016, it waived its home right against Kosovo in the qualifiers for the 2018 World Cup, and instead the two teams met in Krakow, Poland. In June 2019, Ljubiša Tumbaković was fired as Montenegro's national coach. The Belgrade-born coach had refused to stand on the sidelines against Kosovo. Shortly afterwards, he was hired by Serbia as national coach. In September 2019, Kosovar police temporarily arrested eight Czech fans who apparently wanted to fly a drone at the match between Kosovo and the Czech Republic in Pristina, with the words: 'Kosovo is Serbia'.

Other states also express their rejection of Kosovo through football: the federations from Serbia, Russia and Bosnia and Herzegovina, for example, have submitted a request to UEFA that they do not want to play against Kosovo. The Spanish government, which does not recognise Kosovo either, is taking a different approach. Before the 2022 World Cup qualifying match between Spain and Kosovo, the Ministry of Culture in Madrid specifically approached the Spanish television broadcaster RTVE to set out some 'ground rules'. The presenters and commentators then spoke of a Kosovar team, but not of a national team. And the stadium announcer announced the 'anthems for the game' without naming the countries. The reason for this is obvious: the government in Madrid does not want to accept Kosovo's independence because it fears separatist imitators in its own country, in Catalonia and especially in the Basque country.

With the help of Alexander the Great

Wherever you go, whoever you listen to, in the Balkans it is always about symbolism, and this is also true for North Macedonia. The ultras of FC Vardar for example can bring several hundred men onto the streets in a few hours. In recent years, they have often paraded through the Macedonian capital Skopje. Organised, self-confident, loud. On their banners they express an attitude shared by many Macedonians: 'The name is our identity.'

The Republic of Macedonia broke away from Yugoslavia in 1991 and has been independent ever since. In the south, it borders a province of Greece that bears the same name. For decades, the Greek government has feared territorial claims by its neighbour. Athens has long opposed Macedonia's entry into NATO and the EU. The result: provocations, embargoes, referendums. As a compromise, a change of name came into effect 2019: Skopje is now the capital of North Macedonia. For the ultras of FC Vardar this is a nightmare.

More than two million people live in North Macedonia, in the south of the Balkans. Around 65 per cent of the population are Christian Orthodox Macedonians, a quarter are ethnic Albanians. Many of the Orthodox Macedonians stick with FC Vardar, the record-breaking champions with 11 titles since independence. 'The vast majority of football fans are nationalist,' says Macedonian sports journalist Ilcho Cvetanoski. 'The right-wing parties use this potential of football. When they need tough guys for demonstrations or security services, they bring in the ultras.'

This became clear from 2006 after a change of government. At that time, the right-wing conservative VMRO-DPMNE party emphasised the ancient meaning of the name Macedonia and drew a line to the general Alexander the Great, who died in 323 BC. The government had statues erected in the centre of Skopje. An airport and a motorway were named after Alexander the Great, the national stadium after his father Philip II. 'This redesign was meant to make the nationalist ideology visible and provoke Greece,' says Cvetanoski. The government speaks of Macedonia's historical disadvantage and goes on the offensive – with the support of the ultras.

The inferiority complex is deeply rooted: in the 19th and for a long time also in the 20th century, Macedonia was not sovereign, but was claimed by surrounding powers, by Bulgarians, Greeks and Serbs. In 1923, the first football championship was held in the Kingdom of Yugoslavia, and it was not until 12 years later that a team from Macedonia was allowed to play. During the Second World War, Bulgaria annexed its western neighbour Macedonia and took control of the sport there.

After the war, Macedonia was one of six republics in socialist Yugoslavia. Many football fans were interested in the top clubs of other regions, in Red Star Belgrade or Dinamo Zagreb. Macedonian teams have been represented in the

Yugoslav league in 33 of the 45 seasons. Macedonian players also moved to the top clubs. In the successful Yugoslav national team, they were considered well integrated.

Many fans were drawn to politics after Macedonia's independence. The leader of the ultra group 'Komiti', Johan Tarčulovski joined the VMRO-DPMNE party. At the age of 19, he headed a right-wing youth organisation, and soon he was part of the Macedonian president's security team. At the turn of the millennium, the conflict between ethnic Macedonians and Albanians escalated. With a paramilitary unit, Tarčulovski attacked an Albanian village in August 2001, several people died.

The International Criminal Court in The Hague sentenced Tarčulovski to several years in prison as a war criminal. After his release in 2013, he was celebrated in Skopje like a 'war hero', writes the British journalist James Montague in his book *1312: Among the Ultras*. With this support, Tarčulovski was later elected to parliament. The former ultra leader mobilised fans against rapprochement with Greece. In 2016, the Social Democrats took over the Macedonian government. Nationalists stormed the parliament at the inauguration. Tarčulovski is said to have supported them.

The new government approached Greece and removed many of the symbols that reminded us of Macedonia's ancient significance. The stadium in Skopje was renamed after a popular singer. The 'Komiti' ultras provoked protests and riots. There is speculation that the Russian investor Ivan Savvidis has supported the demonstrators financially. Savvidis owns companies, hotels and media houses in Greece. He was known as the owner of PAOK Thessaloniki, the most famous club in the Greek region of Macedonia. Until 2011, Savvidis sat in the Russian parliament for Vladimir Putin's party. Moscow does not want North Macedonia to join NATO. The ultras of PAOK Thessaloniki are also positioning themselves against their neighbour.

Since the change of the country's name to North Macedonia at the beginning of 2019, the situation has been comparatively calm. But other conflicts exist. Around 25 per cent of the population are Albanians of Muslim faith. For many of them, the Albanian nation also extends to those states where Albanian minorities live. 'Many of the Orthodox Macedonians identify strongly with the Macedonian national team, but this is less the case with the Muslims,' explains Ivan Anastasovski, a sports scientist from Skopje. But Albanians also use football as a political and cultural platform. In the city of Tetovo near Skopje, Albanians founded FC Skendija in 1979 to cultivate tradition. The Yugoslav authorities banned the club, fearing Albanian nationalism. After independence, Skendija became champions three times. The ultras call themselves 'Ballistët', in reference to an Albanian fighting organisation in World War II.

Albanian fans in North Macedonia are also pursuing their agenda. Some of them display flags of a fictitious 'Greater Albania'. With banners and chants, they support the Kosovo Albanians against the claims of ownership from Serbia. Researcher Ivan Anastasovski believes that participation in the delayed EURO 2020 (in 2021) strengthened the construction of a separate identity in Northern Macedonia. A symbol of diversity instead of disunity. Like the national team, most professional teams in North Macedonia are ethnically mixed. But there is still no diversity in the clubs' governing bodies and supporters' sections.

'We all speak the same language after all'

After a three-week tour of the western Balkans, after 25 interviews and reading books, studies and articles, many of my questions have been answered, but a number of points remain open. How and when will it be possible for the ethnic groups to reconcile? How can one talk about the war crimes that happened less than 30 years ago?

Perhaps Robert Prosinečki has an answer. The son of a Croatian father and a Serbian mother, he is the only player to have scored World Cup goals for two countries: for Yugoslavia in 1990 and for Croatia in 1998. He won the European Champions Cup with Red Star Belgrade in 1991 and returned as coach in 2010. 'Things happened in the war that we will never forget,' says Prosinečki. 'But we can't let that dominate our lives.' He played for Real Madrid during the war, calling his family and friends in Zagreb every day.

Prosinečki has worked as a coach in Turkey and Azerbaijan, and between January 2018 and November 2019 he was in charge of the Bosnia and Herzegovina national team. In the summer of 2019, he is sitting on the terrace of the training centre in Zenica, an industrial town north of Sarajevo, lighting one cigarette after another. You quickly notice that Prosinečki doesn't really want to talk about politics. 'I never had any problems because of my origin. And I don't give a shit where people come from. We work as a team for good results, because football is the best marketing in the world.'

Perhaps such an attitude would bring some serenity to everyday life, but Robert Prosinečki also had to deal with politics as coach of Bosnia and Herzegovina. One of his national players came under criticism: Ognjen Vranješ, born in Banja Luka, had the border of Republika Srpska tattooed on his upper arm in 2015. Many Bosniak fans called for his expulsion. And their calls grew stronger when Vranješ got a tattoo of Momčilo Đujić in 2018. The Serbian priest had collaborated with the Nazis during the Second World War and was convicted as a war criminal.

Prosinečki prefers to talk about topics that spread hope: in 2014, the national team of Bosnia and Herzegovina played its only World Cup to date, in Brazil. In their very first match, they pressed Argentina hard, but lost 2-1. People in Serbia and Croatia paid respect to this performance.

'There is much more to come,' says Prosinečki. 'We all speak the same language after all.' Maybe there will be solidarity among neighbours again someday. Maybe even with a friendly match or two.

The Most Important
Source of Propaganda

*Vladimir Putin has used football for his
nationalism. Major events such as the 2018
World Cup were expected to bring prestige and
help him expand his security apparatus. With
Gazprom, the Kremlin secured access beyond
classical diplomacy. But after the invasion of
Ukraine, sport highlighted Russia's isolation.
The Putinisation of European football, however,
is likely to continue.*

IT IS an iconographic image of sports history. On cushioned
armchairs, Vladimir Putin, FIFA president Gianni Infantino
and Saudi Crown Prince Mohammed bin Salman watch the
opening match of the 2018 World Cup at Moscow's Luzhniki
Stadium. At this point, Russian forces have annexed Crimea
and fought alongside Syrian dictator Bashar al-Assad. This is
the era when Russian forces stepped up repression against civil
society and [allegedly] interfered in the 2016 US presidential
election. Yet on one of the most important stages of sport, at
the World Cup, Putin is still allowed to present himself as a
citizen of the world.

After the 2022 war of aggression against Ukraine, there
will be no more such images for the time being. After some
hesitation, the International Olympic Committee (IOC) made

the recommendation to move competitions out of Russia and to exclude Russian athletes from its events. One sports association after another took action. FIFA, world football's governing body, barred the Russian national team from qualifying matches for the 2022 World Cup in Qatar. UEFA excluded Russian clubs from its competitions. Russia was isolated in international sport.

There have been few examples of such a move in recent history: in the 1960s, sport stood united against the apartheid regime in South Africa; and a good 30 years ago, athletes were banned from the war-torn country of Yugoslavia. But a political heavyweight like Russia had not yet been hit with such force. On a symbolic level, Russian state propaganda lost one of its most important sources: sport – the platform for heroes and supposedly apolitical patriots.

To grasp the significance of this setback, it is worth taking a historical perspective. Whether it was within the Tsarist Empire, the Soviet Union or the Russian Federation, for more than 130 years sport had an identity-forming effect on many Russians. During the Cold War, the USSR established a system to leave its economically superior rivals from the West behind, at least at the Olympic Games. The Soviet Union collapsed and the prestige sport had gained was lost.

In the chaotic 1990s, the Russian economy shrank by 50 per cent, millions of people became impoverished. In this period of upheaval, a small elite of oligarchs, politicians and security forces came to power and prosperity. In 1999, Vladimir Putin took over the government. He profited from an economic upswing and rising commodity prices. The desire for internal security and global recognition shaped his actions, and sport helped him achieve this.

Gradually, state institutions and companies became involved in sports associations and football clubs: they included energy giants, banks and transport companies. Gazprom, the world's largest producer of natural gas, led the football club from Putin's hometown, Zenit St Petersburg, to the top of the European league. And it took on partnerships with FC Schalke 04 and with Red Star Belgrade, as well as with UEFA and FIFA. In this way, the Kremlin linked politics, state and economy.

As a state-owned corporation, worth billions, Gazprom is not really dependent on advertising abroad. But through the channels of sport, the Kremlin was able to maintain communications with Western politicians that the stricter protocols of diplomacy did not allow. At FC Schalke 04, Matthias Warnig, managing director of the controversial Nord Stream 2 pipeline project, sat on the supervisory board. At UEFA, Alexander Dyukov – the CEO of Gazprom Neft – was on the executive committee. He has been president of the Russian Football Federation since 2019. Warnig and Dyukov will probably no longer hold important positions in international football. But their contacts are likely to continue in the background. And whether international sport actually excludes Russia completely remains to be seen. At the group draw for the Qatar World Cup in Doha, Russia was hardly criticised.

Other examples show how much Vladimir Putin has established sport as a facade for his politics and networks. At the beginning of the millennium, several of his henchmen joined the boards of international sports federations. Putin was still considered open to reforms and concessions to civil society. His government declared a 'Decade of Sport'. Dozens of international events took place in Russia, such as the 2011 World Biathlon Championships in Khanty-Mansiysk, the 2013 World Athletics Championships in Moscow, the 2015 World Swimming Championships in Kazan and the 2016 World Ice Hockey Championships in Moscow and St Petersburg. Formula 1 has been an annual guest in Sochi since 2014.

Thousands of activists gave up or went abroad

Putin was able to present himself to the international public as a cosmopolitan statesman – and to his own people as a hands-on father of the country. This became particularly clear during the 2018 World Cup, both in the stadiums and far beyond. That summer, in a trendy neighbourhood in the centre of St Petersburg, in a backyard, surrounded by cafés and galleries, the Diversity House invited people to discussions, exhibitions and alternative city tours during the World Cup. Its motto: 'Cup for People'. Originally, the name Pride House was intended for this meeting place, but the authorities would have found that provocative because of the reference to LGBTIQ+. And the Diversity House was originally going to be located at another address, closer to the official fan fest, but the landlord cancelled the contract at short notice.

Olga Polyakova, one of the organisers, was glad at the time that the events went off without disturbances and attacks: 'For civil society, the World Cup was a rare opportunity to network. We don't have a big institution behind us. We rely on small and medium-sized partners.' Other groups outside football also experienced a relatively relaxed time in June and July 2018. Fans celebrated peacefully in large groups, even drinking alcohol in public was tolerated, and the police remained in the background. A birthday party for the long imprisoned Ukrainian director Oleg Sentsov was watched by police officers but not broken up. 'What worries us most is the arbitrariness of the state,' said Polyakova in 2018. 'No one knows what is allowed to be said and what is not. Everything is deliberately left in the dark.'

The authorities' serenity, however, was only possible because of their years of preparations. Freedom of assembly had already been largely suspended in Russia during the 2017 Confederations Cup. And so it was before and during the World Cup. Large-scale protests were impossible. The Interior

Ministry ordered the police to cut back on news about crimes, raids and investigations during the World Cup. The regions were also supposed to report mainly on positive things. There were no substantial official comments from FIFA.

Civil society: in many countries of the West, it is a respected partner of the rule of law. In Russia, it is seen as a counter-movement to the Kremlin – and as a projection screen for its worries about losing power. Since Vladimir Putin's re-election as president in 2012, human rights activists have counted dozens of laws and amendments to laws that restrict civil rights. More than 200 organisations have been listed as 'foreign agents', among them well-known institutions like the Levada Centre, Memorial and the Sakharov Centre. Their issues: human rights and a different view of the communist dictatorship. Many have been closed down completely in the meantime. Thousands of activists gave up, exhausted, went abroad or refrained from public criticism.

Soon after the World Cup, correspondents reported on repression again. Protests were regularly dispersed. From the summer of 2019, police detained several thousand demonstrators at various rallies, where they were protesting against the exclusion of opposition politicians in the election to the Moscow city parliament. Criminal proceedings against critical regional politicians have also been on the rise. On 21 July 2019, activist Yelena Grigoryeva was murdered. 'The World Cup was a break from everyday life for us,' says LGBTIQ+ activist Alexander Agapov. 'The government felt even stronger afterwards.'

Most activists have little to do with the glitzy events like the World Cup, as Sorina can tell you. When the doorbell rings in the small community centre on the outskirts of Moscow, she is startled for a moment. She goes to the speakerphone, looks at the screen and is relieved. It's not angry neighbours, not officials, not neo-Nazis, it's a familiar face. She opens the heavy iron door for her colleague as if she were the security guard of a bank. Then she sits back down at the table for the interview. It's about homosexuality, about strong women in football. About topics for which a certain caution is not wrong in Russia.

Sorina grew up in Tomsk, in the western part of Siberia. She doesn't want to give her last name, not even to a journalist from Germany. She weighs every word, her medium-length hair tied in a pigtail. When she was 14, her mother leafed through her diary and found out that she was a lesbian. Since then, their relationship has been strained. Sorina studied architecture and built up a football team with fellow students. They called it 1604, after the founding date of their city.

Football was new for the women. It strengthened their feelings of breaking out, at least for a few hours. They helped each other find jobs and study. Sorina moved to Moscow and joined the LGBT Russian Sport Federation, a network for queer athletes. Again, she formed a team, looked for places and backers. She wanted to motivate others. She transferred her self-confidence in sport to her work and family.

Sorina and her team belong to the generation that can hardly remember life without Vladimir Putin. But she knows from books and stories that the situation of women was not too bad, even long before Putin's term in office. In March 1917, demonstrating women had promoted the fall of the Tsar. In 1917, Russia was the first country to introduce the right to vote for women and the right to abortion. After that, things went up and down, reports Ekaterina Kochergina of the Levada Centre, the only independent opinion research institute in Russia. Women fought on the front lines during the Second World War. In 1972, a football tournament in Dnepropetrovsk was named after Valentina Tereshkova, the former seamstress who was the first woman in space, a heroine of the USSR. The Soviet Union massively restricted civil rights, but women were less disadvantaged than elsewhere. Kochergina says: 'Today, the historical roots of progress are barely perceptible.'

On a conference table, the researcher spreads out tables and diagrams. 'Women belong in the family, many think today. This image of women is politically prescribed.' World power aspirations and nationalism have grown under Putin since the annexation of Crimea in 2014. The giant country with its roughly 100 ethnic groups is looking for an overarching identity, especially as the victory in World War II continues to fade. But, by 2050, the population of 143 million could drop by 20 million. Financial worries connected to this are often alleviated by rejection, especially of immigrants from the Caucasus and Central Asia. Also, of homosexuals, because they cannot bear children, says Kochergina: 'The pressure is also growing for women. But the birth rate in our country is not much lower than in other industrialised nations.' The difference is that the life expectancy of Russian men is lower, they die on average at 64. So, frustration and prejudice are dumped on minorities.

Some hooligans took over security services

In this climate, Putin wanted to use sport to perpetuate his narrative of unity, against the alleged paternalism and arrogance of the West. It is quite possible that the successfully organised 2014 Olympic Winter Games in Sochi reinforced his great power aspirations. A few days later, Putin had Crimea annexed. Few in the political class objected. In the Russian parliament, the Duma, there are 20 sports-related deputies representing Putin's United Russia party, such as Alexander Zhukov, the former president of the National Olympic Committee.

The political embrace of sport has a long tradition, as Martin Brand, Stephan Felsberg and Tim Köhler show in their anthology *Russkij Futbol*. And this tradition applies especially to football. For example, in 1912 at the Olympic Games in Stockholm, the Russian team lost 1-2 to Finland, which at that time still belonged to the Russian Empire. Critics interpreted this as a sign of the downfall of the Tsardom. Two decades later: the Red Army used football to keep its soldiers happy.

Clubs were soon linked to industries. Dynamo Moscow was in the custody of the secret service, Lokomotive belonged to the railways, ZSKA to the army. In the 1930s, arbitrariness and persecution reigned under Stalin. Anyone who came up with new ideas in times of forced collectivisation made himself suspect. Nikolai Starostin, co-founder of Spartak Moscow, was sentenced to camp imprisonment for 'bourgeois working methods'. Whether football was a distraction during the Second World War or a status symbol during the Cold War, *Russkij Futbol* tells Soviet-Russian history through the lens of football.

The state also had a firm grip on fan culture. In the Soviet Union, the supporters of the big Moscow clubs in particular were under surveillance. Their emotions and opaque hierarchies were interpreted as a 'danger to order'; all the more so in tense times, such as after the Soviet invasion of Afghanistan in 1979, the Western boycott of the Olympics in Moscow in 1980 and the rise of Solidarność (Solidarity) in Poland. At times, flags and scarves were banned in stadiums. The Komsomol, the Communist Party's youth organisation, acted against critical supporters.

The police, press censorship and the KGB secret service prevented brawls in the stadium environment from reaching a wider public. Even the mass panic at the 1982 UEFA Cup home match between Spartak Moscow and HFC Haarlem, in which at least 66 people died, was not discussed in detail until seven years later. In the political vacuum of the 1990s, there was no social work done with fans in Russia as there was in Germany, for example, where people tried to attract young men to creative and positive hobbies around their clubs. So hooligans and neo-Nazis networked. Some hooligans took over security services for regional elected officials, others intimidated political opponents.

Football is now a considerable element of the political male alliances. The Russian Federation consists of 85 'federation subjects' – republics, regions, territories – with different faiths and degrees of autonomy. Local elites want freedom, in return they guarantee loyalty. Many first division football clubs are supported by their regional administrations, explains political scientist Martin Brand: 'The regions compete with each other. A successful club can attract investors and secure approval among the population.'

Sport's involvement in politics has to be subtle, in a society where, according to the Lewada Centre, only seven per cent of the population is interested in politics. But after the invasion of Ukraine, it was sport that highlighted the Kremlin's isolation. The British government adopted tough sanctions against Russian oligarchs. These included Roman Abramovich, who had owned Chelsea since 2003. Abramovich's assets, worth billions, were frozen. He was banned from any transactions with people and companies from the UK. On top of this, the government in London charged that Abramovich, through the steel company Evraz, had been involved in 'destabilising, undermining and threatening the territorial integrity, sovereignty and independence of Ukraine'. Abramovich held 28.6 per cent of Evraz's shares and the company may have been involved in 'supplying steel to the Russian military'.

The sanctions hit Chelse hard. The financial institution Barclays blocked its accounts and credit cards. The team's travel expenses were limited. The club had to stop selling match tickets and merchandise, the fan shops were closed. Under Abramovich, Chelsea had won the Champions League twice, now he was being pressured to sell. And he was not the only Russian oligarch in football to feel the international pressure. There was Alisher Usmanov, for example, a financier of Everton, who was more publicly aligned with Putin than the reticent Abramovich. Usmanov was supposed to be involved in the construction of Everton's new stadium, but the plans were put on hold.

The extent to which Russian billionaires represented the Kremlin's interests in Western Europe through football was mostly nebulous. What is certain is that they drove a change for foreign investment. This applies to Maxim Demin, the owner of AFC Bournemouth, and Dmitri Rybolovlev, the owner of AS Monaco in France and Cercle Brugge in Belgium. The same goes for Valery Oyf, who took over Dutch first division club Vitesse Arnhem. And Ivan Savvidis, the long-time owner of the Greek club PAOK in Thessaloniki. When Roman Abramovich grabbed Chelsea a good 20 years ago, only Fulham already had a foreign owner (among top English clubs). By early 2022, 19 of the 20 Premier League clubs were in the hands of major investors.

Ukrainian ultras called for resistance

In the debate after the Ukraine war began, the oligarchs were among Putin's accomplices. However, the emotional nature of football also gave a voice to the victims. In the Premier League, the Ukrainian professionals Oleksandr Zinchenko and Vitaliy Mykolenko solicited support for their country. The media published numerous articles about refugees, not only from Ukrainian footballers, but also from players from Latin America and Africa who experienced racism at the border. And from the Spanish coach Lluís Cortés, who had coached the Ukrainian women's team.

The war presented many Ukrainians with a difficult choice. Former national player Andrei Voronin, born in Odessa, sharply criticised Putin and resigned as assistant coach of Dynamo Moscow. His former colleague in the Ukrainian national team, Anatoliy Tymoshchuk, chose a different path. The former FC Bayern player had been working as assistant coach at Zenit St Petersburg, the most important club from Putin's hometown, since 2017. Even after being asked to do so, the record-breaking international initially refused to condemn the war. As a result, the Ukrainian Football Association banned him from any footballing activity in Ukraine – for life.

But war was not new to Ukrainian football in 2022. Already after the annexation of Crimea in 2014, several clubs from the east of the country had gone into exile. The modern stadium of Shakhtar Donetsk was shelled. Sergei Kurchenko, owner of Metalist Kharkiv, fled to Russia. The insolvent club was banned from playing in 2016. Some representatives of the Russian Football Federation wanted to incorporate the Crimean clubs, Tavriya Simferopol and FC Sevastopol into the Russian league. And so football increasingly became a stage for hostility between Russia and Ukraine.

Nevertheless, both nations share a common and successful history. Between 1961 and 1990, Dynamo Kiev won the Soviet championship 13 times and even the European Cup Winners' Cup twice. For a long time, Ukrainian players formed the foundation of the Soviet national team. In 1988, the USSR reached the final of the European Championship. Of the 20 players, ten came from Dynamo Kiev, and that also applied to the national coach, Valery Lobanovsky.

This established the perception in Ukraine that, in football of all things, it enjoyed a certain sovereignty within the Soviet Union. Many fans wrote letters to local newspapers and sports authorities. In them, they raved about Dynamo Kiev and sometimes made critical remarks about the Moscow clubs.

Some of these letters were written in Ukrainian, which was very unusual at the time, as the Communist Party wanted to impose the Russian language in the republics as well. Most of the letters were never published, writes Eastern Europe expert Manfred Zeller in his dissertation on Soviet fans. But the letters gave the authorities a picture of the mood. And they showed that there was indeed Ukrainian patriotism. But the so-called militias also made sure that it did not turn into violent nationalism in the stadiums.

Some Ukrainians were now playing for Russia

There was great hope in Ukraine that this strength would be preserved, even after the collapse of the Soviet Union. But this hope came to nothing. Of the successor states of the USSR, only the Russian national team was allowed to take part in the qualifiers for the 1994 World Cup. The new Ukrainian team was not allowed to enter until the qualifiers for the 1996 Euros. 'Many Ukrainians thought this was unfair and wrote many letters of protest to FIFA and UEFA,' says Ukrainian historian Kateryna Chernii, who is also researching the transformation of Ukrainian football.

Before the 1994 World Cup, however, there was the 1992 European Championship. The Soviet Union had qualified for the tournament in Sweden. However, the state had ceased to exist. And so the team of the CIS, the Commonwealth of Independent States, played in the European Championship, as a transition. This team included several Ukrainian players: Oleh Kuznetsov, Andrei Kanschelskis and Sergei Juran. They no longer played for Dynamo Kiev, but for Glasgow Rangers, Manchester United and Benfica.

Many players came from mixed marriages, their parents were from places like Lithuania, Georgia or Belarus, and so they could decide which national team they wanted to play for in the future. The newly founded Ukrainian Football Federation had hardly any money and at times could not even provide plane tickets for its team. The prospect of higher bonuses led some Soviet-Ukrainian players to accept Russian citizenship – for example, Sergei Juran, who grew up in Luhansk, in eastern Ukraine. Other players, nearing the end of their careers, turned down the offer – for example, Oleksij Mykhaylychenko, the best player in the USSR at the 1988 European Championship. In Ukraine, these decisions were controversial, Chernii reports: 'Oleksij Mykhaylychenko was described as a good Ukrainian citizen. Sergei Yuran, on the other hand, was criticised. He was considered a Ukrainian who had lost himself. But it was the time when many people in society had to be honest with themselves: who are we? Where will we live? How will we live?'

It took the Ukrainian national team a few years to establish itself at the top level. In 2006, it took part in a World Cup for the first time in Germany. Its peak followed in 2012, when Ukraine hosted the European Championship together with Poland. In an exhibition at the time, famous Ukrainian players such as Oleh Blochin were shown in the jersey of Dynamo Kiev, but not in the jersey of the USSR. Chernii says: 'Ukraine's official history policy today is, after all, based on distancing itself from the Soviet Union – and thus also from Russia.'

The complicated politics of remembrance is illustrated by Valery Lobanovsky. Many Ukrainians associate him with the successes of Dynamo Kiev. His work as Soviet national coach is suppressed. But at the opening of a Lobanovskyj memorial in 2003, one of the speakers was a representative of the Russian Football Association. Today that would be unthinkable. Currently, football is strongly characterised by segregation and even hatred.

Ultras went to war

And brutal violence is also part of it. The Russian invasion of 2022 began in Ukraine on 24 February. Just a few hours later, fans of Dynamo Kiev spoke out on social media. 'We are ready to fight. We kill all occupants who come to our land,' read one post framed by the Ukrainian national colours. 'Call to all people who have honour – go to the Russian embassy and protest. Go to your government and order them to fight against the common enemy. Ukraine is shield of Europe. Together we are power.'

The post spread on Telegram, Twitter, Facebook. Ultras and hooligans from other Ukrainian clubs also called for resistance. They promoted joining the Ukrainian military as volunteers. Broad-shouldered men in uniforms posed in photos. They carried weapons and club flags, and were usually masked. In several forums, ultras circulated videos of soldiers and fleeing people. Football illustrated the broad mobilisation in Ukrainian society, says journalist Thomas Dudek, who deals with politics and football in Eastern Europe. Many ultras already had experience with fighting and weapons.

In 2013 and 2014, hundreds of ultras took part in the protests against the then pro-Russian government in Kiev during the Euromaidan movement. They came from fan groups that were hostile to each other, but together they used their experience in street fighting with the security apparatus. Ultras erected barricades, brought the injured to safety, protected other demonstrators from the thugs of President Viktor Yanukovych, a confidant of Vladimir Putin. The ultras did not play a decisive role in bringing down Yanukovych, but their contribution was not negligible either.

Soon afterwards, separatists in the eastern Ukrainian cities of Donetsk and Luhansk proclaimed so-called 'people's republics'. Hundreds of fans joined the army and fought against the separatists. Others who could not flee in time were imprisoned and, in some cases, only released years later. Numerous ultras died in the war in eastern Ukraine. Many returned, traumatised.

In Western Europe, football fans who take part in protests and revolutions are sometimes glorified and romanticised. This was the case after the Arab Spring in Egypt in 2011, when ultras fought in Tahrir Square against the ruler Hosni Mubarak. Or after the protests in Turkey in 2013, which originated in Istanbul's Gezi Park. Books have been written and documentaries made about the power of the ultras. Ukraine played a central role. But the heroisation also masked dangerous developments.

Dozens of Ukrainian ultras and hooligans have been fighting for the Azov Battalion, one of the paramilitary volunteer forces, since 2014. It is difficult to say exactly how many there are, because the organisation is secretive. The ultranationalist group has links to right-wing extremist movements in Europe. In 2022, neo-Nazis in Western Europe also mobilised for the war against the 'Bolshevist' Putin, who was supported by Muslim fighters from Chechnya. Security authorities assumed that several hundred right-wing extremists wanted to take part in the war in Ukraine.

Beyond Ukraine, thousands of football fans took a very different stance on the Russian invasion. Ultras in Germany, Poland and Croatia expressed their rejection of Vladimir Putin in chants and banners. Many groups collected money and donations in kind for Ukraine, organised the transport of refugees and arranged accommodation. And they mourned war victims and fallen friends.

Sports journalists as a 'national threat'

The networking of the Ukrainian ultras was also closely observed in other Eastern European states, especially Belarus. 'This was a warning for Alexander Lukashenko,' says Eastern Europe activist Ingo Petz, founder of the Fankurve Ost alliance. 'The mobilising power of the ultras is harder to control than some civil society NGOs. So, the regime had large fan groups like those of Dinamo Minsk systematically broken up.' Many ultras were visited by secret service agents, and some of their leaders were imprisoned for years after show trials. Dozens of ultras were arrested before political elections and released weeks later.

This was also the case in the summer of 2020, around the rigged presidential election, after which Alexander Lukashenko, in office since 1994, once again proclaimed himself the winner. In the months that followed, hundreds of thousands of people protested against Lukashenko, and thousands have been arrested to date. Athletes also took to the streets and displayed regime-critical banners. Footballers of the privately financed FC Krumkachy appeared in the streets wearing white T-shirts with the slogan 'We are against violence'. Several of them later reported torture, abuse and threats from officials. 'We athletes were apolitical for a long time, we wanted a simple life,' says Aliaksandr Apeikin. 'But this attitude strengthened the system.' Apeikin and his colleagues have founded the Belarusian Sport Solidarity Foundation (BSSF). With donations, they want to support athletes who have lost everything after protests: their place in the national team, their employment or their studies.

The consequence of the increasing repression was that prominent athletes like the track and field stars Andrei Krauchanka and Yana Maksimava, who had taken part in protests, went into exile. The always critical kickboxing world champion Alexei Kudin was sentenced to two and a half years in prison for allegedly attacking police officers. Wide-ranging sports media such as *Tribuna*, which had reported on protesting athletes, were banned. 'Sports journalists in Belarus never thought it was possible that they would one day be considered a threat to national security,' says sports expert Yagor Khawanski. 'Advertisers and subscribers were asked to cancel their contracts with more critical media,' – a development that we also know from Russia.

Ultras from football were also present at the protests in Minsk 2020, but not in groups with their symbols. They had been warned: in mid-August 2020, the 28-year-old ultra Nikita Krivtsov from the small Belarusian town of Maladzyechna had been found dead in a forest. The police claim he committed suicide. His friends believe he was beaten to death after a demonstration. Some players attended a funeral service in Maladzyechna. Fans collected donations for Krivtsov's family. Others posted themselves in front of prisons and encouraged imprisoned friends with chants.

No signal of regret came from the sport's officials. Like ice hockey, the football association in Belarus is particularly dependent on state support. Its president is the former general Vladimir Basanov. Shortly after the presidential election in 2020, the football association issued a circular demanding political restraint from players and officials. However, the association itself had published excerpts from a speech by Lukashenko on its website before the election.

'Lukashenko perceives demonstrating athletes as a betrayal,' says Vałdzis Fuhaš, co-founder of the Belarusian human rights organisation Human Constanta. 'Sport has long played an important role in state propaganda.' This system had been established over years: in 1997, three years after he became president, Lukashenko also took the helm of the National Olympic Committee. He placed confidants from the military and state enterprises in important sports federations and clubs. This political influence is a violation of the Olympic Charter. Lukashenko nevertheless allowed himself to be filmed guiding a puck in ice hockey and shooting at the goal in football. Similar images exist of Vladimir Putin, Lukashenko's most important supporter.

The champions from a breakaway region

The Soviet Union has been history for more than 30 years, but Vladimir Putin was able to exert influence with his networks in several successor states for a long time, also with the help of football. Moldova offers an interesting example. A conflict that escalated during Perestroika has been smouldering there for generations. The majority in the Soviet constituent republic of Moldova wanted to leave Russian foreign rule behind and oriented themselves towards the pro-European neighbour in the West, Romania. Transnistria, a narrow strip of land in Moldova's east, situated on the border to Ukraine, professed its allegiance to the Russian language and Moscow's politics. Fighting broke out, with almost 600 people killed. Since the ceasefire in 1992, the conflict between Moldova and Transnistria has been considered 'frozen'.

Transnistria is not recognised by any UN state, but has its own government, currency and military. More than 1,000 Russian soldiers with heavy war equipment are said to be stationed in Transnistria, because the networks have been established for a long time. In the largest city, Tiraspol, two former Soviet security forces founded a company named Sheriff in 1993. They quickly established links with the ruling party and increased their influence. With supermarkets, petrol stations, mobile phones and media houses: by now Sheriff is said to influence 60 per cent of the Transnistrian economy and to cover half of the state budget through its tax levies. The ties to the Kremlin are close.

Football lends this network a supposedly apolitical facade. FC Sheriff, established in 1996 in Tiraspol, are allowed to compete in Moldovan football. Sheriff won the Moldovan Cup for the first time in 1999, followed by ten championship titles in a row from 2001 onwards. The Sheriff group financed one of the most modern training centres in Europe and one of the most beautiful stadiums in the region, with an integrated luxury hotel. Between 2009 and 2018, FC Sheriff played in the group stage of the Europa League four times. In 2021, the club competed in the Champions League for the first time and even won at Real Madrid.

'Through football, Transnistria wants to show that it is superior to Moldova,' says Sascha Düerkop, former secretary general of the Confederation of Independent Football Associations (CONIFA, the football association for unrecognised states, minorities and regions). The pro-Western Moldovan government officially has nothing against its country being represented in Europe by a club from a breakaway region. Officials and fans of FC Sheriff abide by the rules at international competitions and refrain from using Transnistrian symbols, chants or flags. Many of them still feel connected to Russian culture. 'You can also see Sheriff as a reconciliation project,' says Düerkop. 'For the home games in Tiraspol, many fans cross the hard border between Transnistria and Moldova, which they might not otherwise cross.'

Internationally, football also provides a stage for diplomatically isolated Transnistria to network. Other members of the Community for Democracy and Rights of Nations founded in 2001, such as the autonomous regions of South Ossetia and Abkhazia, which belong to Georgia under international law, are also hoping for such opportunities.

Football is a platform for territorial claims

In the Soviet Union, Georgia was one of the smaller of the 15 constituent republics. Geographically, politically – but not in football. Alongside the big Moscow clubs, Dinamo Tbilisi established itself as a reliable player, partly because of the support of secret service chief Lavrentiy Beria, a key figure in the terror under dictator Stalin. In 1981, Dinamo Tbilisi won the European Cup Winners' Cup. The Soviet media reported proudly. Thousands of Georgians took to the streets.

Uninhibited, cheerful, self-confident. The state let them go, for the last time.

A few years later, the independence movement grew in Georgia. Several demonstrations against communism were put down by Soviet soldiers, with dozens dead and injured. Football established itself as a symbol of resistance. In 1990, the first national league was formed in Georgia, a year before the official independence of their country. 'This championship was shaped by Georgian nationalism,' says Caucasus expert Rusif Huseynov. 'On the orders of the political leadership, the clubs had to drop their Russian names. The players were also supposed to change their surnames to match Georgian culture.'

Some clubs on Georgian territory refused to join the new Georgian football league in 1990, remaining loyal to the Soviet game, for example Dinamo Sukhumi from Abkhazia. In this region on the Black Sea, many people feel more connected to Russian culture than to Georgian culture. After the final collapse of the Soviet Union, Abkhazia declared itself independent in 1992. Georgia, however, wanted to annex the region by military force. The result was a war of secession, thousands of people died and more than 200,000 Georgians were displaced.

Again, football played a role in the symbolism: sources suggest that Georgian prisoners were also executed in Abkhazian stadiums. The venue of FC Gagra was named after Daur Achwlediani, the Abkhazian player who had joined the separatists and was killed in the fighting. With Russian help, Abkhazia was able to push the Georgian army back and the war ended in 1993.

Since then, Abkhazia has considered itself an independent state, but is regarded as part of Georgia by most governments in the world. The same is true of the mountainous region of South Ossetia, a few hundred kilometres east of Abkhazia. For a few years, the conflict remained calm, but that changed in August 2008: Tbilisi wanted to win back the breakaway regions by force. Once again, Russian troops pushed back the Georgian military. The fighting lasted almost a week, and more than 800 people were killed.

'The Beijing Olympics were taking place at the same time,' recalls British sports scientist Joel Rookwood, who has long studied the Caucasus. 'Governments were using the world stage for their political messages.' At a press conference during the Games, then-Georgian President Mikheil Saakashvili railed against interference from Moscow. Saakashvili was considered a Western-oriented reformer. In his view, Georgian territories were occupied by Russia. Another sensitive time came with the 2014 Winter Olympics in Sochi, Russia, a few kilometres from Abkhazia. Again, there were provocations between Russia and Georgia, but no escalation.

In Soviet times, the path of particularly talented footballers from Abkhazia often led to the Georgian showcase club Dinamo Tbilisi – today that would be unthinkable. There are few personalities who could build a bridge with their life stories, but one is Temur Ketsbaia, who grew up in Abkhazia, later turned professional with Dinamo Tbilisi, became Georgia's national coach in 2009, and has been working abroad for years now. Many people in Abkhazia prefer to look to Russia, for example to Stanislav Cherchesov, the national coach of the Russian national team till 2021, who grew up in the Caucasus, in North Ossetia.

The regions of Abkhazia and South Ossetia, which are not recognised by the United Nations, have a combined population of just under 300,000. Their footballers are integrated neither in the Georgian, nor in the Russian game. Instead, they have joined CONIFA. In 2016, Abkhazia hosted the CONIFA World Cup. 'For the people, it was a rare opportunity for representation,' says Sascha Düerkop. 'In their opening ceremony, they emphasised the long and diverse history, not the conflict.' Abkhazia won the tournament; 10,000 people celebrated in the streets.

The Caucasus is one of the most diverse regions in the world. The conflicts between the population groups are about concepts such as territory, identity, belonging. And football is a platform for territorial claims. In Tbilisi, Georgians who were expelled from Abkhazia have founded FC Gagra, in reference to their hometown. Dinamo Tbilisi's ultras are also considered nationalist. Some of them wave the old Georgian flag, which was valid more than a hundred years ago, before the Russian occupation of Georgia from 1921. They also rail against Vladimir Putin and show solidarity with fans who have been expelled from eastern Ukraine. Tens of thousands of Georgians also protested against the Russian invasion in 2022, against a war that will also occupy football in Eastern Europe for a long time to come.

Even long after Putin's political end, his sports policy is likely to leave its mark on Europe. Even in the EU, his methods have been copied, for example in Hungary. Four European Championship matches were held in Budapest in 2021, a political opportunity that Hungary's Prime Minister Viktor Orbán did not miss. Since he took office in 2010, his government has financed the building and renovation of numerous stadiums, halls and sports schools. Orbán encouraged companies to invest more in sport in return for tax breaks. Leading members of his ruling party Fidesz are on the boards of the big football clubs. The record-breaking champion club Ferencváros Budapest is headed by Gábor Kubatov, a member of the party's board. Kubatov mobilised Ferencváros security guards against anti-government demonstrators, including extreme right-wing football fans.

Viktor Orbán follows a model of sports policy for which Vladimir Putin laid the foundation. Photo opportunities showing Putin in the stands alongside FIFA president Infantino will not be repeated, but other dictators will take his place.

Attackers for Secession

In Spain, football serves as an emotional backdrop for the quest for independence. Especially in the Basque Country and Catalonia, chants and choreographies in stadiums blur political demands, nostalgia and marketing – and sometimes the glorification of terror. How do separatism and the global football industry fit together in places like Bilbao and Barcelona?

THE SCREEN on the outside facade of San Mamés can be seen from far away. Athletic Bilbao's new stadium was built next to the old one in the middle of Bilbao and opened in 2013. The young tour guide Pablo leads the guests through the arena this afternoon. At the beginning, he explains the unique selling point: Athletic's teams have been made up exclusively of Basque players since 1912. Their motto is, *'Con cantera y afición, no hace falta importación'* ('With local talent and local support, we don't need imports'). Pablo puts it this way: 'The club symbolises our values: ambition and a sense of home.' His idol is Julen Guerrero. The midfielder was active for Athletic for 24 years, both as a youth player and with the professionals. One of his contracts was for ten years; he turned down lucrative offers. Only three clubs have never been relegated from the

74

Primera División, which was introduced in 1929: Real Madrid, Barça and Athletic Bilbao.

Spain is one of the most diverse countries in Europe. The autonomous communities have regional parliaments and governments. Their self-government and cultural differences have evolved over centuries. But dictator Francisco Franco, who ruled for almost four decades until 1975, brutally suppressed autonomy. He centralised the state, banned symbols and languages.

The consequences can still be felt today. In some parts of the country, people are striving for independence: for example in the north-west in Galicia, in the north in the Basque Country, in the north-east in Catalonia. In politically turbulent years, the subject of secession is topical again for other population groups in Europe: for Scots in Great Britain, for Flemings in Belgium, for Corsicans in France. The causes are complex, but in no other country is it as emotional as in Spain. This is also evident in football, as this chapter will illustrate with the example of two cities: Bilbao and Barcelona, in regions where affection is also measured by the origin of the players.

In Athletic's club museum, the tour begins in front of a wide video wall. A steam locomotive rattles through the picture. Blast furnaces, factory chimneys, hard-working men. Hammer blows and ship sirens boom from the loudspeakers. The museum is reminiscent of the late 19th century, when Bilbao, with its shipyards and mines, was one of the industrial centres. The economically flourishing port city was also attractive abroad. It was British immigrants who founded Athletic in 1898, with an English club name.

Conservative Basques saw football as a danger. They were worried that the youth would stay away from the churches, instead they preferred the Basque game of pelota. This changed: pro-independence supporters also used Athletic's networking power to fight for more autonomy in the 1930s. In

1936, José Antonio Aguirre, a former Athletic player, became the first president of the Basque Country. Aguirre initiated the creation of a Basque national team, as an ambassador for a possible secession from Spain.

'*Gloria y guerra*', 'glory and war', is the line used to headline the Spanish Civil War between 1936 and 1939 in the Athletic Museum. Posters, tickets and a patched leather ball are displayed in the glass case. 'It's hard to find memorabilia for that period,' says Asier Arrate. The museum director used to work as a history teacher. In recent years, he has been looking for flags, jerseys, documents and letters. 'There was no real archive for decades,' Arrate says. 'It's a Basque tradition to remember history with stories and less with objects.'

Asier Arrate interviews eyewitnesses, archives objects and plans collaborations with schools. The museum, which opened in 2017, focuses on fans and members; it is modern without seeming superficial. It is not only intended to list club successes, but to depict Bilbao's history with the help of Athletic. This includes disappointments and contradictions. For example, many of Franco's supporters were active at Athletic. The dictator banned foreign club names – Athletic became Atlético. The Basque roots faded into the background.

The fascist regime installed new club presidents

'The whole stadium loudly cheers,' is how FC Barcelona's club anthem begins. 'It doesn't matter where we come from.' The founder, however, had little to do with Catalonia. The Swiss Hans Gamper had already founded FC Zurich in 1896, so when his uncle got him work in Barcelona, he set up another club there in 1899: Football Club Barcelona. 'The first club statute was in German, and the team mainly included foreign players,' recounts political scientist Klaus-Jürgen Nagel, who taught at Pompeu Fabra University in Barcelona for more than two decades, and also has an interest in football. 'Barça helped many Spanish internal migrants integrate into Catalan society.'

From 1923 to 1930, Miguel Primo de Rivera ruled Spain in a military dictatorship. The general curtailed Catalonia's special historical rights and pushed back regional cultural assets, explains Julian Rieck, a historian at the Humboldt University in Berlin. Rieck cites football as an example: At a friendly match of FC Barcelona in 1925, a naval band played first the English, then the Spanish anthems. In the stadium Les Corts, the forerunner of the Camp Nou, the spectators demonstratively applauded the English anthem, but whistled during the Spanish one. As a result, FC Barcelona was banned from operating for six months and its stadium was closed. Hans Gamper had to leave the country temporarily.

Things became even more difficult during the civil war. Barça's club leader Josep Sunyol, a member of the independence party ERC and founder of the sports magazine *La Rambla*, was shot by Franco's henchmen. Membership declined and the club faced ruin. The team went to America for ticket revenue, and several players remained in exile. In 1938, the FC Barcelona grounds were shelled. After Franco's takeover, the Catalan symbolism had to be removed from the coat of arms. The name was changed to Club de Fútbol Barcelona. In 1943, Barça won the first leg of the cup semi-final against Real Madrid 3-0. Before the second leg, police officers allegedly intimidated the Barça players – Real won 11-1. Riots ensued and both club leaders were forced to resign. The fascist Falange installed new presidents: at Real, their choice was Santiago Bernabéu.

Events become myths and shape identity. Even today, many Catalans justify their dislike of Madrid and the central government with the events of several decades ago. Probably no one has found better words for this than the Barcelona-born writer Manuel Vázquez Montalbán. For him, Barça was 'the unarmed army of Catalonia' and a 'republican and secular religion'. At a time when Catalan history and language were not allowed to be cultivated, Montalbán described the Camp Nou as a rallying point for feelings of independence: with handkerchiefs in Catalan colours, also with shouts of protest against the regime. As early as 1960, 15 years before Franco's death, Barça's New Year's greetings in the club newspaper were written in Catalan.

A projection for protest

Was FC Barcelona a victim of the dictatorship and Real Madrid its beneficiary? Sid Lowe shakes his head vigorously: 'There was not only black and white, but also contradictions that fans today find difficult to endure.' Lowe, an Englishman, lives in Madrid and reports on Spanish football for *The Guardian* newspaper; for his doctoral thesis he studied the Spanish Civil War. 'In the dictatorship it was often hard to draw the line between regime supporters, hangers-on and resisters. If you wanted to get to the top in football, you had to be subordinate, otherwise you were threatened with dismissal.'

Fear and Loathing in La Liga, the name of Sid Lowe's book about the rivalry between Barça and Real Madrid, has also become a Spanish history of the 20th century. In it, Lowe writes about the Francoist governors at FC Barcelona. The regime allowed the club to exist in order to counteract social tensions. Francesc Miró-Sans, Barça president for many years, came to terms with Franco and linked up with Real Madrid. Some fans wanted to name their new stadium after founder Hans Gamper, but politicians refused. The name remained uncontroversial: Camp Nou, new pitch.

Spain was classified as a fascist state by the United Nations, and only five countries – all predominantly Catholic – maintained diplomatic relations with Franco: Italy, Portugal, Ireland, Argentina and the Vatican. In 1948, the Spanish Foreign Ministry banned the national team from playing international matches against non-aligned nations. In the 1960 European Championship, Franco banned the national team from travelling to Moscow, fearing a surge of leftist currents on the Iberian Peninsula.

And the narrative about Franco's favourite club being Real Madrid? 'There is no simple answer to that either,' says historian Julian Rieck. For his doctoral thesis on Real during the Franco era, he was allowed to spend weeks researching in the club's archives – a rarity. Franco had already been in power for a decade and a half when Real advanced to the top in sporting terms in the mid-1950s. At a European Cup match in Geneva in 1955, some Real players even met members of the royal family who were living in exile.

The Spanish Cup competition was dedicated to the *Generalíssimo* as early as 1939, and Franco usually handed over the trophy in person. But, according to Julian Rieck, one has to abandon the idea that Franco had a long-term plan with football: 'There were ministers and officials in Real's management, but that was also the case with other clubs.' Arguably, it was the club's five European Cup triumphs between 1956 and 1960 that piqued the interest of politicians. 'During that period, Real secured prestige and revenue for the government.' With international players like the exiled Hungarian Ferenc Puskás and Alfredo Di Stéfano, who was born in Argentina and later naturalised, the appearance of 'a free and cosmopolitan country' emerged, according to Rieck. Compared to other European countries, Spain had an underdeveloped infrastructure. Franco needed investors from abroad for modernisation.

Santiago Bernabéu, Real's president between 1943 and 1978, brought together representatives from politics, the monarchy and the judiciary in the VIP stand. At European Cup matches, he established contacts in countries that rejected diplomatic relations with Spain. On the other hand, Real was used as a projection screen for protest on trips abroad. For example, in Vancouver, demonstrators displayed a slogan: '*Real si, Franco no*'. In Turin, left-wing groups protested in front of the team hotel and in Brussels, spectators in the stadium waved the flag of the Spanish Republic (thousands of exiles and migrant workers from Spain lived in Belgium at the time). Dutchman Johan Cruyff chose a move to Barcelona over one to Real in 1973, saying he could not play for a club associated with Franco.

'Real propped up the dictatorship and perhaps made it more durable,' says Julian Rieck. 'But you shouldn't overinterpret that either.'

ETA sent blackmail letters to wealthy players

José Maria Etxebarria leans forward on the conference table when he thinks of the end of the dictatorship, speaking louder and faster. Etxebarria works for the PNV, the Basque Nationalist Party, founded in 1895. In his youth, shortly before Franco's death, Athletic Bilbao once played with mourning flags, officially in memory of a club member who had died – actually in protest against death sentences. Etxebarria also tells of a Basque derby he watched as a young man in 1976. Before kick-off, the captains from Bilbao and San Sebastián, José Ángel Iribar and Inaxio Kortabarria, stuck the flag of the Basque Country in the centre spot. 'This is an image that every child in Bilbao knows today,' says Etxebarria. 'It was like a revival, because for 40 years our symbols were banned.'

The PNV is the most influential party in the Basque Country. Its overriding goal is separation from Spain, and it takes moderate conservative positions. The PNV has always tried to maintain good contacts with Basque associations, and several of its top leaders have been active on the executive boards. This was the case before the dictatorship – and even more so afterwards: Athletic now used the English club name again. In 1977, the PNV politician Jesús María Duñabeitia took over as president. Basque singers and dancers again performed confidently in the stadium.

More and more club members supported the campaign for autonomy, with success: Basque was established as a nationality and elevated to an official language alongside Spanish. Thanks to new self-government rights, the Basque Country was able to develop better financially and in terms of infrastructure than other regions. Football, according to the narrative, provided the emotional backdrop. 'Athletic brought people from all social classes together,' says José Maria Etxebarria. 'Young and old, left and right.'

Real Sociedad from San Sebastián won the Spanish championship in 1981 and 1982, Athletic Bilbao the following two years. Politicians and economists interpreted these four Basque titles as an encouragement, because the region was struggling with increasing unemployment and a sharp decline in industry. In the suburbs, many young people suffered from drug addiction. In 1984, more than a million people stood on the riverbanks of Bilbao as their players sailed towards the city centre on a launch. In total, the Autonomous Community of the Basque Country has only 2.2 million inhabitants.

One often comes across these triumphant images in Bilbao, whether in tourist offices or in the Museum of Fine Arts, but another current of nationalism tends to be suppressed: *Euskadi Ta Askatasuna*, Basque Country and Freedom, or ETA for short. The underground organisation killed more than 800 people between 1959 and its dissolution in 2018. ETA turned its attention to football in January 1986, when it kidnapped the businessman Juan Pedro Guzmán, a member of Athletic's board of directors, but released him days later. It also sent blackmail letters to wealthy Basques, including Bixente Lizarazu, born on the French side of the Basque Country. ETA's accusation: as a national player he had chosen an 'enemy nation', France. They demanded a 'revolutionary tax' from Lizarazu to 'protect his family from consequences'. The latter then received police protection.

ETA had a few hundred members but tens of thousands of sympathisers. Therefore, institutions weighed opinions carefully. In the stands of Athletic, too, fans sometimes demanded the release of imprisoned ETA fighters, some displaying their logo, an axe with a snake coiled around it. Interspersed with the loud fan chants were isolated shouts of 'Let's kill a Spaniard'. In March 2008, Athletic held a minute's silence for Isaías Carrasco, the Basque social democrat who had been murdered two days earlier. Part of the crowd disturbed the silence with whistles. 'They were small minorities,' says Mikel Burzako of the PNV party. 'Athletic was a place of peaceful encounter even in heated times. Everyone could agree on football. It will always be like that.'

No broad debate in the media

Ernest Pujadas pays less attention to diplomatic words. For the location of the interview, he suggested a rustic tavern near the Camp Nou. Pujadas has been a fan of FC Barcelona ever since he can remember. He can well remember his first *Clásico* in 2000. He was six years old, sitting on his father's lap, with his grandfather next to him. It was the season when former Barça icon Luís Figo returned to the Camp Nou, wearing a Real Madrid jersey. Ernest Pujadas still has the deafening whistles in his ears. Coins flew onto the field, mobile phones, stones, even a pig's head.

Ernest Pujadas underwent his fan socialisation at the beginning of the millennium, when Catalan nationalism turned into an independence movement, supported by the lawyer Joan Laporta, who lead FC Barcelona as president between 2003 and 2010. Laporta campaigned for a separate state and valorised the Catalan language in club life. His fans chanted: 'Laporta president – Catalunya independent.' And he found a prominent supporter in team captain Carles Puyol. His colleague Oleguer Presas turned down a call-up to the Spanish national team in 2006.

This also pleased Ernest Pujadas' family. His grandparents told him how they had suffered under Franco, the Camp Nou was a retreat. But which events actually indicate that Barça was critical of the regime? Historian Julian Rieck reports on an increase in ticket prices for trams in 1951. After an FC Barcelona home game, numerous fans went on strike. Rieck says, 'The narrative of Barça as an opposition club is a backward projection'.

Ernest Pujadas refers to the man who gave his name to Real Madrid's stadium: Santiago Bernabéu fought as a volunteer on Franco's side during the civil war. One of his closest confidants had been a member of the Blue Division, a Spanish volunteer group that fought with the Nazis in the Soviet Union during World War II. But it is also true that Bernabéu, as Real boss, threw former Franco generals out of the stadium. And he built up relations with Barça. There is no broad and differentiated debate about this in Spain, neither in the media nor in academia, and certainly not in the chronicles and museums of the big clubs.

'We cannot separate football and politics in Barcelona,' says Ernest Pujadas. Since the age of 18, he has followed home matches in the north stand. He is a formative figure in an influential fan group, the *Penya Almogàvers*, founded in 1989 and now with several hundred members. They design choreographies, and the hard core is present at every away game. Pujadas spent two years drumming in the corner, two games a week; he got blisters on his hand and could hardly write. Now he takes care of the fan group's social media and says: '95 per cent of our members are for Catalan independence, that's what we're for. We want this attitude from new members as well.'

Ernest Pujadas studied political science, he has travelled a lot and likes to watch political series from the USA on TV. He has distributed leaflets for the separatists, and also promoted discussion groups and fund-raising concerts. He took part in dozens of demonstrations, wearing his old Barça away jersey in the Catalan colours. This was also the case in September 2017 at the away game in Girona. Carles Puigdemont, the then president of the Catalan autonomous government and former mayor of Girona, was celebrated in the VIP stand. Thousands of spectators chanted, 'We vote!'

On 1 October 2017, the regional government held a referendum on independence – against the veto of the Spanish Supreme Court. The police unit Guardia Civil wanted to prevent the vote and took action against those involved. The pictures went around the world, hundreds of people were injured. Ernest Pujadas observed the referendum in his hometown of Malgrat, 80 kilometres from Barcelona. The police intervened five times at the polling station, Pujadas recounts, and ten people were injured. 'I wanted my family and friends to be able to vote safely. Without fear for their health.' A total of 3,000 people voted in the school premises, 87 per cent for independence.

Pujadas made dozens of phone calls that day, initially to other polling stations, later to FC Barcelona fans and staff. As the escalation became apparent, the club asked to postpone the home match against Las Palmas scheduled for the same day. The league refused; its managing director Javier Tebas is considered a conservative anti-separatist. Several groups of fans threatened to storm the pitch, so Barça opted to play in front of empty stands. 'That way we could show the world for 90 minutes how much Catalonia is suffering,' said then club boss Josep Maria Bartomeu.

A football federation for non-recognised states

Among the players, it was Gerard Piqué who was the most outspoken: 'The use of violence was one of the worst decisions in the last 40, 50 years. It has further separated Catalonia and Spain.' Piqué, born in Barcelona, active for Barça since 2008, has never publicly spoken out in favour of independence, but for '*dret a decidir*', meaning the right to self-determination. According to polls, 70 to 80 per cent of Catalans want to be able to decide freely, including many opponents of secession. This is similar to the situation in Great Britain: there, the Scots voted in 2014 to remain in the United Kingdom. The Spanish constitution, however, forbids such a referendum.

In the days following the 2017 vote, the Spanish national team gathered for international match preparation, with their defender Gerard Piqué among them. During a public training session, right-wing extremists mingled with the audience, singing songs from the civil war. Dozens of spectators chanted: 'Pique, asshole, your nation is Spain.' Coach Julen Lopetegui stopped training.

Piqué had endured a lot in the past, even being accused of once cutting off long jersey sleeves because of Spain's national colours. After the 2018 World Cup, he ended his career in the national team at the age of 31. He now has more time for his side-line activities as a businessman and investor, including tennis and developing e-sports events. In March 2019, Piqué played for the Catalan national team, which has played around 200 matches since 1904 but is not recognised by FIFA.

According to political scientist Ryan Griffiths, there have been around 400 secessionist movements worldwide in the past two centuries. Of these, 60 are still active today. Some of these movements want to make their voices heard in football, with CONIFA, the football association for non-recognised states, minorities and regions. Teams from Tibet, Kurdistan, Northern Cyprus and Somaliland are all involved, but perhaps the most well-known ones are based in the Basque Country and in Catalonia.

The Camp Nou's exterior facade features the logos of the fans' groups, the one of the *Penya Almogàvers* above the entrance gate 48. Diagonally above it hangs a huge banner with a photo of the combative-looking Piqué, complemented by the club's mantra: '*Més que un club*', 'More than a club'. Piqué played 102 international matches. Spain became World Champions in 2010, won the European Championship in 2008 and 2012. Among the leading figures were several FC Barcelona professionals: Carles Puyol, Xavier Hernández, Sergio Busquets, Andrés Iniesta and David Villa.

Temporarily, it looked as if the national team could reduce regional tensions. This had already happened in 1992, when the Spanish team won gold at the Olympic Games in Barcelona, with 95,000 spectators cheering at the Camp Nou. But at that time, the situation was not yet so messed up. Beyond that tournament, the national team has not played a home match in Barcelona since 1975, and television ratings for international matches in Catalonia, the Basque Country or Galicia are ten to 20 per cent below the national average.

When Spain failed to reach the last 16 against hosts Russia at the 2018 World Cup, Ernest Pujadas and his friends had a party with fireworks. Pujadas also mentions the Copa del Rey, the Spanish cup under the patronage of the king. Traditionally, Barça supporters whistle the national anthem before the finals. The dislike was particularly loud in 2009, 2012 and 2015, because the fans of the opponents joined in: Athletic Bilbao.

Twenty scouts are on the road in the Basque Country

One of the centres of Basque football is the *Cantera*, the so-called quarry of Lezama, an idyllic community ten kilometres from Bilbao. Surrounded by hills and meadows lies Athletic's training ground. There are well-tended grass pitches and glass office buildings, in front of which is the archway from the old

San Mamés stadium, as a reminder of eight championship titles. Families watch their sons' game from the small stands. '*Vamos!*' they shout, 'let's go!' Down by the pitch, the then sports director pulls up the zip of his jacket and takes notes. José María Amorrortu is to make the seemingly impossible possible for the future: First Division football – exclusively with players of Basque origin.

Amorrortu was born in Bilbao in 1953 and grew up near the stadium. As a player, coach and manager, he spent almost his entire professional life in the Basque Country, in Bilbao, Eibar, and San Sebastián. For a time, he coached the unofficial Basque national team. 'In this region, the identification with football is particularly high,' says Amorrortu, who has a degree in economics. 'People work hard. They don't always have to be the best, but they want to be able to look in the mirror.' Honesty, down-to-earthness, identity. These terms are often mentioned by fans and staff of Athletic, also as a distinction from the capitalist football industry. Is it nostalgia, social marketing or naivety?

For more than 100 years, Athletic has relied on players with Basque roots. Only a few clubs in the world engage in comparable regional recruitment, such as Deportivo Guadalajara in Mexico. In Spain, many of Franco's supporters had rejected FC Barcelona as a symbol of internationalism, but even the dictator is said to have identified with Athletic: for the 'preservation of the Spanish race', for 'keeping the blood pure'.

In times of sporting failure, this search for talent was criticised by fans, who feared for the club's competitiveness. In 1959, Miguel Jones Castillo, born in Equatorial Guinea and raised in the Basque country, was considered for a contract. Jones was not considered good enough. Some still think it was because of his black skin. Jones moved to Atlético Madrid and was successful. In the 1980s and 1990s, radical nationalists also used football as an outlet. A popular slogan was: 'God created only one perfect team, he heaped strangers on the rest.'

Society changed, and so did Athletic Bilbao. For a long time, only players from the three provinces of the Autonomous Community of the Basque Country were admitted. Later, the search was extended to the neighbouring area and the French part of the Basque Country. These rules are not laid down in any statute, presumably otherwise they would attract the attention of the Supreme Court for structural discrimination.

Athletic acquired a reputation as a 'training' or 'nursery' club; outstanding players moved on. As the years have passed, the players' birthplace has become less central, but their 'growing up in Basque football' is still a key factor. In 2000, Blanchard Moussayou became the first black player to join the youth team. After injuries, he had to end his career early. Years later, he admitted that he had had it twice as hard as a black player at Athletic. In 2008, the Cameroonian youth player Ralph N'Dongo was racially insulted by a spectator during a training session, and Athletic filed charges. In 2011, a black player played for Athletic in the Primera División for the first time, accompanied by an intense debate in the media. Jonás Ramalho, the son of an Angolan, was unable to establish himself in the starting line-up.

The breakthrough came in 2014, when Iñaki Williams, born in Bilbao to a Ghanaian father and Liberian mother, became Athletic's first black goal-scorer in the Europa League. The media described his biography in great detail: his parents' jobs and the support of the priest with the Basque name Iñaki, who he was named after. Williams developed into a popular striker. And he was considered a symbolic figure for modern Bilbao. With architectural highlights like the Guggenheim Museum, the city has reinvented itself as a cultural metropolis. In August 2019, Iñaki Williams extended his contract with Athletic until 2028.

'It is not a given that we play in the first division with our model,' says club icon José María Amorrortu. 'So, we have to be focused and professional.' Athletic has 150 partner clubs in the surrounding area that make Bilbao aware of their greatest talents and receive financial support in return. They have 20 scouts on the road in the Basque Country. A database stores candidates from other countries with Basque ancestry.

In the meantime, there are quite a few players in the youth teams who were born in Africa or Latin America. Hardly any of them speak Basque. About 30 per cent of the regional population speak this language, which has unknown origins and nothing in common with any other European language. Athletic were keen to delay commercial developments, but had to adapt. Athletic was one of the last professional clubs to allow advertising on jerseys and stadium boards. And what would happen to the promotion of talent if the club were to be forced into the second division for the first time? The approximately 50,000 members would then discuss whether they could continue to deviate from their anthem, 'Because you are born of the people, the people love you'.

The best-known supporter is Pep Guardiola

FC Barcelona, with more than 150,000 members, reaches other dimensions. This morning, a queue has formed in front of the club's museum. Groups of tourists push their way through the three-storey club shop, jersey prices of £140 are no deterrent. They quickly upload their mobile phone photos of advertising banners to the internet. There is sparkle on every corner, with chart music blaring from the loudspeakers; the visitors speak English, Japanese or German. Barça generates a quarter of the turnover in Spanish professional football and is aiming for an annual turnover of more than one billion euros in the medium term. The *Clásico* against Real Madrid is one of the most-watched football matches worldwide on television. What would *La Liga* be without this duel?

Hardly any club has benefited as much from globalisation as FC Barcelona, so how is it that many fans describe themselves as Catalan nationalists? As defenders of a region of 7.5 million inhabitants who are not oppressed within Spanish democracy? 'We are not dealing with an ethnic blood and soil nationalism here,' says journalist Florian Haupt, who lives in Barcelona and reports for German newspaper *Die Welt* among other publications. 'Many Catalans are regionally and globally oriented. Many independence supporters want a cosmopolitan nation that stays in the EU.' With terms like 'offside', 'penalty' and 'corner', Catalan everyday language is more mixed with English football vocabulary than Spanish.

The fronts are contradictory, the camps divided, also within families, circles of friends and among FC Barcelona supporters. The club supports the right to self-determination. The press releases are diplomatically formulated, mentioning 'dialogue', 'respect' and 'sport'. The club is apolitical, but is 'on the side of the Catalan people'. When the police used violence during the referendum in 2017 and Catalan politicians were arrested for alleged rebellion, the Barça leadership expressed itself more offensively, but it does not advocate secession from Spain, out of consideration for fans in other regions. And how would sympathisers in China, India or Turkey, who associate the struggle of minorities with something else, react?

The Spanish league, the football association and the sports media also seem to weigh their statements carefully. According to Florian Haupt, however, Barça's board seems to be fine with voices from within the club taking a more uncompromising stance. Fans are allowed to unfurl banners that read: 'Welcome to the Catalan Republic' or 'SOS Democràcia'. During home matches fans watch the clock. After 17 minutes and 14 seconds of play, they shout 'Independencia!' with fervour. This ritual recalls the year 1714, when Catalan troops were defeated by the Bourbon army and the region of Barcelona was incorporated into the central state. In their eyes: the loss of freedom.

Probably the best-known supporter of independence is Pep Guardiola, former Barça player and coach. In 2015, he stood for the separatist party *Junts pel Sí* in the regional elections. On several occasions he recited poems by the Catalan poet Miquel Martí i Pol at events. At his current employer Manchester City, Guardiola has worn a yellow ribbon on his lapel in 2017, a show of solidarity with imprisoned independence supporters. He was warned and fined by the English FA for wearing 'political symbols'. Its then chief executive Martin Glenn said, 'Where do you draw the line – should there be someone wearing an ISIS badge?' And he gave examples he didn't want to see in football: 'Strong religious symbols, the Star of David, the hammer and sickle, the swastika and something like Robert Mugabe on a shirt.'

Martin Glenn apologised for this 'offensive comparison', but his remarks highlight the awkwardness with political issues. What is football allowed to take a stand for? What should it take a stand against? 'I'm not just a coach, I'm a human being first and foremost,' Pep Guardiola said. 'It's not about politics, it's about democracy.'

In October 2019, several separatist leaders were sentenced to prison terms, some of them long. Large demonstrations and riots followed in Barcelona, with several hundred people injured. On social media, the group 'Tsunami Democràtic' also mobilised for protests, such as a blockade of the airport. In one of their videos, Pep Guardiola criticised the court rulings. When Guardiola used to play with Barça in Madrid or Seville, opposing fans would passionately wave the Spanish flag. They wanted to provoke Guardiola, and he accepted that. Because he was free to express his opinion.

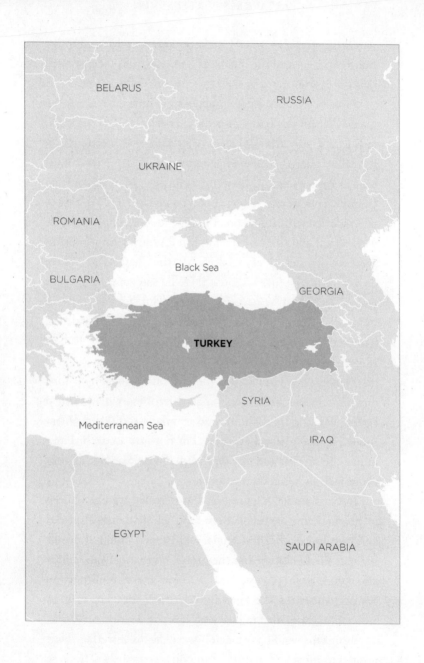

The Power of Imam Beckenbauer

*Turkish President Erdoğan is networking in
football to stay in power. Politicians from his
Justice and Development Party (AKP) sit on
club boards. Conservative entrepreneurs receive
preferential treatment when stadiums are built.
Erdoğan repeatedly poses with prominent players
like Mesut Özil. Critical ultras, on the other
hand, are monitored and suppressed – there is
hardly any space left for protest.*

HUNDREDS OF football fans in black and white shirts
crowd through the narrow streets of Beşiktaş, a five-minute
walk from the Bosporus. They clap, sing, toast their club
with raki. Young men stand next to the statue of the eagle in
the heart of the neighbourhood and light Bengal flares. The
thunderous cheering echoes over to the small market where the
social democratic Republican People's Party (CHP) has spread
its flags. There are not many neighbourhoods in Turkish cities
where the largest opposition party can appear so confident. In
Beşiktaş, the conservative AKP government with its president
Erdoğan traditionally does badly.

Supporters of Beşiktaş proudly declare their allegiance
to Çarşi, probably Turkey's best-known fan group. They are
committed to environmental projects and animal welfare and
regularly collect donations. Their logo shows the crossed-

out A, the symbol of anarchy. On the pub benches in their neighbourhood, they talk passionately about politics, about Erdoğan, repression, about the increasing religiosity in everyday life. These are topics they would have taken to the stadium a few years ago, with angry chants and banners. 'But those days are over,' says Bariş, a member of Çarşi. He wears a full beard and black clothes. 'Nobody wants to go to prison for football.'

From the eagle statue, fans head towards Taksim Square before home games, past the impressive Dolmabahçe Palace, towards Beşiktaş's stadium. Those who want to attend matches in Turkey have had to use an electronic ticketing system since 2014 and reveal personal data. The only operating company is a bank with links to the AKP. Even more surveillance cameras have been installed inside the stadiums, and political messages are prohibited. 'Many of us don't want to go along with this,' says Bariş in his smoky voice. 'It's sad that even in football we are being harassed by the state.' Some friends now only watch matches in the pub.

Civil society, freedom of the press, demonstration rights: in the wake of Recep Tayyip Erdoğan's rise to power, freedoms have become narrower. As if under a magnifying glass, this has been evident in football for years. Politicians and entrepreneurs use the sport for their own purposes. But football also offers activists a platform for resistance. There are examples of this in Turkey's recent history that have made headlines around the world.

It started in May 2013 with rallies against a construction project in Gezi Park, in the heart of Istanbul. The police responded with violence, but the demonstrators refused to be intimidated. The movement grew, spreading to other cities. In Taksim Square, different groups opposed the government of then Prime Minister Erdoğan, including hundreds of fans of the otherwise rival clubs Beşiktaş, Fenerbahçe and Galatasaray. They had often encountered aggressive police officers in their everyday football life. With their experience, they now protected demonstrating youths and senior citizens from tear gas and water cannons.

Erdoğan insulted the fans as looters. Hours later, they joined together, clapping in rhythm, stamping their feet and chanting: 'The looters are coming.' And, 'Send in the water cannons. We haven't showered in three days.' Some days the mood was not at all aggressive, Emre, a member of Çarşi, tells us: 'For a long time it was peaceful, even humorous. There were lectures, concerts, discussions. In the neighbouring houses, banners expressing solidarity were hung from the windows. But our expectations were probably too high, and the problems too complex.' Some groups protested for the Kurds, others for LGBTQI+ or the refugees from Syria. The demonstrators soon went their own way and dispersed.

An estimated three million people took part in around 5,000 protests in 2013. Even afterwards, resistance stirred, especially in the stadiums. A popular chant was, 'Everywhere is Taksim, everywhere is resistance'. Fans in Istanbul displayed anti-government banners and sang the praises of Mustafa Kemal, also known as Atatürk, Father of the Turks, the founder of the modern republic after the First World War. In Beşiktaş, Atatürk is visible everywhere: photos on house walls, quotes on walls, a huge banner in the stadium: 'The greatest Beşiktaşli.' Fans often drowned out the national anthem before matches with Atatürk chants.

But the AKP networks recovered from the Gezi protests – and wanted to prevent a flare-up. Beşiktaş fans stormed the pitch at a derby. The game was stopped, the club punished. Later it became known that the perpetrators had connections to the government. They called themselves '1453 Eagles', after Beşiktaş's heraldic animal and the year Christian Constantinople was conquered by the Ottomans. 'These people wanted to pit the Gezi demonstrators against each other and ruin our reputation,' says Bariş from Çarşi. Other fan groups also reported the presence of troublemakers with contacts to the AKP.

New stadiums for a conservative middle class

'For a long time, stadiums were among the hardest places to control,' says journalist Patrick Keddie, who has written a book on Turkish football, *The Passion: Football and the Story of Modern Turkey*. Keddie says: 'The state is looking with concern at the mobilisation of fans.' The government went on the offensive with the electronic ticketing system, officially as a preventative measure against fan violence. Hundreds of fans were temporarily arrested and 35 Beşiktaş supporters stood trial in 2015. The accusation: terrorism and plans for a *coup d'état*. 'We can't even overthrow our unpopular club leader,' joked one accused at the hearing. 'Then how are we going to bring down the government?' The charges were dropped, but many fans were intimidated in their daily lives, on the street or at work. They have since been cautious or stay away from the stadiums altogether. In 2014, the *Süper Lig*'s average attendance was 14,000, and it has dropped in the years since.

But politics has not disappeared from the stadiums. In July 2014, the Başakşehir stadium was inaugurated, in a conservative suburb of Istanbul. The then Prime Minister Erdoğan led a selection of politicians onto the field, scoring three goals in the opening match. His shirt number 12 is no longer used at the club. Erdoğan had already campaigned for Başakşehir's urban development as mayor of Istanbul in the 1990s. The club has advanced to the top of the *Süper Lig* in just a few years and won its first national championship in 2020. It is well connected with the Ministry of Sport, the Football Association and the sports media. Başakşehir wants to establish one of the most modern training centres. The construction of the stadium took only 16 months.

'The AKP government wants to build its own conservative middle class. One way to do this is through the construction industry,' says reporter Patrick Keddie. For decades, Turkey's economic elite had been guided by the secular values of the state's founder Atatürk. Erdoğan and his henchmen then transferred more construction contracts for airports, roads, mosques and stadiums to Islamic conservative firms from Anatolia. 'This is an easy way for politicians to spread their ideology,' says Keddie.

Until the currency collapse in 2018, Turkey had above-average economic growth. Since the beginning of the millennium, Keddie says, the construction of 30 stadiums in 27 cities has been set in motion, along with 1,000 halls and 400 other sports facilities. The government confidently announced its contribution of more than £1bn. But due to the bankruptcy of some companies, construction was sometimes delayed. In regions where Erdoğan is controversial, the AKP increased the pressure before elections; the American-Turkish blogger John Konuk Blasing wrote: 'The new stadiums should secure affection.' The social-democratic CHP, however, is taking a similar approach in those regions where it has the greatest influence.

Often the arenas are owned by the regional administrations. Especially in medium-sized cities, they have a special value far beyond sport, says Turkish sports journalist Volkan Ağır, who reports for *Deutsche Welle*, among others: 'Many old stadiums were located in the city centres. They were demolished and shopping centres and residential buildings were then built on the valuable plots of land. Above all, the AKP's networks benefit in the long run.' The new stadiums are built in conservative outer districts, which are also upgraded as a result. Residential complexes and cultural centres are often built next to the stadiums, and the tourist trade increases.

Twelve of the old stadiums were named after Atatürk and his companions. They had separated state and religion in Turkey after the collapse of the Ottoman Empire. There is hardly any trace of this in the new buildings. In Istanbul, the old Beşiktaş stadium was named after İsmet İnönü, a friend of Atatürk's; the new one bears the name of a mobile phone company. Erdoğan even decreed that stadiums could no longer be called arenas. That sounded too American to him.

Turkey has bid four times to host the European Championship, with no success. Most recently, in 2018, the 2024 European Championship was awarded to Germany. If Turkey had won the bid, the tournament would have taken place in ten stadiums, in conservative cities like Konya and Trabzon, but not in western-oriented Izmir. In Istanbul, two arenas were planned. The homes of the clubs with critical fans, like Beşiktaş and Fenerbahçe were not among them. And without the Euro? In an economic crisis, the operating costs of stadiums could become a burden. 'The debt of many companies is enormous,' says Felix Schmidt, long-time office manager of the German Friedrich Ebert Foundation in Istanbul. 'The consequences could be a wave of bankruptcies and higher unemployment.'

Nevertheless, the arenas are needed. In December 2016, the new stadium of Trabzon was inaugurated, in north-eastern Turkey on the Black Sea. An Imam read verses from the Quran in front of 40,000 spectators and commemorated the victims of terrorist attacks. He called for solidarity with Turkish soldiers on war missions, especially in Syria. Again and again, the television cameras showed Erdoğan in the VIP box. 'Such prayers are part of everyday life, but in a football stadium it was the first time,' says journalist Volkan Ağır. 'Religion and politics were brought together in front of a large audience.'

It was a new dimension in Turkish football history, which had never been free of political influences, writes author John

McManus in his book *Welcome to Hell? In Search of the Real Turkish Football*. British merchants and seafarers had imported the game to the Ottoman Empire in the 1870s, to port cities like Istanbul, Izmir and Thessaloniki. Minorities of the giant empire such as Greeks, Armenians and Italians quickly fell for football, but it was initially forbidden for Muslims. The autocratic Sultan Abdülhamid II believed the game would undermine moral values. And he was worried that strong men might conspire against the rulers in a team sport. The first Turkish club to rebel against this was the 'Black Stockings' around 1900, its English name intended to prevent a pitch ban.

By the early 20th century, the passion for football was unstoppable, writes McManus. After the defeat in the First World War, games were seen as patriotic events. Several clubs supported Mustafa Kemal's independence movement and smuggled arms during the war of liberation. Professionalisation with leagues began in the 1950s. Since the 1980s, politicians and entrepreneurs have taken advantage of football's reach. Regional administrations acquired clubs, mayors took over board positions, government officials intervened in promotions and relegations. Corruption and match-fixing led to heated debates.

It was a time when violence between fans also became commonplace. Time and again, fans were killed in the stadium environment. The Turkish sports sociologist Ahmet Talimciler put it this way in a study: 'Football is just a reflection of the growing violence in society, whether in traffic, at home or in schools. Fans used to want to try each other, now they want to destroy each other.'

Recep Tayyip Erdoğan, like an estimated three-quarters of all Turks, felt an early attachment to football. He played at a good level in his youth; a professional career seemed possible. His nickname was Imam Beckenbauer. As a politician, Erdoğan lets himself be seen in stadiums or players' dressing rooms, especially in Islamic-conservative cities like Trabzon, Konya and Bursa. The stadium from his Istanbul home district of Kasimpaşa bears his name. Representatives of the regional administrations and the mosques meet in the VIP stands. And sometimes they become places of diplomacy: in 2008, Abdullah Gül, then Turkish president, visited the first international match of his homeland in Armenia. Hundreds of people in Yerevan demanded that Turkey recognise the Armenian genocide of 1915/16.

Turkish fans could join riots with Azerbaijanis

During the 2021 European Championship, the Turkish national team played two group matches in Baku, the capital of Azerbaijan, an important partner of Erdoğan. A few months before, in autumn 2020, however, playing football in the region was almost unthinkable. Once again, Azerbaijan and Armenia were fighting over the region of Nagorno-Karabakh by force of arms. The autonomous region was for a long time inhabited by a majority of Christian Armenians. Under international law, however, it belongs to Azerbaijan, which is dominated by Muslims. Several hundred people were killed in the attacks.

Football was used as a platform for hostile propaganda. In the capital Baku, the Zira club raised a banner for Ilgar Burcaliyev. The former youth player had been drafted into the army and died in combat. Azerbaijani flags were draped over the stands. In Azerbaijan, teams wore jerseys with the inscription: 'Karabakh is Azerbaijan'. Players saluted cameras and spread military videos on social media, reports Yossi Medina. The Israeli writer for the website Babagol is an expert on the conflict in the Caucasus: 'Some players showed pictures of teenage war victims.'

The conflict between Armenians and Azerbaijanis has been simmering for more than 100 years. In Soviet times, they lived side by side instead of with each other, but there were hardly any outbreaks of violence. In the 1980s, Ağdam, one of the largest cities in the region, was home almost exclusively to Azerbaijanis. One of their most important symbols: the local football club.

During the disintegration of the Soviet Union, the dispute over Nagorno-Karabakh culminated in war. Armenia won and expelled almost all Azerbaijanis from the region. Ağdam was destroyed. The local club adopted the name Qarabağ in 1987, in reference to its home region. 'The footballers also fled to Baku,' says publicist Yossi Medina. 'They were without a permanent home there for a long time, but now they have their own stadium.' The roots in the symbolically important region of Nagorno-Karabakh ensure support for the Qarabağ club in Azerbaijan. The result: seven championship titles in a row recently.

Azerbaijan has created considerable economic growth with its oil and gas reserves. The authoritarian government wants to publicise this through sport, so it hosted the European Games in 2015 and, since 2016, has been home to a Formula 1 race. In the times of the Soviet Union, there had been some integration in football, even in Nagorno-Karabakh. Armenians played sporadically in predominantly Azerbaijani clubs – and vice versa. 'Today that would be completely unthinkable. There are no Armenians in the Azerbaijani league,' says Sascha Düerkop, who has travelled to the region several times. 'There were huge problems around the 2015 European Games: in the end, a tiny contingent from Armenia was allowed to participate under military protection.'

On the Armenian side, too, sport is part of a political strategy. A football association was founded in Nagorno-Karabakh in 2012. Because the region is not an independent state, it is denied FIFA membership. Instead, the federation joined CONIFA, the international football association for unrecognised states, minorities and regions. The first general secretary of the Nagorno-Karabakh Football Federation worked for the Armenian Foreign Ministry. 'The association was close to politics,' says Sascha Düerkop, co-founder of CONIFA. 'Football should make Nagorno-Karabakh more visible internationally, even away from the conflict.' In 2019, Nagorno-Karabakh hosted the European Championship of unrecognised states.

Attention is mainly focused on the big football stage. A special UEFA clause has prevented direct clashes between clubs and the national teams from Armenia and Azerbaijan. Nevertheless, there are chants of hate and hostile banners at international matches. When teams from Armenia or Azerbaijan play in European competitions, mobilisation of local communities is likely. Turkish fans might join riots with Azerbaijanis against Armenians. Some far-right groups are already showing solidarity with Armenia, as an alleged bastion of Christianity against Muslims.

Turkey is seen as an important party in the conflict. President Erdoğan refuses to address the Turkish genocide of Armenians more than 100 years ago. He stands by Azerbaijan. During EURO 2021 Erdoğan visited Azerbaijani President Ilham Aliyev around the matches in Baku. Together they wanted to symbolise political and economic strength.

A former icon becomes enemy of the state

In Turkey, too, many fan groups follow the symbolism of the president. They use symbols of Ottoman culture in their coats of arms and anthems. Ankaraspor in Ankara is leading the way. Opposing fans, in turn, use this to provoke the club in the capital city. They sing about the Battle of Ankara in 1402, when the Ottoman Empire suffered one of the heaviest defeats and the Sultan was captured: unique in history. 'Secular Turkey is decreasing and religious Turkey is increasing,' summarises Felix Schmidt of the Friedrich Ebert Foundation. 'In schools, the teaching of Islam is coming to the fore. More and more religious schools are also being founded. And that will produce a generation that is much closer to religion.'

The consequences? In September 2019, the German club Borussia Mönchengladbach hosted Başakşehir in the Europa League. Some fans from Germany were turned away with their flags outside the stadium because Mönchengladbach's city emblem includes a Christian cross. Max Eberl, then Borussia's sports director, commented: 'I don't know Turkey like that, I know the people in Turkey differently: they are nice and polite people. But if I may say so: this is police dictatorship.'

The Turkish authorities seem to want to restrict the opportunities for dissenters as much as possible. Possibly they have memories of 2011, when Galatasaray's new arena was opened in an Istanbul suburb. Erdoğan was booed and angrily left the stadium before kick-off. Since then, he has not been seen at matches of the big Istanbul clubs. Even the Turkish national team hardly ever plays home games in Istanbul any more, but rather in conservative strongholds like Konya, as it did in October 2015 against Iceland. Before kick-off, a minute of silence was planned for victims of an Islamist suicide bomber. Hundreds of spectators disturbed the silence with whistles, thanking the 'martyrs' and praising Allah as the 'only God'.

The social climate has intensified, especially since the failed coup attempt in 2016 and the state of emergency that followed. Even in football, Erdoğan only distinguishes between friends and enemies. Among the friends is Yildirim Demirören, who was appointed president of the Turkish Football Association in 2012. The entrepreneur, whose conglomerate also manages high-circulation newspapers, spoke out in favour of Erdoğan in the 2017 constitutional referendum. Current and former national players such as Arda Turan, Burak Yilmaz and Ridvan Dilmen did the same. In this way, Erdoğan secured even greater political influence. The powers of the parliament were curtailed.

Other supporters hold back on words – and let pictures do the talking. The long-time German national player Mesut Özil met Erdoğan several times. The most discussed meeting took place in London in May 2018, a few weeks before the World Cup in Russia and the presidential election in Turkey. In addition to Özil, German international İlkay Gündoğan and Turkish international Cenk Tosun presented one of their jerseys to Erdoğan. After a controversial debate that extended beyond Germany's early World Cup failure, Özil resigned from the national team. Erdoğan described the move as patriotic: 'I kiss his eyes.' In Devrek, Özil's parents' hometown on the Black Sea, a poster of Özil in a German jersey was replaced by the picture with Erdoğan.

In June 2019, Özil got married in a luxury hotel in Istanbul, with Erdoğan as one of his guests of honour. Erdoğan had already been best man at the wedding of national player Arda Turan. His presence at Özil's wedding triggered strong reactions in Germany, also because of a song that was played at the ceremony: 'Ölürüm Türkiyem' by Mustafa Yıldızdoğan is considered an anthem of the far-right, the title translates as 'I die for you, my Turkey'. At Özil's wedding, Erdoğan is also said to have spoken out against contraception. German politician Cem Özdemir commented: 'Erdoğan interferes in all areas of life. Obviously, he needs such appearances, because his popularity in the country is declining.' One indication: the election of CHP politician Ekrem İmamoğlu as Istanbul's mayor in 2019.

There has long been speculation about how close Özil and other footballers actually are to Erdoğan. The Turkish-born basketball player Enes Kanter attempted to explain in an interview with the English *Daily Mail*. Kanter has been playing in the North American professional league NBA since 2011. He professed his support for the Islamic preacher Fethullah Gülen, who is considered a central enemy of Erdoğan and has been living in exile in the USA since 1999. Again and again, Kanter sharply criticised the Turkish head of state, for example 'as the Hitler of our century'.

The Turkish government cancelled Kanter's citizenship in 2017. His father was arrested twice in Turkey, Kanter says. His family broke away from him, his sponsors were put under massive pressure from Turkey. Kanter was described as a terrorist by Turkish politicians and put on the wanted list. He avoids travelling abroad for fear of being extradited to Turkey. Even in New York, the Turkish consulate-general has been making moves against charity events involving Kanter. He told the *Daily Mail*: 'If Özil and Gündogan presented a different view of things from the prevailing public opinion in Turkey at the moment – they would meet the same fate as me.'

Or like Hakan Şükür, Galatasaray icon and record top scorer of the Turkish national team. Şükür, who entered parliament for the AKP in 2011, left the party in 2013. He is considered a supporter of the Gülen movement, which is regarded as a terrorist organisation in Turkey. In 2016, Şükür was indicted for allegedly insulting the president and was put on notice. He has been in the USA since 2015. Under pressure from the sports ministry, his membership of Galatasaray was revoked in 2017, against the majority vote of the fans. Şükür told the German newspaper *Welt am Sonntag* that he had to work as an Uber driver in Washington. Much of his property in Turkey has been confiscated, and potential tenants of his properties are being intimidated.

The anti-terror police investigate a Kurdish club

But the 'enemies' mainly include less prominent people, young men like Rızgar. It is a cold day in February 2019. Rızgar is tired, he leans on the table with both arms, for a moment he closes his eyes. In front of him in the VIP room of SV Babelsberg in the German city of Potsdam near Berlin, sit around 100 guests. They are watching a film with violent scenes, many of the audience seem disturbed. The clip shows the everyday life of Rızgar and his friends, the fans of Amedspor. The club has become a symbol of Kurdish identity in Turkey. But the price is high.

Chants of hatred against Amedspor blast from the loudspeakers. Opposing fans call it a club of 'terrorists' and 'traitors to the fatherland'. They threaten violence, throw bottles on the pitch, wave the Turkish flag demonstratively. And the police watch or participate. This hatred is state-sponsored, says Rızgar, a formative head of the group Direniş, in English 'resistance'. 'The government wants to suppress Kurdish culture. Parties, media, our language: everything is criminalised. But Amedspor is a bastion against racism.'

In Turkey, probably no ethnic group has to struggle with as many problems as the Kurds. The language and culture of the 15 million Kurds is being pushed back. Time and again, state authorities equate them with the underground organisation the Kurdistan Workers' Party (PKK). The hatred is also unleashed in football. But some fans are fighting back: Direniş, for example, collected donations on their 2019 tour of Germany. More than 600 guests attended the six events.

The second division club Amedspor is rooted in south-eastern Turkey, in Diyarbakır, the unofficial capital of Kurdistan. This is how the Kurds refer to their territories, which extend into four countries, including Syria, Iran and Iraq. Amedspor has borne its Kurdish name since 2015, when the decades-old conflict was in an easing phase. Erdoğan and the Kurdish freedom movement were moving towards each other. Diyarbakır was administered by the left-wing People's Democratic Party (HDP). Thus, Amedspor received better promotion – and its fans confidently displayed the Kurdish colours of red, green and yellow again. The name Direniş was granted to their group by the football association, several requests had been rejected before.

But the situation changed after the coup attempt in 2016 and the state of emergency. In several cities, including Diyarbakır, hundreds of mayors and deputies were arrested and replaced by governors loyal to the regime. The new regional government dropped Amedspor. Funding was frozen and sponsors intimidated. Employees of the club lost their jobs. The team was denied hotel rooms at away matches. Fans are no longer allowed to display flags in Kurdish. Some stadium announcers refuse to pronounce the Kurdish club name. 'Meanwhile, our matches are accompanied by 1,500 police officers,' says Rızgar. 'At checkpoints, our flags are confiscated. Once our club board in the VIP stand was damaged.'

The situation came to a head in 2016 when the Turkish army advanced against the PKK with tanks and snipers. Hundreds died in battles in Kurdish towns like Cizre, Silopi and Diyarbakir. At that time, Amedspor attracted attention in the sporting arena, becoming the first third-division team to reach the quarter-finals of the Turkish Cup. German-born Amedspor player Deniz Naki dedicated this success to Kurdish victims. He was banned for 12 games for 'ideological propaganda' and later for life. Naki had to leave the club and Turkey to avoid a prison sentence.

The state intensified the repression against Kurds, with restricted areas, curfews, arbitrary arrests. Direniş wanted to emphasise in banners and chants that not every Kurd was a terrorist; one of their slogans at the time was, 'Don't let the children die, but go to the stadium.' Afterwards, several fans were arrested, says Vedat, a member of Direniş: 'The anti-terror police investigated our club premises. And we have not been allowed to attend away matches since then.'

During the fighting, parts of the old city of Diyarbakır were destroyed. Tens of thousands of people fled the region, going to Germany, including Vedat. But even there they have to be careful. At the beginning of 2018, Deniz Naki's car was shot at, and he keeps receiving threats. But especially in Germany, Kurdish players and fans experience a lot of support, through donations, stadium banners and petitions on the internet. 'We long for normality,' says Vedat. Their opponents say that aggression usually comes from Amedspor; for example in March 2019, at the match against Sakaryaspor, Amedspor player Mansur Çalar allegedly attacked opponents with a razor blade. Heated debates followed. Amedspor spoke of a conspiracy and accused the opponent of 'slander with unfounded allegations'. Calar was banned for four years.

The salute of players is taken for granted

The next stage of the escalation came in October 2019. In 'Operation Peace Spring', the Turkish army advanced in northern Syria against the Kurdish militia YPG, the Syrian arm of the PKK. Many Western politicians called the offensive illegal under international law. At the same time, the Turkish national team was playing Albania and France in the European Championship qualifiers. At both games, several players saluted and the Turkish fans chanted: 'The greatest soldiers are our soldiers.'

Almost all Turkish newspapers reproduced the military salutes on their front pages. 'Stand to attention Europe!' wrote the sports paper *Fanatik*. In the German newspaper *Frankfurter Rundschau*, journalist Timur Tinç gave the salute some context: 'In times of war, the nation stands together, it has always been like that in Turkey. And the louder the international criticism gets, the closer the country moves together.' But some national players, including Düsseldorf professionals Kaan Ayhan and Kenan Karaman, rejected the military gesture, at least against France. Tinç commented that Turkish players with German roots were caught between two stools: 'If they remain silent or refuse to support Turkish soldiers, they are branded as traitors to the fatherland by Turks.'

The German national players Emre Can and İlkay Gündoğan also felt this. On social media they 'liked' a photo of the military salute posted by player Cenk Tosun, but after great outrage they withdrew the tag. FC St Pauli's Cenk Şahin took a clearer stance, writing on Instagram: 'We are by the side of our heroic military and armies. Our prayers are with you.' Because of this and 'further misconduct', the club released him. This, too, probably contributed to the controversies in the German-Turkish community spilling over into amateur football. In the following days, numerous footballers saluted, others criticised the gesture and showed solidarity with Kurdish demonstrations in German cities.

In Turkey, on the other hand, saluting was taken for granted. Hostility and the cult of masculinity mean that fewer and fewer liberal people go to the stadiums. This is highlighted by a visit to Kadiköy, a district on the Asian side of Istanbul. Between flea markets, bookshops and music shops, the rustic pubs show Fenerbahçe matches. 'We hold back on political messages, even on social media, people are afraid of the government,' says Sener from Vamos Bien. The left-wing Fenerbahçe fan group has boycotted Turkish stadiums since the introduction of the electronic ticketing system. Instead, they travel abroad to European matches or attend basketball games.

In 2014, Vamos Bien still had 100 active members; now there are fewer and fewer. Groups like Vamos Bien used to publish messages of support for arrested scientists and journalists, but that is too delicate for them now. 'For a long time, everything revolved around Fenerbahçe,' says Sener. 'We miss that time very much.' He is continuing his studies in Germany, other friends have also left Turkey. They wish for a football where freedom of expression is not punishable.

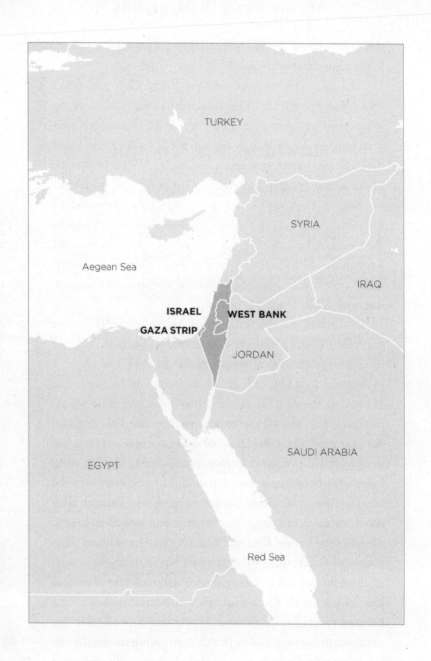

Instrument of Control

In Israel, the national team is considered one of the few symbols of harmony between Jews and Arabs. In Palestine, the national team is seen as a symbol of statehood. But often an escalation in the conflict in the Middle East is also reflected in stadiums. Among the fans on both sides, the lines of conflict run between secular, conservative and radical groups. But some players and projects show a rapprochement is possible.

'FREE PALESTINE'. With this writing on their T-shirts, the players of Fenerbahce Istanbul prepared for their game in May 2021. In other countries, too, in Scotland, Qatar and Chile, players and fans showed Palestinian symbols. On social media, some professional footballers showed solidarity with the Palestinians. For example: the Algerian Riyad Mahrez of Manchester City and the Frenchman Paul Pogba of Manchester United.

Mohamed Salah's statement received particular attention. On Twitter, the Egyptian Liverpool striker posted the following message: 'I call on all world leaders, including the Prime Minister of the country that has been my home for the last four years, to do everything in their power to ensure that the violence and killing of innocent people stops immediately. Enough is enough.' Salah refrained from using terms like

Israel, Palestine and Gaza in his statement. Instead, he showed an older photo of himself in front of the Dome of the Rock, a holy site of Islam in Jerusalem. Hamza Choudhury and Wesley Fofana of Leicester City went one step further. After their FA Cup Final win in 2021, they waved a Palestinian flag.

In the spring of 2021, the conflict in the Middle East had escalated once again. Israel launched a military offensive against Hamas in the Gaza Strip. The radical Islamic organisation fired rockets back. More than 200 people were killed. The conflict was – as always – controversial, and it had prominent supporters on both sides – including in football.

Munas Dabbur also spoke out. On Instagram, the TSG Hoffenheim striker posted a photo of the Al-Aqsa Mosque, a holy site of Islam in Jerusalem, accompanied by a quote from the Quran: 'Do not think that God will ignore the deeds of evil people. He will only postpone their judgement until the day when the gaze is frozen.' Dabbur grew up in Nazareth and is considered Israel's most successful national player with Arab roots.

Quite a few players, fans and officials criticised Dabbur's statement, reports Israeli journalist Yossi Medina of the website Babagol: 'Some members of parliament called for his exclusion from the national team. But we are not surprised by this development. After every escalation there is political commentary in football, sometimes with strong reactions, sometimes not.' During one match, former player Frédéric Kanouté lifted up his playing shirt to reveal a T-shirt supporting Gaza. Many people in Israel were then against Kanouté for a few days. 'But soon it was all forgotten,' says Medina.

'Athletic people to defend the country'

Around 20 per cent of Israelis are Arabs. On average, they have a higher standard of living than the Palestinians in the West Bank and Gaza Strip. But compared to the Jewish majority, they are disadvantaged when it comes to education and jobs. According to government figures, almost half of Arab families in Israel lived in poverty in 2016, compared to 13 per cent of Jewish families. The 2018 Nation-State Law declared Israel the 'national home of the Jewish people' and Hebrew the sole national language.

Football is a different story. In recent years, the number of Arab-based teams in the Israeli game has increased. The Israeli national team in particular is regarded as a stage for peaceful coexistence. Recently, there have been five or six Arab players in their starting 11. The most prominent: Munas Dabbur.

But this is not exclusively a positive sign. 'Many Israelis who see themselves as liberal use football to ease their guilty consciences. They can show others and themselves how equal Israel is,' says sociologist Tamir Sorek, who researches football in Israel. 'Many Israelis are happy to see Arab players who quietly submit. But when the players criticise structures, that's the end of tolerance.' For Tamir Sorek, football in Israel is not only a place of encounter, but also a disguised instrument of control by the majority over the minority. A system that has grown over decades.

In the first half of the 20th century, Jewish and English teams had initially dominated football in the British Mandate territory of Palestine. The clubs' followings were segregated along sectarian lines, writes Palestinian sports historian Issam Khalidi in his book *One Hundred Years of Football in Palestine*. Many Arabs of the Muslim faith resisted the 'western import' of football. The first football association in the region, founded in 1928, initially named its team Land of Israel and used Zionist symbols. Arab players also played no role in the qualifiers for the 1934 and 1938 World Cups.

Due to the immigration of Jewish refugees from Europe during the Second World War, many Arabs felt marginalised. Muslim politicians took teachers and athletes to task in a 1946 appeal: 'As soldiers, you should be active on the sports field for many years.' And preachers in mosques added: 'Remember that you are forming an army of well-educated and athletic people who will defend the country against the demons of colonialism.'

The establishment of Israel in 1948 and the war of independence against neighbouring Arab states put a stop to Palestinian sports culture. The Arabs who did not flee Israel stayed away from state sports organisations. Issam Khalidi describes the fine line walked by the Israeli authorities in the 1950s and 1960s. On the one hand, they wanted to limit the founding of Arab sports clubs because they feared a mobilisation of young men against the state. On the other hand, they tolerated tournaments in Arab villages because they saw football as less threatening than parties or mosque communities.

The 1967 Six-Day War between Israel and its neighbours intensified the conflict between Jews and Arabs. Many Palestinians also interpreted footballers as 'resistance fighters', such as the first Arab professional in the Israeli league, Hassan Boustouni at Maccabi Haifa. Rifaat Turk provided the breakthrough. He was the first Arab national player to represent Israel at the 1976 Olympics. Turk was regularly insulted by Jewish nationalists, even by players like Shlomo Kirat, who was expelled from the national team because of it.

With the commercialisation of football, the boundaries blurred. The big clubs from Tel Aviv, Jerusalem and Haifa extended their search for talent to Arab communities. And by 1998, four of the 16 second division teams came from majority Arab cities. But there were setbacks: During the so-called Second Intifada, violence erupted between Palestinians and Israelis from 2000 onwards. Football matches in Arab villages in Israel were cancelled or overseen by the police.

The confrontations dragged on. On 18 May 2004, Israeli troops stormed a Palestinian refugee camp in the Gaza Strip because they suspected terrorists were there. On that day, FC Bnei Sakhnin from northern Israel became the first Arab club to win the national cup. Israeli Prime Minister Ariel Sharon interpreted the victory as a symbol of diversity. And Yasser Arafat, President of the Palestinian Authority, spoke of 'pride for the Arab nation'.

Of the 30,000 inhabitants in Sakhnin, 95 per cent are Arabs. The captain of FC Bnei was Abbas Suan. The midfielder of Muslim faith also caused a stir in the Israeli national team in 2005. He signed advertising contracts, was featured in films and songs, and so FC Bnei also aroused the interest of Jewish fans. 'Bnei and Suan have performed a miracle for Palestinian pride,' writes James M. Dorsey in his book *The Turbulent World of Middle East Soccer*. Abbas Suan illustrates the complex identities in Israel. He calls himself a Palestinian because he has many relatives and friends in the Arab world. And he calls himself Israeli because of his nationality and because of his connections in Jewish milieus. Nevertheless, Suan did not want to sing the Israeli anthem 'Hatikwa' as a national player, because it only emphasises Jewishness.

Some groups felt provoked by Abbas Suan: first and foremost the fans of Beitar Jerusalem. 'Suan, you don't represent us' was written on one of their banners during a match against FC Bnei. They also chanted, 'We hate all Arabs'. At Beitar, many supporters are proud of their club's roots as a rallying point for resistance against the British almost 100 years ago. In 1940, a passage in the club's anthem read, 'With blood and sweat, a race is established by and for us'. Later, in the then long socialist state of Israel, Beitar was a meeting place for nationalists. In 1976 the club won the cup for the first time, and in 1987 the championship. Beitar helped mobilise right-wing voters and this continued through 1977 when, in

Menachem Begin, a conservative became Israeli prime minister for the first time, and during the term of Benjamin Netanyahu, who became prime minister again in 2009.

Beitar fans regularly sing racist and anti-Arab songs, for which they accept fines and point deductions. Many of them even reject Jewish immigrants from Eastern Europe. The most radical group around Beitar calls itself 'La Familia', in reference to the Italian mafia. Some of its members have cultivated contacts with Kach, a far-right movement in Israel that has since been banned. They disrupted a minute's silence for Prime Minister Yitzhak Rabin, assassinated in 1995, who had been a strong supporter of the peace process. After Beitar announced the signing of two Chechen players of Muslim faith in 2013, fans set fire to a club office. Other groups from Jerusalem, Haifa and Netanya sharply criticised this behaviour. Fans of Hapoel Tel Aviv chanted against Beitar: 'Give Jerusalem to Jordan, there is nothing worthwhile there anymore.'

Football as a sign of statehood

The hatred of Beitar makes many officials and politicians in the Palestinian territories feel vindicated in their actions. Probably the most prominent representative is Jibril Rajoub, president of the Palestinian Football Association. In 2015, Rajoub applied to FIFA for Israel's exclusion. *Vice Sports* magazine quoted Rajoub as saying: 'I think that the Israelis should no longer exploit the Holocaust thing – which, of course, no one in their right mind can condone – in order to be able to inflict the same on others. We Palestinians suffer, we are humiliated. We are subjected to a racist policy on the part of Israel that does not even stop at sport! I say: those who do not grant us the right to play football without obstacles and harassment will never recognise a separate, independent Palestinian state alongside the state of Israel. Let us and our children just play football.'

After long mediation, Jibril Rajoub withdrew his application to FIFA. The multi-functionalist has learned that he can use sport to generate extra attention for his criticism of Israel. Rajoub, who is also head of the National Olympic Committee, has long been a member of the Fatah party. Under its leader, Yasser Arafat, he was head of security for the Palestinian Authority, then National Security Commissioner from 2003.

Jibril Rajoub fondly remembers 26 October 2008, a historic day for the Palestinian Territories, which are not recognised as a state by the United Nations. For more than ten years, the Palestinian national team had played its home games abroad for security reasons, but on that day it celebrated its home debut against Jordan. Almost 7,000 spectators watched the 1-1 draw in Al-Ram, a small town north-east of Jerusalem, the stadium was named after the Palestinian nationalist Faisal al Husseini. Present at the premiere was the then FIFA President Sepp Blatter as well as journalists and non-governmental organisations. 'Palestine has joined international organisations in culture and sport,' says political scientist Danyel Reiche from Georgetown University in Doha.

Palestine has participated in the Olympic Games since 1996 and has been a FIFA member since 1998. 'For the Palestinians, this is a sign of statehood,' says Reiche. 'In sport they get recognition that they are otherwise denied.' But the breakthrough only came from 2006 onwards through the influence of politician Jibril Rajoub. The federation's annual budget and staff have grown enormously since then. Stadiums and training facilities have been built, also with the support of other Arab states.

But the development has reached its limits. According to Jibril Rajoub, the government of Israel is to blame, especially its border controls on the Gaza Strip and its settlement policy in the West Bank. Time and again, Palestinian players have been prevented from leaving the country. As a result, Palestine was unable to participate in some international matches. In July 2019, the Palestinian Cup Final had to be postponed at short notice. Quite a few professionals ended their careers prematurely. In 2009, striker Mahmoud Sarsak was arrested by Israeli officials on his way to training, on suspicion of terrorism. He was kept in 'administrative detention' – without charge. Sarsak went on hunger strike and was released after a campaign in 2012, backed by US philosopher Noam Chomsky and former French professional Éric Cantona, among others.

'The players can't move freely,' says publicist James M. Dorsey, who has been observing football in the Middle East for years. 'The separate leagues in Gaza and the West Bank symbolise the division of the Palestinian movement, geographically, but also politically, because they are under different claims to power.' Whether arresting Palestinian players, searching their football association or preventing them from sending material, Israeli security agencies always describe this as a prevention of terror.

Sports fields named after suicide bombers

British author Nicholas Blincoe analyses the tension between Israel and Palestine using football as an example, in his book *More Noble Than War*. Blincoe also looks at a temporary rapprochement: Palestinian athletes could call an emergency hotline in case of delays at checkpoints. National players stayed overnight at training facilities to save time. International donations supported the development of Palestinian football. But federation head Rajoub saw no progress. He opposed Israeli clubs in settlement areas, the legal situation of which is internationally disputed.

Rajoub's statements have also received support from other countries, such as some members of the European Parliament. But many Israeli politicians call him a terrorist. As a youth,

Rajoub had thrown a grenade at Israeli soldiers. During his several years in prison, he organised protests and hunger strikes, reports the Palestinian philosopher Sari Nusseibeh in his book *Once Upon a Time There Was a Country. A Life in Palestine.*

For his involvement in the first Intifada starting in 1987, a violent uprising by Palestinians against Israel, Jibril Rajoub was imprisoned again. During the Second Intifada, in 2001, his house was shelled by Israeli forces. In 2013, Rajoub told a television station, 'If we had nuclear weapons, we would use them'. He also reportedly accepted that sports fields and tournaments in the Palestinian territories were named after suicide bombers.

In June 2018, Argentina planned a Test match against Israel in Jerusalem. The status of the city is a central point of contention in the conflict between Israel and Palestine. The mood at the time was charged; a few weeks earlier the US embassy had moved from Tel Aviv to Jerusalem. Jibril Rajoub called for Lionel Messi jerseys to be burned. The match was cancelled and Rajoub was banned by FIFA for a year. Moreover, some of his players are said to have violently attacked Israeli police officers in recent years.

The disadvantages of the Palestinian population have been documented many times in terms of care, education and mobility. This is also reflected in their participation in society.

In football, talents need long-term support, finds Sameh Masri of the Palestinian non-governmental organisation Sport for Life: 'Ten years ago, our national team was still dependent on players from other countries. They had Palestinian roots but lived in Lebanon, Chile or the USA. It is important that we provide regular training for our young people. It strengthens the community.' Activists like Sameh Masri rely on international support. But as is so often the case in global development cooperation, projects cannot always rule out the possibility that the funding is also being used to support fundamentalists.

On the Palestinian side, too, football offers a forum for different currents: for example, Fatah in the West Bank or the radical Islamic Hamas in the Gaza Strip. Within this spectrum, a few personalities received broad support. The aforementioned Abbas Suan, who was with FC Bnei Sakhnin until 2010, campaigned for an independent state of Palestine and was antagonised for it. Rifaat Turk, the first Arab player in the Israeli national team, had similar experiences in the 1970s and 1980s. Turk won the championship with Hapoel Tel Aviv in 1981. He mediated between Jews and Muslims, joined the left-wing Meretz party and became deputy mayor of Tel Aviv in 2003. In football, Palestinians can gain the acceptance of Israeli majority society more quickly, writes Jewish publicist and human rights activist Uri Davis, 'regardless of the fact that they have been disadvantaged for decades'.

Israel was isolated in international sport for decades

Among Israel's Jewish majority, however, the long exclusion has also been etched into the memory of many representatives of football. 'In sport, states can easily and quickly express their rejection of Israel,' says German sports and cultural scientist Robin Streppelhoff, who has been working on sports issues surrounding Israel for more than ten years. 'In Lebanon, the law was passed as early as the mid-1950s that athletes were not allowed to compete against Israelis.'

In 1955, the football federation of the young state of Israel had asked to be admitted to European competition structures, but FIFA and UEFA refused. Again and again, Arab states boycotted matches against Israel or demanded that they be transferred to neutral countries. Time and again, Israeli delegations were excluded from sporting events, for example from the 1962 Asian Games in Jakarta. 'In football, FIFA delayed a clear position for a long time,' says Robin Streppelhoff.

For years, Israel had to switch structures for qualifying rounds, between Asia, Oceania and even South America.

The Six-Day War in 1967 and the Yom Kippur War in 1973 intensified Israel's isolation in the Middle East. This was also evident in sport, as German sports historian Manfred Lämmer shows in his book *German-Israeli Football Friendship*. At the 1974 Asian Games in Tehran, representatives from Kuwait and Iraq organised protests against Israel, with the People's Republic of China, Pakistan and North Korea joining in. Their athletes refused to compete against Israeli opponents. In the mixed doubles tennis final, the Chinese team idly conceded gold to Israel.

Also in 1974, two years after the attack on Israeli athletes at the Munich Olympics, the Asian Football Confederation (AFC) expelled the Jewish state. Opposition grew in other sports as well. Before the 1978 Asian Games, Arab investors offered support to hosts Bangkok. Their condition: the exclusion of Israeli athletes. This is what happened, officially because of the high security costs for the Israeli team. Manfred Lämmer writes that countries like Japan also followed this policy of exclusion, their dependence on Arab oil exports was too strong.

FIFA threatened the Asian Football Confederation with suspension, but in the end the newly elected president of the federation, João Havelange, did not want to risk a conflict with Arab countries. Applications for Israel to join the European UEFA were rejected under pressure from the socialist Eastern Bloc countries. 'It was above all the West German Football Federation (DFB) with its president Hermann Neuberger who stood up for Israel,' says Robin Streppelhoff. Günter Schneider, president of the East German Football Association of the GDR between 1976 and 1983, did not want Israel in the European structures, out of concern for the 'unity of UEFA'. Only in 1991, after the collapse of the Soviet Union, was it possible to get the association accepted into UEFA. Since 1994, Israel has been a full member and is now a permanent fixture in European competitions, even hosting the European Under-21 Championship in 2013.

But in world sport, events are increasingly taking place in countries that are hostile to Israel. These states have less and less to fear from democracies. Often they even feel legitimised by European contacts. Moreover, Qatar, for example, has invested billions from state funds and state-related organisations in European football, especially in Paris Saint-Germain. FC Bayern has already been to a training camp in Doha and has partnerships with the airport there and with the airline Qatar Airways.

Publicly, no top European club would admit to foregoing the signing of Israeli players for fear of dwindling revenues in the Arab markets. On several occasions, however, Israeli professionals were not granted visas for their clubs' training camps in the United Arab Emirates: in 2014 Vitesse Arnhem travelled to Abu Dhabi without Dan Mori, in 2017 Red Bull Salzburg without Munas Dabbur. Eintracht Frankfurt went a different way in 2017. The club looked for an alternative in Spain. The Emirates relented and allowed Taleb Tawatha to enter the country. All three cases made international headlines.

Hatred of Israel is particularly pronounced in Iran. Bibras Natcho also felt this. When the then captain of the Israeli national team moved from ZSKA Moscow to Olympiacos Piraeus in August 2018, it became a political issue. The Greek club also had Ehsan Hajsafi under contract, a top performer for the Iranian national team. In the Islamic Republic, leading political and clerical forces do not recognise Israel's right to exist. Since the 1979 revolution, Iranian athletes have been banned from competing against Israelis. Never before have players from the hostile countries been on the same team. After Natcho's transfer to Olympiacos, religious leaders in Iran were

122

furious. A goal celebration of their compatriot with an Israeli? In their eyes: treason.

Ehsan Hajsafi has been criticised by the clerics before, as has his national team-mate Masud Shodjaei. Both had played in the Europa League qualifiers against Maccabi Tel Aviv in 2017 with their then club Panionios Athens. They were banned from 'Team Melli', as the national team is called by Iranians, due to political pressure. Only after fan protests was their exclusion lifted. In sporting terms, they were indispensable for the 2018 World Cup in Russia. But in the shadow of this debate, anti-Semitic comments were dismissed worldwide. Hardly any region is as marked by tensions as the Middle East. Football is often a magnifying glass for moods, fears and conspiracy theories.

Election campaign in Beitar's stadium

Is there hope? At the age of 27, Dia Saba became a historic figure. In 2020, the Israeli international footballer moved from Guangzhou in China to the Al Nasr club in Dubai, the largest city in the United Arab Emirates. Dia Saba was the first prominent sportsman from the Jewish state to play in an Arab league. The basis was a historic agreement: Israel established diplomatic relations with the Emirates and with Bahrain.

'For the first time, Israel will be open to investment from the Middle East,' said then Israeli Prime Minister Benjamin Netanyahu. Israeli football has also been discussing possible investors from the Emirates, for example at Hapoel Tel Aviv. The club, founded in 1927, has roots in the labour movement, and its supporters look back on a long history of cooperation between Jews and Arabs. 'There could be friendly matches between the two countries,' says Middle East expert James M. Dorsey. 'For the Emirates, football is a kind of soft power. They seem to want to soften anti-Arab attitudes in Israel, including in the complicated relationship with the Palestinians.'

The extent of this change is likely to be demonstrated by another club. Beitar Jerusalem had been formed in the 1930s in British Mandate Palestine to resist the occupiers. After the founding of the state of Israel in 1948, Beitar established itself as a network of Jewish nationalists. As the only professional club in Israel, Beitar has not signed an Arab-Muslim player to date. Can the rapprochement between Israel and the Emirates change that?

Moshe Hogeg wants to try. The IT entrepreneur has been Beitar's owner since 2018 and is looking for investors in the Emirates. In doing so, he is supporting the course of the Israeli government. 'In right-wing political circles, Beitar is an important factor,' says Israeli journalist Felix Tamsut. 'Every election campaign includes a visit to a Beitar home game.' Benjamin Netanyahu has met fellow members of his Likud party several times in the VIP stand. President Reuven Rivlin used to be president of the club.

But not all fans support the new contacts in the Arab world. Beitar's fan group La Familia is one of the most influential far-right structures in Israel. In 2018, supporters praised Donald Trump, the US president, who announced the relocation of the American embassy from Tel Aviv to Jerusalem. In 2019, Beitar signed Ali Mohamed from Niger. La Familia demanded that the Christian player drop his Muslim-sounding name.

Beitar's owner Moshe Hogeg positions himself against racism like few other officials. He threatened hostile fans with charges and claims for damages. By opening up to Arab investors, he wants to strengthen seemingly moderate and less audible groups. Hogeg has received encouragement for this even in liberal circles.

'For us, money doesn't matter, principles do,' La Familia countered on Facebook. 'We want to remember that Jerusalem is a holy city for Jews and that Beitar is the only team in the world that has the Jewish menorah as its symbol.' This refers to one of the most important symbols of Judaism. La Familia ended its statement with a biblical battle cry calling on soldiers to fight for the Jewish people. The group often justifies itself by referring to the exclusion that Jewish athletes have experienced since the founding of Israel.

Jewish players feel threatened every weekend

There are still several states in Asia that clearly reject Israel: Iran, Lebanon and Malaysia. But Israel also has powerful allies like China and India. And in the Arab world, too, more governments are following a pragmatic course. Publicist James Dorsey believes, 'If there was a new vote in the Asian Football Confederation to admit Israel, Israel could win that vote.' The Israeli team has qualified for the World Cup only once, in 1970, but never for a European Championship. Their chances would probably be better at the Asian Cup.

'Football can unite us. Let's play!' With these words, the Israel Football Association headlined a message on social media in 2020. Its logo was framed by the emblems of the Emirates and Bahrain. It was accompanied by the word 'peace' in Arabic, Hebrew and English. It is likely that symbolism like this is coordinated with the great power Saudi Arabia, says scholar Danyel Reiche: 'All four countries have the same goal: isolating the common enemy, Iran.' Reiche does not consider it out of the question that Saudi Arabia will also establish diplomatic relations with Israel in the coming years.

Around 20 per cent of the Israeli population are Arabs. For decades, however, football has been centred in the majority Jewish cities of Jerusalem, Tel Aviv and Haifa. A central role in future partnerships with the Emirates is likely to lie with the City Football Group. This Abu Dhabi group is known for investing in Manchester City. But beyond sporting success, it pursues three major goals with football, says sports economics expert Simon Chadwick. First, the promotion of talent, in locations such as Lommel in Belgium or Girona in Spain. Second, networking in the entertainment industry, in locations like New York and Mumbai.

'The third pillar aims at political and trade relations,' says Chadwick. 'This is clearly illustrated by the Chinese location in Chengdu. And it's quite possible that in two or three years another site will be added in Israel.' Israel is touting itself as a centre for technological innovation and was also a guest at the 2021/2022 World Expo in Dubai, home to Emirates, the largest state-owned airline which is among the most influential sponsors in football, and perhaps might become involved in Israel at some point.

Many politicians in the Palestinian territories do not want to imagine that. According to them, Arab investments in Israel would endorse the settlement policy in the West Bank. 'The Emirates are not only betraying the Palestinians, but also their own roots,' said Jibril Rajoub, head of Palestinian football. Rajoub criticised Israeli security measures as harassment, such as the arrest of Palestinian athletes in the Gaza Strip or the search of his association's premises. In 2015, Rajoub welcomed the Emirates national team with the Palestinian footballers in the Jerusalem suburb of Al Ram. More than 10,000 spectators cheered and railed together, including against Israel. Will the Emirates now be able to mediate between Israelis and Palestinians in football? At least it no longer seems to be an illusion.

It is probably only a matter of time before the situation in the Middle East escalates again. And that also has consequences for the diaspora. Often football highlights those facets of anti-Semitism that are disguised as brutal criticism of Israel. Sometimes they are violent, as in August 2015, when hooligans from ZSKA Sofia threw bottles at players from the Israeli club FS Ashdod and chased them across the pitch. Or as in July 2014, when 20 youths, mostly of Turkish origin, stormed a match between the Israeli team Maccabi Haifa and their French opponents OSC Lille near Salzburg.

Similar scenes were repeated in the spring of 2021, after the escalation in the Gaza Strip. Anti-Semitic shouts could be heard at demonstrations in German cities against Israel's policies: 'A bomb on Israel' or 'Jews out of Palestine'. The football clubs of the Jewish-based sports movement Maccabi hear such hate slogans almost every weekend. Sometimes their players are threatened with knives, often the police have to come. They have got used to the fact that their hobby is dangerous.

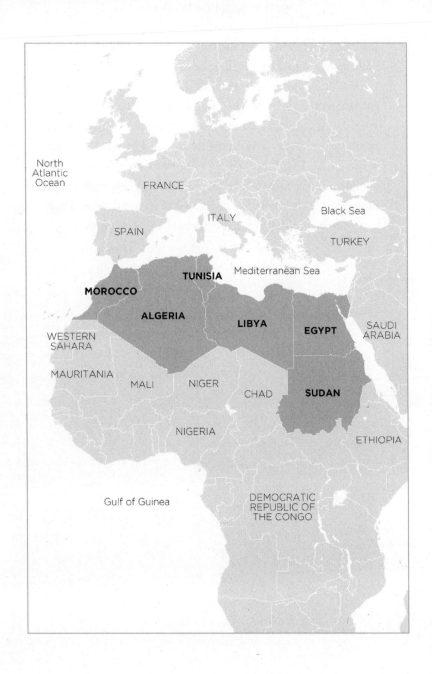

Playground of the Generals

For more than 100 years, Arab rulers have used stadiums for propaganda, including in Egypt. In the new millennium, ultras in Cairo developed a protest culture that played a role in the 2011 revolution. This was followed by a split in the movement and violence with many fatalities. In the meantime, fans are closely monitored by the secret service and many groups have disbanded.

THEY CALL it a revolution, but it doesn't feel like a change for the better. A decade after the Arab Spring, Tahrir Square is a place of tension. Few tourists come to Cairo. There is hardly any activity outside the old Egyptian Museum, the country's treasure trove. If you stop on Tahrir as a foreign-looking guest and look around curiously, not five minutes pass before a man in dark clothes approaches. 'What brings you to Cairo?' he asks in a firm voice. 'Where are you from?' Then, introducing myself as a tourist, ending the conversation; walking further through the centre, past ministries and government offices, this scene is repeated much the same way twice more in one afternoon: 'Where are you from? What are you doing here?'

You can have a wonderful time in Cairo with hospitable people, in the alleys of the Islamic Quarter, in the bazaars, in the restaurants and museums, but as soon as you turn to politics, things get tricky. Many state buildings and embassies are surrounded by massive protective walls, soldiers with machine guns patrol in front of them, there are bollards and police patrols on many streets. In Tahrir Square, it is mainly men who are on the move, also on the southern edge in front of the Mogamma, one of the most important administrative buildings, a concrete block with 14 floors. Two burly men hold up a banner that can be seen from a distance. On it: Abdel Fattah al-Sisi, Egypt's president since 2014. He is smiling in the picture, looking into the distance as if he is looking forward to the future.

But in Egypt, only a small elite has reason to rejoice. 'President Sisi considers human rights defenders his biggest enemies,' says Egyptian Amr Magdi, who works for Human Rights Watch in Berlin. 'The persecution of civil society is profound, brutal and merciless.' Organisations such as Human Rights Watch and Reporters Without Borders estimate that around 60,000 people are in Egyptian prisons for political reasons. At least 300 are believed to have died there after being tortured, without medical care. The most prominent death of a detainee occurred in June 2019: Mohammed Mursi, the former president of the now banned Muslim Brotherhood. Abdel Fattah al-Sisi justifies his crackdown by saying it is part of the fight against terrorism.

The repression extends far into everyday life, reports Amr Magdi: 'Thousands of alliances and NGOs have been dissolved. Journalists, lawyers and human rights activists can be arrested at any time. They are often banned from travelling, their bank accounts are frozen and their families intimidated.' Activists like Magdi avoid returning home. But even abroad, he believes, the initiatives of many exiles are monitored by intelligence services: 'The embassies write reports about what they do and who they meet – and then send them to Cairo.

Sometimes they even try to prevent meetings of activists with international institutions at an early stage.'

New forms of protest in a frustrated generation

Millions of Egyptians took to the streets across the country in 2011. They protested and fought for free elections, independent media, demonstration rights, but above all, for an economic upturn and a life with dignity. None of this has become reality. Egypt is a military dictatorship with powerful secret services. The population is strictly monitored in the public sphere and on social media. Critical voices are silenced. At least 2,000 people died in riots and clashes with the security apparatus after 2011, including at least 150 active football fans.

Ultras: in probably no other country does this term stand for the politicisation of a society as much as it does in Egypt: for hope, sacrifice, even revolution. But the term is also a symbol of disappointment, trench warfare and repression. The government has long regarded ultras as terrorists, their groups are officially banned. And so, once again, it is football that expresses political developments. In Egypt and in the Arab world.

To this day, it is disputed where and when the first ultra group was founded in north Africa, whether in Tunisia or Libya. Fans from Cairo came into contact with ultras from Europe at the beginning of the millennium, from Serbia, Italy, Russia, but also with supporters from Argentina. They discussed choreographies (visual displays created by fans holding up pieces of card, to create one huge image), pyrotechnics and violence. Young men formed small alliances in Cairo's neighbourhoods, which led to Egypt's first official ultra groups in 2007: 'Ahlawy' of the Al Ahly SC club and the 'White Knights' of Zamalek SC.

At that time, the ultra movement also spread to Algeria and Morocco. The members, mostly between 16 and 30 years old, came from different social classes, including workers and students, Salafists and Muslim Brothers. They contributed their talents to sub-groups, painted banners, composed songs, organised trips. By 2011, ten groups had emerged in Egypt with tens of thousands of members, exact numbers are not available.

'The basic motivation of the ultras was not political at the beginning,' says Philip Malzahn. The Islamic scholar from Germany evaluated Arabic sources, such as the central ultras source by Mohamed Gamal Beshir, the former leader of the White Knights of Zamalek. Malzahn spent half a year in Cairo in 2015 researching and writing his bachelor's thesis on Egyptian ultras, and he repeatedly gives lectures on the topic: 'In football, young men were virtually forced to become political. Because the authoritarian state denied them any freedom.' The ultra movement emerged at a time when Egypt was in a phase of stalemate. President Hosni Mubarak had ruled with emergency laws for more than a quarter of a century since 1981, which gave him far-reaching powers. Important reforms failed to materialise, the gap between rich and poor grew, the all-powerful military was considered a haven of corruption and self-enrichment.

In 2005, 75 per cent of Egyptians were under 30 years old. 'In this frustrated generation, new forms of protest have emerged,' Malzahn tells us. Whether bloggers, Muslim Brothers or the grassroots movement Kafaya: the state arbitrarily imprisoned critics and intensified surveillance, for example in universities. According to the Egyptian Organisation for Human Rights, at least 167 people are said to have died in prisons after torture between 2003 and 2007. In addition, harassment by police officers has been documented: they demanded protection money, harassed women, planted drugs on critics.

In their early days, the state did not regard the ultras as opposition, but as petty criminals. But more and more young men recognised the stadiums as their most important and perhaps last public space. They sang and drummed for their teams, they insulted their opponents, they could block out fear of the future and financial worries. They felt stronger in the anonymous crowd than in the workplace or on the street. 'The ultras brought together social groups that otherwise did not get along. Their common ground was football. Any statement on specific political parties would have jeopardised this cohesion,' Malzahn explains. 'With their basic anti-authoritarian stance, the ultras opposed commercial and corrupt football, but not necessarily the state.' But football and the state cannot be separated in Egypt.

The first club by Egyptians for Egyptians

Hosni Mubarak had recognised the value of football for his propaganda early on. During his 30 years in office, the Egyptian national team won the Africa Cup of Nations five times. Before important matches, Mubarak met with the players; after winning titles, he hung medals around their necks. In his speeches, he interpreted the team as a symbol of the country's growth and historical significance. State media described him as a fatherly advisor. His speeches in the dressing room were often filmed, but only broadcast after victories.

The cords between government, security agencies and big corporations penetrated deep into football, writes blogger and scholar James M. Dorsey in *The Turbulent World of Middle East Soccer*. When his book was published in 2016, half of Egypt's 16 premier league clubs were owned by the Interior Ministry, police and army. They have names like Border Guard or War Production. Military-owned construction companies had built 22 stadiums.

The Cairo ultras of the Al Ahly club were thus regularly opposed by football representatives of the state. From 2009

onwards, they boycotted international matches, because for
them the national team was 'Mubarak's team'. At that time,
confrontations between fans and police intensified. The ultras
had only been in existence for a few years, now they were
adopting tactics of street fighting. They erected barricades,
threw stones, protected themselves from tear gas. In an
interview with German outlet *Zeit Online* in February 2013,
two ultras look back on that time: 'The Ahly ultras have been
around since 2007 and since then we have been arbitrarily and
brutally beaten up and arrested by the police,' says Ahmed
M.. 'The police can do whatever they want with us, they don't
face any punishment, that's how our legal system works. So
we have to fight for justice ourselves.' His comrade-in-arms
Mohamed A. reports: 'The constant, brutal violence of the
police has changed us over time, it has politicised us. You could
say we were converted by police batons, from simple football
fans to revolutionaries.'

At the headquarters of the Al Ahly club, this past has left
no visible traces. The club offices are located on the southern
side of Zamalek, the largest city island in the Nile, a 20-minute
walk from Tahrir Square. The area is surrounded by parks,
upscale hotels and embassies, in the neighbourhood of the
opera and museums. At weekends, the limousines pile up;
wealthy Egyptians like to spend their free time on the tennis
courts and at sports facilities. Many of them visit the Al Ahly
fan shop, buy jerseys, marvel at trophies. The club was named
Africa's Club of the Century in 2000. Al Ahly has won the
Egyptian championship 42 times and the African Champions
League ten times.

No club, no party, no other movement is identified with
by as many Egyptians as Al Ahly. The reasons for this lie far
back in the country's history. 'After centuries of foreign rule, a
strong urge for self-determination developed in 19th century
Egypt,' writes Philip Malzahn in his bachelor thesis. The urban

middle class with higher education grew, but the economic boom was heavily dependent on foreign investors, for example in the construction of the Suez Canal. Britain occupied Egypt in 1882 and made it a protectorate in 1914.

Memberships of prestigious sports clubs were reserved for citizens of the colonial power. Egyptian nationalists like Omar Lotfy, president of a student club, did not want to accept this, and with friends he founded Al Ahly in 1907. 'It was the first club by Egyptians for Egyptians. An essential element of emancipation and separation from the British colonial empire,' says political scientist Jan Busse from the University of the German Bundeswehr in Munich. Al Ahly organised gatherings for resistance against the British, but also against the Egyptian monarchy, which was subordinate to the British colonial rulers. Club members participated in the 1919 revolution that led to formal independence in 1922. Club president Abdel Khalek Sarwat Pasha rose to become prime minister in 1922. Even today, a century later, Al Ahly play in red jerseys, the colour of the pre-colonial Egyptian flag.

But football also became more popular under occupiers and monarchists, says Jan Busse, who has been studying this topic for years and gives lectures on it time and again. Busse is referring to the second major Cairo club, Zamalek SC. The Belgian lawyer George Marzbach created a sporting organisation in 1911 that was also popular with Egyptian intellectuals. The club was called Al Muhtalat and played in white, the colour of colonialism; it came under the rule of the unpopular King Farouk. In 1952, the 'Free Officers' overthrew the monarchy and the club was renamed after its place of origin, the Nile island of Zamalek.

A testing ground for police tactics

In the young and independent Republic of Egypt, politics, culture and sport changed fundamentally. Army officer Gamal

Abdel Nasser, became prime minister in 1952 and president two years later. Nasser also made an impact on the population as honorary president of Al Ahly. Field Marshal Abdal Kakim Amer became head of the Egyptian Football Federation. General Abdel Aziz Salem became the first president of the new African Confederation CAF in 1957. High ranking members of the military showed up in the stands, also attributing victories of their teams to the government. Nasser lobbied for the establishment of the Africa Cup, also as a prop for his vision of supra-regional 'Pan-Arabism'. In the absence of success, he interfered in the running of Al Ahly. In times of conflict, he had matches cancelled or postponed for fear of protests, for example during the Six-Day War against Israel in 1967. 'Nasser set a course that many more regimes in the Arab world were to follow,' says publicist James M. Dorsey.

In *The Turbulent World of Middle East Soccer*, Dorsey analyses dozens of examples of the intertwining of politics and football in north Africa and the Middle East: in Algeria in the 1950s, for example, national players took part in the liberation struggle against the French occupying forces. In Jordan, the successful Al Wehdat club became a symbol of the Palestinian minority. In Lebanon, the long-time Prime Minister Rafiq al-Hariri took clubs into state ownership in order to emphasise the unity between the religiously separate followings. Whether in Tunisia, Morocco or Iraq, ruling families, state organs and the clergy secured influence in clubs and associations – and thus a sensorium for social moods.

On the other hand, young men in the supporters' terraces brought about one of the most important shifts. A shift in mood from subservience and acceptance to determination to question and challenge the system. They developed this new determination outside the stadiums in other areas of life: liberals took a stand against conservatives, sons against parents, Muslims against Islamist hardliners.

Since their foundation in 2007, the ultras Ahlawy of Al Ahly and the White Knights of Zamalek had fought many battles with the police. 'The stadium has long been a testing ground for police tactics that could later be used on opponents who are taken more seriously,' says political scientist Jan Busse.

Probably the biggest show of force occurred in Egypt in early 2011. At the beginning of the protests against Hosni Mubarak, the ultras emphasised their political neutrality: they did not want to appear as a unified bloc with an agenda, but individual members were free to participate in demonstrations. Alongside the new generation of the Muslim Brotherhood, ultras became an important shock troop. They knew each other and could quickly identify spies from the secret services in their ranks. The ultras threw stones, broke through police chains, used overturned cars as a protective wall, carried the injured to safety on mopeds. They gave security to people who had never taken part in demonstrations.

'The ultras were well organised,' says Jan Busse. 'They were important in holding the symbolically important Tahrir Square.' This became clear on 2 February 2011: government-paid thugs rode camels into the crowd. 'The ultras pushed these thugs back using sophisticated fighting techniques.' On 11 February, Mubarak finally resigned. How great the influence of the ultras actually was in this is difficult to say. In any case, their impact radiated far beyond the country's borders. In some countries of the Middle East, ultras took part in protests as well: in Algeria, Tunisia and Morocco.

In Egypt, it looked for a while as if the Arab Spring might usher in democratisation. The military's interim government announced the first free elections would take place in six months. 'People were looking for orientation, we saw this as an opportunity for civil society,' says Joachim Paul, expert of the German Heinrich Böll Foundation on the Arab world. Paul wanted to set up a foundation office in Cairo with local partners after the revolution in 2011. 'But very quickly we realised that this would only be associated with great difficulties. We would have been mainly concerned with protecting our staff from the secret service.' The security apparatus was less concerned with civil rights than with economic and political gains.

Civil society was in upheaval. The common opponent Mubarak was history, so now fractions joined different parties. New hierarchies were forming in trade unions, alliances and loose groups. This also applied to the ultras, who were celebrated in many media as heroes of the revolution. Ahlawy and the White Knights were very popular, and internal tensions grew as a result. 'New members provoked acts of violence that were not agreed upon,' says Philip Malzahn. A section of the White Knights stormed the pitch in the African Champions League and threatened opposing players. Police and military used this as an excuse to crack down on the ultras. Fans were arrested and their homes searched. Around the matches, the groups intensified their stance against the police from mid-2011. There were regular street fights and demonstrations with fatalities. The military banned all forms of protest. The ultras were no longer considered petty criminals, but agents who want to destroy Egypt.

Attacks with sticks, knives and broken bottles

The history of the Arab world is rich in demonstrations of power in football, and James M. Dorsey has analysed events for this as well: in Jordan, the Al Wehdat club was temporarily shut down in 1986 after fan chants against the monarchy. In Iraq, Udai Hussein, son of the former dictator, gave his favourite players money, cars and flats. He shaved the hair of disliked athletes, sometimes forcing them to play barefoot on asphalt in the summer heat. In Libya, Al Saadi al-Gaddafi, son of the former head of state, was the most powerful string-puller in football. His club in Tripoli almost always won because Gaddafi bribed referees. Fans from Benghazi were so angry that they sent a donkey with Saadi's shirt onto the pitch. Saadi ordered the destruction of their clubhouse and had dozens of fans arrested. In Bahrain, henchmen of the royal family are said to have arrested and even tortured critical athletes.

But all this is overshadowed by 1 February 2012, when Al Ahly met hosts Al Masry in the port city of Port Said, almost a year after the fall of President Hosni Mubarak. Before the previous meeting between the two teams at the same venue, Cairo ultras had rioted in the city. Now, eight months later, the Green Eagles, the ultras of Al Masry, threatened retaliation. Beyond these usual threats, the circumstances were unusual even before the match. Home supporters were hardly checked at the entrance, so they were able to bring batons, knives and fireworks into the stadium. During the match, some barriers between the blocks of fans were opened, there were brawls. But the police did not stop the match, it was broadcast live on TV, and Al Masry surprisingly won 3-1.

After the final whistle, the stadium lights were switched off early. Hundreds of Al Masry fans stormed the pitch and the opposing stand. They threw devices at the ultras of Al Ahly, attacked them with sticks, knives and broken glass bottles; the police let them go. The visiting fans fled, panic ensued. Some were violently pushed from the stands, others met locked gates in narrow exits – and were trampled to death. Players and fans fled to the dressing rooms, where they held out for hours before being flown out by helicopter. In the end, 72 people were dead, other sources say 74, most of them between the ages of 15 and 20. Many of the almost 1,000 injured did not want to be treated in Port Said for fear of further attacks.

In the days following the disaster, fans, players and the media speculated about the causes and motives of the escalation. Did the army want to teach the rebellious ultras of Al Ahly a lesson that got out of hand? Were followers of Hosni Mubarak planning to destabilise the new military council? There were street battles all over the country. In Cairo, ultras attacked some police stations and paralysed the metro. They demanded 'justice for their martyrs,' otherwise they would continue to throw the country into turmoil. 'This behaviour went too far for many people,' says Jan Busse of the Bundeswehr University in Munich. 'Public approval for the ultras slowly declined.' The government announced a comprehensive investigation of Port Said. The board of the Egyptian Football Association had to go, and league operations were suspended.

In June 2012, four months after the stadium massacre, Mohammed Mursi was elected president in the first free elections. His Muslim Brotherhood had rarely had an easy time of it in the six decades under military governments, and now Mursi announced reforms for the huge security apparatus. But the Port Said investigation showed how intertwined politics and the judiciary are. Many of the 73 defendants complained about arbitrary arrests, one-sided investigations, untrustworthy evidence. The Al Ahly ultras threatened violence if the verdict was lenient. In the days leading up to the announcement, they protested against the military council and paralysed traffic in some places. The courthouse was guarded by 4,000 police.

On 26 January 2013, the second anniversary of the start of the revolution, 21 defendants were sentenced to death, most of them ultras from Al Masry in Port Said. 'High-ranking military and police officers did not have to answer charges,' says Jan Busse. 'Impunity for security forces is a common phenomenon in Egypt.' Defence lawyers spoke of a political verdict: young fans had to be used as scapegoats to avoid chaos in the capital. In Port Said, where many people feel economically isolated from Cairo anyway, riots followed with several deaths. People demonstrated against the verdict for months. International non-governmental organisations demanded clarification.

Football exposes the ideological rifts in society

In Egypt, the frustration of the population grew, because their standard of living had deteriorated further. Prices were rising, inflation too, the currency was losing value against the dollar, plus there were regular power cuts. The military was still an important power factor, there was no trace of a functioning separation of powers. The ultras stood symbolically for resistance against a corrupt regime. New groups with political overtones were forming all over the country, even without ties to clubs. Their relationship with the Muslim Brotherhood is complicated.

In 2013, there were growing impressions that Mohammed Mursi also had little interest in real reforms; he came to an agreement with the military. From then on, the internal conflicts of the ultras became palpable: at a demonstration, ultras sang songs against Mursi, other group members resisted with violence. 'Part of the population began to wonder whether the ultras had been infiltrated by the Brotherhood,' writes Islamic scholar Philip Malzahn. Dissatisfaction with Mursi was expressed in nationwide uprisings – but the ultras did not take a unified stance. On 3 July 2013, the military staged a coup against the democratically elected president. Mohammed Mursi was imprisoned and later sentenced first to death, then to several years in prison; he died in mysterious circumstances in 2019.

One of the main perpetrators of the coup was General Abdel Fattah al-Sisi, who has held the presidency since 8 June 2014. More than three years after the revolution, Egypt was far from democratic government, the economy was stagnating, and Sisi continued to intensify repression against marginalised civil society. Sometimes, however, he presented himself as willing to compromise, for example in football. After the furore over Port Said died down, league play resumed – in front of empty seats. A few months after taking office, Sisi contacted a television programme by telephone. He offered to talk to the leaders of the ultras to discuss their return to the stadiums. The ultras refused, saying they did not want to be taken over.

On 8 February 2015, the government wanted to test the social mood and allow fans back for one match. The Ministry of Interior limited the crowd for the match between Zamalek and ENPPI to 10,000. However, far more people turned up outside the Air Force Stadium on the outskirts of Cairo. Thousands crowded outside the narrow entrance. The atmosphere became more aggressive, suddenly the police fired tear gas into the crowd. There was mass panic, fights, burning cars, in the end 20 people were dead, most of them members of the revolutionary ultras White Knights.

Once again the legal process became politically charged, once again football exposed the ideological rifts in society. The prosecution labelled the Zamalek ultras as terrorists and enemies of the state because of their alleged proximity to the Muslim Brotherhood, which had been banned after the coup. The White Knights accused Mortada Mansour, the chairman of Zamalek. Mansour, a lawyer and member of parliament, had been a loyal supporter of Mubarak, always speaking out against the ultras in drastic terms; for him, the beginning of the revolution was the 'worst day in Egyptian history'. Between these extreme positions, however, the incompetence of security forces and stadium management is considered the probable cause of the disaster.

League matches continued to take place without spectators, and the ultras were demonised as terrorist organisations. Some members have since chosen to watch basketball, handball or volleyball matches. Or they travel with their clubs to away games in the African Champions League. More often, they put their experiences into songs and blog entries. 'The ultra leaders who are not in prison are being watched by the secret services,' says Egyptian Hussein Baoumi, who works for

Amnesty International in Tunis. He says it is likely that phone calls are tapped and emails checked, so ultras keep a low profile on social media. Baoumi says: 'The government is afraid of organised groups, so they want to nip any mobilisation in the bud.'

A song of the ultras becomes an anthem of protest

The situation in Egypt seemed hopeless. But other examples in north Africa show that the protest of the ultras can fundamentally change a society: we can observe an impressive example in Algeria. In February 2019, the long-term ruler Abdelaziz Bouteflika announced his candidacy for a fifth term in office. Due to a stroke, Bouteflika had been confined to a wheelchair for years, he had hardly appeared in public and was considered a puppet of a corrupt power elite. Soon after his announcement, hundreds of thousands of people in Algeria demonstrated against the regime.

The song 'Ultima Verba' became an anthem of the protest movement, saying: 'We are the obstacle for you, oh government. And our fire will never be extinguished.' The song is a tribute to the poem of the same name by Victor Hugo. In it, the French writer described the craving for recognition of Napoleon III, who had himself proclaimed emperor, while in exile in the mid-19th century. More than 170 years later, men and women, children and senior citizens were singing 'Ultima Verba' in Algeria. The composition did not come from musicians or intellectuals. It came from the ultras of USM Algiers, perhaps the most important football club in Algeria.

'The stadiums in Algeria have long been a free space for young men who yearned for belonging,' says journalist Maher Mezahi, who studies fan cultures in north Africa. 'At football they could talk about their concerns, there was no censorship.' The first Algerian ultra groups after the turn of the millennium sang about their love of football. But after the

Arab Spring, their issues became more political. They talked about corruption and unemployment, rising rents and attempts to flee across the Mediterranean, drug use and hopelessness. The songs were sometimes vulgar, but they soon became part of pop culture. The Algerian rapper Soolking released a version of the ultra-protest song 'Ultima Verba', which has had more than 300 million views on YouTube.

In an essay, the reporter Maher Mezahi describes the musical traditions of the Algerian fans and also mentions differences to Europe: the repertoire of songs sung by German or Italian ultras usually consists of shorter chants for their teams; the ultras in Algeria, on the other hand, compose songs with several verses, some of which are longer than four minutes. The most famous is probably 'La Casa del Mouradia', in reference to the presidential palace in the El Mouradia district of the capital, Algiers. The song is a parody of the Spanish TV crime series *La Casa de Papel*, (*House of Money*). In Algeria, tens of thousands sang the song, including the line, 'We're sick of the life we live'. It echoed particularly loudly through the streets when Algeria's national team won the 2019 Africa Cup of Nations.

'This music culture does not arise spontaneously, it is well organised,' says Mezahi, who reports for the BBC and Al Jazeera, among others. Often musicians among the ultras join together to form bands. The icons of the scene from the USM Algiers club call themselves 'Ouled El Bahdja', children of the radiant ones. Ultras record songs in recording studios, create videos and publish them on social media so that other members can learn the lyrics. With the sale of CDs, posters and flags, they also finance aid campaigns for the disadvantaged. Forty-five per cent of the Algerian population is younger than 25, and a third of this age group is without a job.

Football with social power has a tradition in Algeria. From the 1930s onwards, many workers, artists and sportsmen had met in cafés to listen to football commentaries on the radio. These cafés were centres of Chaabi music, a mixture of popular Arabic and Andalusian melodies. Chaabi comes from Arabic and means people. 'These songs were about cohesion, politics and, early on, football,' says Mezahi. 'There was a spirit of resistance back then, and that also plays a role for the ultras today.'

From 1830, Algeria was increasingly under the control of France. By the mid-20th century, more than 20 Algerian footballers were playing in the French league, receiving lower wages than the locals. In 1954, the National Liberation Front (FLN) was formed in Algeria. Its contacts travelled through France in secret to recruit fighters. Shortly before the 1958 World Cup in Sweden, 12 Algerian players defected. 'A national team was formed,' recounts north Africa expert James M. Dorsey. 'The players travelled around the world promoting the struggle for independence.' One of the songs the team sang before their matches later became Algeria's national anthem.

Even after independence in 1962, a stable democracy did not emerge in Algeria. Uprisings, economic crises, in the 90s a civil war. Time and again, authoritarian presidents sought proximity to prominent footballers. Again and again, chants of protest and sport echoed through the stadiums. 'The ultras want to remain innovative and combine many elements of pop culture,' says Algerian-born sports scientist Mahfoud Amara from Qatar University in Doha. 'Many ultras have shown themselves to be more politically mature than some intellectuals.'

During the Coronavirus pandemic, the ultras' chants fell silent for a while, but videos circulated on social media, also showing graffiti in the streets and 'Tifos', the stadium choreographies with huge banners and fireworks.

And in 2019, long-time ruler Abdelaziz Bouteflika bowed to public pressure and renounced a fifth term. However, many of his comrades-in-arms are still in high positions. So, the ultras will continue to sing.

Mo Salah rarely talks politics – yet he is political

Such a development is very unlikely to happen in Egypt. The regime is afraid of losing power. Even national heroes are punished. Mohamed Aboutrika is considered one of the most important players in Egyptian history. In 2006 and 2008, he led the national team to win the Africa Cup of Nations, and he scored 39 goals in his 100 international matches. For almost ten years he played for Al Ahly, the club that has been hijacked by politics for more than 100 years. But Aboutrika, who studied philosophy, made his own decisions: he positioned himself against the high salaries in football, collected donations for disadvantaged people, openly sympathised with the population in the Gaza Strip.

Associations and politicians let him play for a long time, but that changed after the revolution. In September 2012, Al Ahly played against ENPPI in the Egyptian Super Cup, the first official match after the Port Said disaster seven months earlier. The Ahlawy ultras boycotted the match, as a protest against the slow process of coming to terms with the past. Aboutrika did the same and refused to play against ENPPI. He was temporarily suspended. Months later, members of the military regime felt snubbed because Aboutrika would not let them put a medal around his neck. Aboutrika ended his active career in 2013, and two years later his bank assets in Egypt were frozen. He now lives in Qatar and works as a television commentator. According to his lawyer, he has been on a government terror list since 2017. Just like several hundred other prominent compatriots.

President Abdel Fattah al-Sisi chooses other leading actors for his football stage. In October 2017, the Egyptian national team qualified for a World Cup for the first time in 28 years by beating the Republic of Congo, with the winning goal scored in injury time by Mohamed Salah, the national football icon of Liverpool FC. The excited TV commentator shouted: 'Congratulations to the Egyptian team. Congratulations to the President of the Republic. Congratulations to the Egyptian people.' For the first time since the military coup in 2013, tens of thousands of people were allowed to stream into the squares of Cairo, cheering, with police officers and soldiers. However, international matches have not taken place in the capital for years, but in coastal cities like Alexandria or Borg El Arab.

Abdel Fattah al-Sisi received the team a few days later in an exhibition centre. In his speech, he linked sport, economy and politics. 'Sisi wanted to sell the team's success as the success of his government,' says Amr Magdi of Human Rights Watch. 'For him, football is a PR campaign to distract from negative issues.' Sisi's predecessors, all generals – Gamal Abdel Nasser, Anwar al-Sadat and Hosni Mubarak – argued similarly.

The Egyptian squad also came under political pressure during the 2018 World Cup, especially at their base in Grozny, capital of the Russian constituent republic of Chechnya. The autocratically ruling president Ramzan Kadyrov, himself an active football official and fan, attended an Egypt training session. Kadyrov, who is accused of murder and torture among other things, named Mo Salah an honorary citizen of Grozny, and the photos of them together made international headlines. Salah is said to have been furious about this. He has long been perceived as an idol in other Arab countries beyond Egypt. His likeness adorns advertising banners, house walls, fan articles – and in April 2019 also the cover of *Time*. The American magazine named him one of the 100 most influential people in the world.

At Mo Salah's club, Liverpool, one song has become part of the fans' repertoire: 'If he scores another few then I'll be Muslim too. He's sitting in the mosque that's where I wanna be.' Are homages like these meant ironically or is there a hint of seriousness in them? 'Salah gives Islam, which for many seems abstract, an everyday face,' says sports scientist Mahfoud Amara from Qatar University in Doha.

A study by Stanford University and the Zurich University of technology backs up statements like this. The researchers analysed hate crimes in 25 English counties between 2015 and 2018, and found that attacks and discrimination against Muslims had fallen by 19 per cent in Merseyside, the home of Liverpool, while the rate for other hate crimes remained about the same. In addition, anti-Muslim tweets from Liverpool fans fell by 53 per cent. 'We live in a time when young people often look up to gangsters or reality stars,' says Birmingham imam Obayed Hussain. 'Mo Salah is very talented, humble and brings people together. And yes, one of his qualities is being Muslim. It's important to have role models like him, who stand out because of their character – without making big speeches.'

In the area close to the home of first division club Aston Villa, Obayed Hussain organises a midnight football league during Ramadan. During the games, Muslim and non-Muslim youth get closer. 'I often mention Mo Salah in my workshops. The players then immediately have a concrete image in mind.' And sometimes it is then easier for young Muslims to come to terms with their own origins. Salah makes no secret of his faith: after successful games, he sometimes assumes a Muslim prayer posture. Seven points of his body touch the grass at the same time. On social media, he showed himself breaking his fast. His wife attends matches wearing the traditional headgear.

Salah rarely talks politics – yet he is political. In Egypt's presidential election in March 2018, one million people reportedly voted for Salah even though he was not even a candidate. The voters thus invalidated their votes; in the vast majority of cases, this was probably a sign of protest against the president. After the Champions League victory with Liverpool in 2019, Salah posed for a photo with the 'enemy of the state' Mohamed Aboutrika. Salah is among the few who do not face punishment for this.

'Football needs an iron hand'

Abdel Fattah al-Sisi won the presidential election with more than 90 per cent of the vote; potential opponents had previously been arrested or pressured to withdraw. The only competitor was Moussa Mostafa Moussa, an avowed friend of Sisi. A constitutional amendment passed in April 2019 could keep Sisi in office until 2030. Criticism of these events from the USA and the European Union was muted. Many Western countries describe Egypt as a strategic partner against terrorism. Several times their governments have received Sisi, and often Sisi himself has publicly rejected moderate criticism of human rights abuses. 'We are not calling for the end of diplomatic relations with Egypt,' says Amr Magdi of Human Rights Watch. 'But the US and Europe can put pressure on in other ways, such as limiting military aid and trade relations.' Western companies are present in Egypt with investments worth billions. In addition, several EU countries supply weapons and espionage technology to the army and police. 'These deliveries should be stopped,' says Magdi. 'Because they intensify the repression against the population.'

How can democratic states stand up for Egyptian civil society despite economic ties? With what demands can institutions put pressure on the military government without the population feeling its wrath? 'We should keep the dramatic situation in the public eye. Because human rights defenders are afraid of being forgotten,' says Margarete Bause, former member for the Greens on the Human Rights Committee of the German parliament. 'MPs from democratic countries should always ask questions and observe court proceedings in Egypt.' Bause travelled to Cairo with a delegation from the committee in 2018. The parliamentarians met officials and lawyers, but some activists cancelled at short notice. They and their families were threatened. Activists and lawyers are often arrested for having contact with foreign politicians or journalists.

In the 30 years under Mubarak, the human rights situation is said not to have been as dramatic as it is now under Abdel Fattah al-Sisi; this assessment is given by experts again and again. When the president deals with sport, he does not talk about problems, but about visions. He held out the prospect of a new stadium in Port Said and appeared with club officials calling for his re-election. He supported a multi-million dollar bid by a major Egyptian entrepreneur for TV rights to international matches. And he pledged his support to Coptic Christians like no other president. Christians make up ten per cent of the population and are often the target of attacks. In everyday life, they complain of exclusion, even in football, where Coptic players and coaches do not feature. Hany Ramzy, formerly with Werder Bremen, was one of a handful of Egyptian national players of Christian faith.

Despite the human rights violations, in 2018 Egypt was selected as the host of the Africa Cup of Nations for 2019; the tournament had been withdrawn from Cameroon due to organisational problems. The Egyptian government followed tradition and used the event as a stage. The draw for the groups was a pompous show in front of the pyramids and before the start of the tournament president Abdel Fattah al-Sisi made a visit to national training, wearing a white T-shirt and blue casual trousers. He walked onto the stadium turf in Cairo with a smile. The national players presented him with a red jersey signed by them. The head of state was surrounded by cameras when he said: 'More important than the game for me and all Egyptians is how we present ourselves to the spectators around the world. Therefore, you must pay great attention to your behaviour.'

The Egyptian team won all three of their preliminary matches without conceding a goal, but were eliminated by South Africa in the round of 16. The board of the Egyptian federation resigned. Deputy Parliament Speaker Soliman Wahdan called for a legal investigation into the officials for corruption. Former coach Farouk Gaafar called on the military to take over the federation: 'Football needs an iron hand.'

Beyond this excitement, the tournament was significant for fan culture. After years of repression, a free space opened up again. The large ultra groups had officially disbanded in 2018, possibly to protect their young members from the secret services. But every now and then, small groups or individual members drew attention to themselves with protests, for example on the sidelines of Champions League matches. Since 2018, a few thousand spectators had been allowed to attend selected league matches again. However, they had to register in advance with their identity cards and undergo extensive checks, so the noisy atmosphere of the past was in danger of being forgotten.

In 2019, at the African Championship, all four of the host nation's matches took place in the Cairo International Stadium, where the national team had not appeared for years. With more than 70,000 spectators, the atmosphere was like in the old days. And some of them even voiced criticism, with chants for the outcast hero Mohamed Aboutrika and with action in the round of 16: in the 20th and 72nd minutes of the match, tens of thousands of spectators showed the bright lights of their mobile phones – a reminder of 2012 and 2013, when 72 fans died violently in Port Said and 20 in Cairo. It was a silent commemoration, but it could also be interpreted as a loud protest against the government.

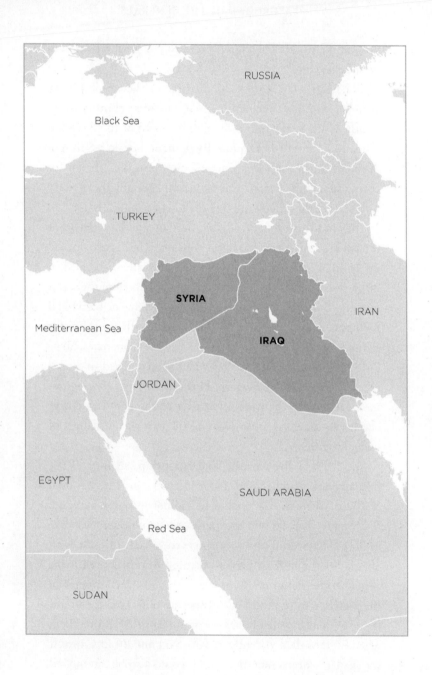

War Players

In the war zones of the Middle East, football is a contested commodity: dictators brutally bring players into line and use stadiums as military bases. For terrorists, games are high-profile targets for attacks, but also places for recruitment. On the other hand, the national teams in Iraq and Afghanistan are among the rare symbols with which hostile ethnic groups can equally identify. The situation is similar in Syria, where President Assad wants to convey normality – because rebuilding the country will be expensive.

ALMOST EVERY day, Rami travelled north from Damascus to Homs, two hours there, two hours back. Together with other young people, from 2009 onwards, he built up one of the first ultra groups in Syria, around the Al Karamah club. In addition to school, he went to work to finance his passion. He travelled to Algeria, Tunisia and Egypt to be inspired by the ultras there. He followed his favourite club everywhere, borders only existed in the Asian Champions League, as he did not get a visa for Singapore and Kuwait. The ultras of Al Karamah rehearsed chants, designed banners, organised away trips. They found something that was rare in Syrian society:

unity and confidence. Until 2011, Rami missed only one of his club's matches, and he is still angry about it today.

With the beginning of the civil war, the six ultra groups nationwide took a break. Rami went to the stadium once more, in 2014. Many seats remained empty. Friends who had joined the rebels were dead, in prison or at the front. 'I stayed there for five minutes, then I walked out,' Rami says. A few months later, he fled to Germany. According to estimates, more than 500,000 people were killed during the war. Twelve million, about half of all Syrians, are on the run.

Even during the civil war, Syrian President Bashar al-Assad wanted to convey normality. Despite terror, despite torture and despite chemical weapons: football league operations were kept up in a reduced form, the teams played out their championship in the supposedly safe cities of Damascus and Latakia. 'Football shows the disunity of our country,' says Rami. He is in his mid-20s now, lives in the Ruhr area and is continuing his film studies. He follows the games of the Syrian national team on the internet, but stays out of the debates on social media: 'Many people claim the team for their political opinion, the tone is very harsh and often hurtful.' For millions of Syrians, football is a distraction from terror – for others, it is a tool of dictatorship.

Bashar al-Assad had not stood out as a football fan before the war. But in recent years he allowed himself to be filmed with the national team, after they won the West Asian Championship in 2012, but also after they narrowly missed qualifying for the 2018 World Cup. Videos show Assad receiving the players in a prestigious hall in October 2017, wearing a light grey jacket, shirt collar open.

Assad signed players' training jackets and said into the camera: 'Your performance is a proof of the Syrian people's vitality, determination, stability and patriotism.' He praised the army, without which such a performance would not be possible.

Football as a showroom

The Syrian team used to play its home matches in Damascus or Aleppo in front of 40,000 fans, but since the war began it has played in exile, often thousands of kilometres away in southeast Asia in front of a few hundred spectators. Sometimes Syrian government supporters sit in the stands next to dissidents, exchange students and descendants of emigrants. As a rule, it remained peaceful.

Sometimes, however, players and officials there wore T-shirts with photos of Assad; former coach Fajr Ebrahim called him the 'best man in the world'. In 2015, Syrian spectators in Malaysia displayed a huge banner with a portrait of Assad. The mass phenomenon of football is an important support for the regime, says freelance German journalist Kristin Helberg, who has written several books on Syria: 'Assad wants to get back into the international community. He needs funds to rebuild the country. A symbol like the national team can help him in his search for investors.'

In Syria, military and police clubs have long had a systemic advantage. The most important and most successful club, with 17 championship titles, comes from Damascus and is called Al Jaish, which translates as 'the army'. It was founded in 1947, a year after the last French occupation troops left and the Syrian Republic was proclaimed. The club's leadership was recruited from military cadres, the team trained in barracks, and the best talents were assigned to it from all over the country.

At the beginning of the millennium, in the initial climate of reform under Bashar al-Assad, privately owned football clubs became more common. Al Karamah, an ambitious club from Homs, reached the final of the Asian Champions League in 2006. Even today, the pictures of the cheering spectators in the VIP stand can be viewed on YouTube: Assad laughs and applauds standing, surrounded by supposed admirers. 'The Assad regime has brought society into line for decades,' says Helberg, who lived in Damascus from 2001 to 2008. 'All aspects of everyday life are taken over by the regime. Whether it's a women's union, a student association or a chamber of commerce and industry: anyone who wants to get involved ends up in the structures of the Assad party. This also applies to football.' Assad is said not to be really interested in football. Yet he invites popular players to receptions and parades. This goes down well with many people.

Several players are still missing

Many top players are under contract abroad. They can earn financial security in Kuwait, Jordan and Qatar. But even there, they are under the influence of the Syrian government, especially since the civil war. Firas al-Khatib, for example, has been a role model since his youth. He played in China and for more than ten years in Kuwait. He sent part of his salary to his home town of Homs, to finance roads and mosques. In 2012, a year after the war began, Khatib announced his resignation from the Syrian national team in Kuwait, declaring his allegiance to the opposition. Team-mate Omar al-Soma did the same. It was a propaganda setback for Assad.

In spring 2017, Firas al-Khatib returned as captain for the crucial qualifying matches for the 2018 World Cup. His statements were no longer combative but mild, thanking Assad: 'We play for all Syrians. We want our country to have happy moments again.' A former friend wrote to him, saying he would end up 'in the dustbin of history'. There was intense discussion on social media: was the government pressuring Khatib? Was his family in danger? Did close friends have to surrender their passports?

The US sports outlet ESPN researched the subject for months and published a long report in May 2017, in which journalist and Pulitzer Prize winner Steve Fainaru wrote: 'The Syrian government has used sport for its brutal repression. At least 38 players from the top two leagues and dozens more from the lower leagues have been shot, bombed and tortured.' Former national player Jihad Qassab, who was involved in Al Karamah's successes, was arrested in Homs in 2014. He was accused of constructing car bombs – which he denied. Qassab died after severe torture in a Saidnaya military prison in 2016. His former colleague Ahmad Hesham Swedan was killed in a shootout in 2012.

Several players are still missing, Anas Ammo told ESPN. The Syrian sports reporter grew up in Aleppo, has lived in Turkey since 2012 and documents human rights violations against Syrian athletes from there. His network is large, including fugitive footballers like Firas al-Ali. At a training camp of the Syrian national team, the defender learned that his 13-year-old cousin had been killed by government troops. Half an hour later, Firas al-Ali overheard another national player taunting the rebels over dinner. After an argument, he called his family, and the next day they drove towards the border. Soldiers who recognised his face let him pass. Firas al-Ali fled to Turkey. There he fared the same as many other refugees: his accounts in Syria were frozen, his property confiscated, his houses destroyed.

The Syrian civil war was influenced by more and more interests as it progressed, including from abroad: Assad received support from Russia and Iran. There were shifting alliances and rivalries among the opposition. Gradually, religious and ethnic motives came to the fore, especially through the terrorist groups al-Qaida and the so-called Islamic State. Both terrorist groups gained enormous power in Syria from 2013 onwards, also through the recruitment of thousands of mercenaries abroad.

IS wanted to use violence to impose its own interpretation of Islam. Its fighters killed tens of thousands of people, destroyed centuries-old cultural sites and relied on martial propaganda, including in football. In July 2016, a video from Rakka, then the IS capital in Syria, went viral. It showed five blindfolded men kneeling, with IS fighters behind them. The men were accused of espionage and executed on camera. Four of them had played for the Al Shabab football club in Rakka.

A league for al-Qaida's fighters

The Austrian football magazine *Ballesterer* dedicated a cover story to 'Football in War' in 2017, in which the author Clemens Zavarsky also mentions attacks in the football environment: in January 2015, IS fighters shot 13 young people in Mossul, Iraq, because they had been watching an Asian Cup match. Two months later, the city derby between Al Zawraa and Al Quwa al-Jawiya took place in the Iraqi capital Baghdad. A series of attacks around the stadium killed 30 people. In November 2015, attacks in Paris killed 130 people and injured nearly 700, including outside the international match between France and Germany at the Stade de France. In June 2016, a suicide bomber killed 41 people 50 kilometres south of Baghdad, during a cup presentation at a stadium.

'Football is a high-profile target for IS,' writes Zavarsky in *Ballesterer*. 'Nevertheless, even for the terrorist group, sport cannot be dismissed as a mere symbol of the secular West.' Terrorist organisations have also used football for networking and mobilisation: on 5 July 2014, leader Abu Bakr al-Baghdadi proclaimed the IS caliphate in Mosul, framed by a Quran quoting contest and a football match. Self-proclaimed Imam Abu Otaiba, who recruited IS fighters, told the *Wall Street Journal* in 2016, 'We can't go to the mosques anymore. There are too many agents there. So, I go to football fields. We take recruits to our training farms. Through organised football matches, we bind them closer to us.'

Osama bin Laden had already taken a similar approach in the 1980s and 1990s, writes scholar and blogger James

M. Dorsey in his book *The Turbulent World of Middle East Soccer*: Bin Laden organised football matches as a youth in his native Saudi Arabia. Later, he preached on the sidelines of tournaments and organised a league for al-Qaida's fighters.

Whether the Islamic State, the Taliban or al-Qaida, different sources suggest that the fundamentalists tolerated the game only under strict and sometimes contradictory conditions: sometimes without hugs between players, sometimes without sponsors' logos and referees' whistles because their sounds supposedly awaken demons. In Kandahar, Afghanistan, the Taliban arrested a Pakistani team for playing in shorts. In Somalia, football was banned as 'satanic' and 'un-Islamic'.

Punishment with electric shocks

But football in the Middle East does not only cause headlines about violence and terror. Proof of this was the triumph of the Iraqi national team at the 2007 Asian Cup. 'For a few weeks, the bloodshed of previous years faded into the background,' says Iraqi journalist Rafeq Alokaby, who emigrated to Australia. Alokaby still carries the 2007 final ticket in his mobile phone case. 'After winning the title, we felt like a normal country. But the circumstances surrounding it were brutal.'

Alokaby has made several documentaries about Iraqi football, which is also a magnifying glass for one of the largest countries in the Arab world, with a population of almost 40 million. There have always been tensions between Arabs, Kurds, Turkmen and Assyrians, also between the two major Muslim sects, Shiites and Sunnis. From 1979 to 2003, Saddam Hussein ruled the country dictatorially. Wars against the neighbouring states of Iran and Kuwait prevented an economic upswing, despite considerable mineral resources and an impressive history with the earliest advanced civilisations in the Middle East.

The Iraqi national team qualified for a World Cup only once, in Mexico in 1986. Hussein Saeed is considered the greatest player in their history, with 78 goals in 137 international matches. After the World Cup, Saeed received several offers from European clubs, including Real Madrid, but the government did not want to let him go. Their hatred of the West was too great.

Under Saddam Hussein, only a small elite benefited. Among them was his family, including the eldest of his five children. Udai Hussein dominated Iraqi sport like no other, as president of the Football Federation, the National Olympic Committee and as minister of sport. The British author Simon Freeman describes Udai Hussein's despotism in his book *Baghdad FC*.

After great victories, he gave players houses and bonuses. After defeats, he sometimes had them arrested and punished with caning or electric shocks. Freeman documented murders, torture and match-fixing. In 2003, a military alliance led by the USA overthrew Saddam Hussein's regime; his sons Udai and Qusai died in attacks in Mosul on 22 July 2003. Iraq's infrastructure was largely destroyed. Conflicts between ethnic groups grew, Islamist groups were on the rise, poverty prevailed. The consequences: thousands of terrorist attacks, kidnappings and injuries from landmines.

Few thought of great football success at the time. Most of the national players were under contract abroad. For security reasons, they did not want to travel to Iraq before international matches. Their football association moved into offices in the Jordanian capital Amman. Iraq played home matches in Dubai, Doha or Aleppo. The British journalist James Montague describes in his book *When Friday Comes. Football, War and Revolution in the Middle East* an eventful preparation for the Asian Championship 2007. Among the players were Sunnis, Shiites and Kurds. Many of them had lost

During the Bosnian war, French soldiers land in April 1994 in the stadium of Goražde to rescue injured civilians.

Many fans in Serbia glorify the Yugoslav wars, for example with a tank at the Red Star Belgrade stadium.

In Croatia, football supported nation building, also with murals in the capital Zagreb.

Vladimir Putin harnessed football for his power networks like no other. Here he spends the victory ceremony after the 2018 World Cup in Russia with FIFA president Gianni Infantino.

In Ukraine, hundreds of ultras and hooligans have joined the military since 2014. Many of them belong to nationalist groups.

FC Barcelona fans repeatedly display flags for an independent Catalonia – here against Real Madrid in October 2021.

Time and again, Turkey's President Erdogan poses with security forces in stadiums, here in December 2016 in Istanbul at a friendly match dedicated to terror victims.

After the escalation in the Gaza Strip in May 2021, many footballers are showing solidarity with the Palestinians. These include Paul Pogba (left) and Amad Diallo of Manchester United carrying a Palestinian flag.

In Egyptian football, there are repeated outbreaks of violence with many deaths. Here in 2016, the ultras 'White Knights' of Zamalek commemorate their friends who died.

During the war in Syria, stadiums were part of the military infrastructure. In Idlib, refugees spent months sleeping in tents.

Iraq has long been marked by war and terror. In July 2007, however, the whole country celebrated the sensational victory of their team in the Asian Cup, including many security forces.

The religious leaders in Iran also control football. At an international match in Tehran in 1998, a member of the national team shows a photo of Ayatollah Khomeini.

Before their match against Iceland in March 2021, German national players are campaigning for human rights. Nevertheless, many of them travel with FC Bayern to the training camp in Qatar.

Football is a frequent topic at political meetings of China's President Xi Jinping. In September 2017, Brazilian head of state Michel Temer presented him with a jersey signed by Pelé.

Goalkeeper Eric Murangwa was lucky to survive the genocide against the Tutsi in Rwanda. For his commitment, he was appointed a Member of the Order of the British Empire in London in 2018.

The 1978 World Cup took place under the military dictatorship of Argentina. Thousands of people protested against it in Paris – one of only a few demonstrations.

friends and relatives in attacks and kidnappings, some received death threats and were afraid of blackmail, others drove to training with a gun. Goalkeeper Noor Sabri had to watch his brother-in-law being killed. His colleague Haitham Kadim witnessed gunmen storming a pitch and shooting players. A few days before the Asian Cup, a physiotherapist left the preparation camp in Jordan to visit his pregnant wife in Iraq. He was killed there by a car bomb.

In his book, James Montague describes a team atmosphere between dejection and anger, between a sense of duty and confidence. He gives special credit to the Brazilian coach Jorvan Vieira, who had taken charge of several teams in the Middle East since 1980. Vieira took over the Iraqi team only two months before the Asian Cup. He encouraged his players in their intention to put religious and ethnic differences in the background. They refrained from prayers in the dressing room.

At first, the Iraqis' interest was limited, but that changed after their team beat Australia 3-1 in the second preliminary round match. The mood increased in the semi-final: Iraq defeated the favourites South Korea in a penalty shoot-out. Tens of thousands of people poured into the streets of Iraq. And then the shock: two suicide bombers killed 50 people during the celebrations in Baghdad, three times as many were injured. In the days that followed, the media reported that some players were thinking about disbanding the national team. It was reportedly emotional accounts from families of the victims that motivated them to move on.

Too many people have a say in coaching decisions

On 29 July 2007, Iraq won the final against three-time Asian champions Saudi Arabia 1-0 in the Indonesian capital Jakarta, with goal scorer Younis Mahmoud voted the tournament's best player. The striker of Sunni origin hails from the northern Iraqi city of Kirkuk, where Arabs, Turkmen and Kurds have often been at loggerheads. Mahmoud had a tattoo of an Iraqi map on his arm as a sign of unity. After the final, tens of thousands of people who otherwise hardly ever meet because of religious differences, celebrated in Baghdad. Even Kurds, who want their own state, waved Iraqi flags. The prime minister then received the team in a massively guarded security zone without civilians, but some players stayed away from Iraq.

The joy did not last long. In the years that followed, football matches and their TV broadcasts were repeatedly the targets of attacks. The organisation Iraq Body Count recorded around 4,000 acts of violence in 2016, seven times as many as in 2003, when Saddam Hussein was toppled. Will the country stabilise in the medium term? The national team has played home games in Iraq again since 2017. However, not in Baghdad, but in Basra, 500 kilometres to the south-east, which is considered safer since the IS has been pushed back.

For the first time since the US invasion in 2003, Iraq was able to hold the national cup competition again in 2016. Nevertheless, several players, coaches and trainers repeatedly apply for asylum abroad. Muayad Khalid, for example, played with Iraq in the Confederations Cup in South Africa in 2009, and now lives in Vienna. In *Ballesterer*, Khalid explained how tensions between the ethnic groups shape the Iraqi teams: 'One player is not nominated because he comes from a certain family or group. Unfortunately, not everything depends on playing ability. There are too many emotions involved, too many people have a say in coaching decisions and line-ups. It's about friendships that are cultivated. Or giving in when certain sections of the population demand a certain coach.'

FIFA's statutes prohibit political appropriation of football, and it has temporarily suspended national associations more than 20 times, including Nigeria in 2014, Sudan in 2017 and Sierra Leone in 2018. After Iraq's conquest of Kuwait in

1990, the Iraqi national team was not allowed to participate in international competitions for three years. In 2009, FIFA again excluded the Iraqi Football Federation for a short period. The reason given: state interference. The Iraqi Olympic Committee had previously dissolved the football federation and government security forces occupied its headquarters. The Iraqi officials bowed to the pressure, at least officially.

But FIFA does not always seem to apply the same standards. In the case of Syria, human rights activists and campaigners called for tougher action against the national football federation. Ayman Kasheet, a former Syrian league player who has been living in Sweden for several years, compiled facts in a detailed report, about the murder of Syrian players and about the compulsory participation of athletes in political events. Kasheet said that the stadiums in Aleppo, Latakia and Homs were used as military bases, prisons or refugee camps. Rockets were fired from the Abbasiyyin stadium in Damascus. Yet Ayman Kasheet did not feel taken seriously by FIFA, wrote US journalist Steve Fainaru in his report on ESPN in 2017.

In different statements, world football's governing body formulated the same thought: such 'tragic circumstances' as in Syria went far beyond football's sphere of responsibility. But did FIFA then have to describe the Syrians' sporting upswing in such flowery terms in its association media? Without an appropriate assessment of the political situation? Was it possibly showing consideration for the most important Assad ally, Russia, the host of the World Cup in 2018?

The Asian Football Confederation (AFC) had Syria's 2017 success assessed by Mosab Balhous, who had played 88 international matches as national goalkeeper until 2016. Balhous was quoted on the federation's website as saying that it was an honour for any player to represent his country. What was not mentioned: according to ESPN, Balhous was arrested by government forces in 2011 for offering sanctuary to rebels.

There was no trace of him for almost a year, and many fans thought he was dead. In 2012, he surprisingly returned to the national team. Since then, he has not commented on politics.

A hero of a country he never lived in

How political are players allowed to be, how political should they be? It is a question that Mansur Faqiryar did not ask himself as a young man; he wanted to play successful football, preferably internationally. Faqiryar was born in Kabul, the capital of Afghanistan, but he came to the German city of Bremen with his parents as a baby. As a youngster, Faqiryar developed into a goalkeeper with prospects for the future. At home, his parents cultivated Afghan culture, but Faqiryar had no memories of the country where one conflict followed another. In 1979, the Soviet Union had occupied Afghanistan, fearing the emergence of another Islamic power centre alongside Iran. After their withdrawal in 1989, Afghanistan plunged into civil war, followed by the rule of the radical Taliban. The country disintegrated into politico-religious areas.

Professional football structures were unthinkable during this time. A few months after the occupation by the USA in 2001, a national team was formed again in Afghanistan; it had played its last competitive matches in 1984, before the birth of Faqiryar. The formation of the team also met with great interest in Europe, especially in Hamburg, where one of the largest communities of exiled Afghans had emerged, and where Mohammed Saber Rohparwar had also found a new home during the civil war. The former Afghan national player built up a taxi business in the Hanseatic city. He founded the football club Ariana SV and looked for talents with Afghan roots, potential national players for his homeland.

In 2007, Mansur Faqiryar was playing for FC Oberneuland in the fourth division when he received a call from Rohparwar. With pride and curiosity, Faqiryar agreed to play, but many difficulties came along with it. In his biography *Heimat Fußball* (*Home Football*), Faqiryar describes the trips to Afghanistan, which sometimes took several days. In Kabul, players were often transported in armoured cars for fear of attacks. Within the national team, 'foreigners' like Faqiryar were critically eyed by the 'locals'. 'Several languages were spoken in the dressing room,' Faqiryar recounts. 'There was friction at first, even scuffles. Over time, we got to know each other better.' Around 50 languages and over 200 dialects are spoken in Afghanistan. The largest ethnic groups in terms of numbers: Pashtuns, Tajiks, Hazara and Uzbeks. Faqiryar says: 'I was often told in detail where my family and I come from. But I didn't get involved in that.'

It is a tradition that the spokespersons of ethnic groups want to have a say in the composition of the Afghan national team. Rarely are they equally satisfied with the outcome, but there are exceptions, like the 2013 South Asian Cup. In the semi-finals, the Afghan selection knocked hosts Nepal out of the tournament. The outstanding goalkeeper Mansur Faqiryar and his team-mates were subsequently banned from going out. A few days earlier, some Nepalese workers had been beheaded by the Taliban in Afghanistan, and now the team feared revenge.

Three days later, their worries faded into the background. Almost ten million Afghans watched the final of the South Asian Cup on television. In the Nepalese capital Kathmandu, their national team defeated India 2-0, a sensation. Mansur Faqiryar was voted the best player of the tournament; under his jersey he wore a T-shirt with the words 'Peace for Afghanistan' printed on it. Suddenly, Faqiryar was the hero of a country he had never lived in.

The day after, tens of thousands of people lined the streets of Kabul to celebrate the return of their team, many of them painting the black-red-green national flag on their cheeks.

The biggest celebration was to take place at Ghazi Stadium, Afghanistan's national stadium, opened in 1923. The Taliban had used the stadium for detentions, torture and executions. They had dangled cut-off arms and legs from the goalposts, burned books and films of 'infidels'. Many Afghans avoided the area around the stadium for years, fearing the ghosts of the dead.

Mansur Faqiryar was happy that Afghans could associate something positive with their national stadium. 'All of us together were proud of our team's performance,' he says. 'Everyone, not just some provinces or family clans. There were no big clashes in the country during the final.' Some newspapers celebrated the players as ambassadors of a country that had to stand up to foreign powers for a long time, against the British, the Russians, the US – to finally be independent and victorious.

But even the victory celebration in the Ghazi stadium made Faqiryar realise that joy can quickly be masked by fear in Afghanistan. Police officers made it clear to him that they could not guarantee security because of the angry crowds. Faqiryar and his team-mates were literally pushed out of the stadium by stewards and attendants. Soldiers with machine guns were also on the alert outside. Officials of the football association always kept their own security guards.

After the title win, Afghanistan's politicians spoke more intensively about football than ever before. Hamid Karzai, president between 2001 and 2014, told Mansur Faqiryar: 'What you've achieved, we politicians haven't managed with billions spent over the years.' Faqiryar received dozens of honours and invitations, including for campaign appearances. 'Everything in Afghanistan is political, I was aware of that. But I filtered carefully. When the president invites me, it is an honour. Not only for me, but also for my family, who gave up a lot so that I could grow up in safety and play football.'

How long will it last? Faqiryar and many of his friends were devastated when the Taliban took power in Afghanistan again in August 2021. Overnight the hope was gone.

Footballers as taxi drivers

Perplexity and powerlessness, that is also true for players in other parts of the Middle East. And probably few could express this feeling as well as Sami Hasan Al Nash, the former national coach of Yemen. This became clear in November 2019, when Qatar was hosting the Gulf Cup, a national tournament on the Arabian Peninsula. The Yemen team did not score a single goal in three matches, but did manage a 0-0 draw against Iraq. Al Nash held three press conferences in a luxury hotel in Doha within a week. These Q&A sessions were supposed to be about the team and tactics, but he seemed to have a different plan. He spoke about the suffering of his compatriots and the power of football: 'I don't think any other national team has such difficulties as we have. It's a miracle that we can play at all.'

Sami Hasan Al Nash said that the civil war in Yemen does not receive adequate international attention. But he said emotionally charged football, the world's most popular game, can make the conflict's consequences, which seem abstract to many, more understandable. 'Our players can rarely train together,' he said. 'Some of them don't play a single game for many months. And even if the war eventually ends, it will take a long time to rebuild our infrastructure.'

The foundations of football in Yemen have been almost completely destroyed. The domestic league has been on hiatus since 2014. Several stadiums have been bombed, many club headquarters looted. The Huthi rebels use clubhouses and team buses for their own purposes. A few national players are active abroad, in Qatar, Oman and Malaysia. Their colleagues in Yemen often have to earn extra money as civil servants, taxi drivers or cashiers in supermarkets. 'Our home games have had to be played abroad for years,' said Sami Hasan Al Nash in Doha. 'It takes a lot of strength physically and mentally.'

During the bombardments, national players were unable to leave from home airports to play abroad. A few times they crossed the Gulf of Aden on hours-long boat trips, their flights then starting in Djibouti in east Africa. Many players ended their careers by necessity, some joining the military, others the Huthi militias. 'Some footballers have been killed in battles,' says Yemeni sports journalist Yahya Alhalali. 'Others have been kidnapped during fake security checks and only released for ransom.' Alhalali also reports that athletes and fellow reporters have drowned while fleeing to Europe.

Yahya Alhalali does not want to only talk about death and terror, instead he recalls January 2019: for the first time, Yemen's squad took part in the Asian Cup. At the tournament in the United Arab Emirates, they didn't register a goal or a point. 'But even qualifying was celebrated like a miracle,' says Alhalali. 'Fear is a constant companion in our country. Unemployment is high, many people suffer from malnutrition. Football can provide a bit of a distraction.'

As in other countries in the Middle East, football is a contested symbol in Yemen, and has been for decades: from the 1960s, the country was divided, into a nationalist-ruled north and a socialist south. Both states promoted sports clubs to help spread their ideologies, both used chants and banners in stadiums for their propaganda. Unification as the Republic of Yemen followed in 1990. 'The new government also sought to symbolise harmony in football,' write US anthropologist Thomas B. Stevenson and Yemeni sociologist Karim Abdul Alaug in an essay for the Middle East Institute: 'The sports ministry created new teams so that both sides were equally represented in the league. The new national identity was also evident in the selection of the national team: both former states were represented by 16 players each.'

But this was soon followed by tensions between the population groups, terrorist attacks and, since 2014, civil war. 'Despite all the crises, the national team was supported by the government,' says sports scientist Mahfoud Amara from Qatar University in Doha. 'In the Arab world, many examples show football can provide a sense of normality where normality no longer exists.' Yemen is experiencing one of the biggest humanitarian disasters in recent history, exacerbated by Coronavirus. The energetic national coach Sami Hasan Al Nash died from the virus, in May 2021, at the age of 64.

English messages are banned from the stands

Meanwhile in Syria, it has become apparent that Bashar al-Assad will remain in office, but his government wants to prevent protests from flaring up in the long term. 'In regimes with a repressed civil society, football is probably the last arena for expressing social and political identities,' says Middle East expert James M. Dorsey, citing examples from which Assad's confidants may have learned: in Tunisia, in Turkey, but especially in Egypt during the Arab Spring in 2011, it was ultras who fanned the flames of street protests against governments. They were trained in hand-to-hand combat with the police. They knew how to dodge water cannons and break through blockades.

As these images resonate, the police want the ultras in Syria to call themselves fan clubs rather than ultras, and since 2017 they have gradually returned to the stadiums. Flags with English messages are also banned. 'People have tried to sneak into the fan groups and throw stones at the police,' says Nadim Rai, a supporter of the Hutteen club in the port city of Latakia. 'Then there would have been an excuse to ban the ultras.' Rai was among the first ultras in Syria, he developed choreographies, wrote blog posts, took photos.

'We couldn't act politically like German or Italian ultras,' says Rai. 'If we wanted to express protest, we had to be very sensitive. In Syria, it can happen that you disappear overnight and never reappear.' Rai lives in south-west Germany after fleeing Syria. He studies IT and uses his season ticket for the train to watch as many games in the region as possible.

Football in Syria won't let him go. With friends, he collaborated on a film for the online outlet Copa90, *The Secret Life of Syrian Ultras*, which is on YouTube. 'I have already been asked if there is beer and PlayStations in Syria. It's sad that many Europeans reduce our country to war and terror.' Rai also educates people in lectures about the complex background and the rapid developments in Syrian football, for which he has to update his presentation almost monthly. The title of his lecture: 'Fan culture in the war zone – football is our weapon.' He says: 'For years the ultras let their rivalries rest during the war, now they are becoming more aggressive again.' For him, this is also a good sign. For far too long, everyday life has revolved around survival.

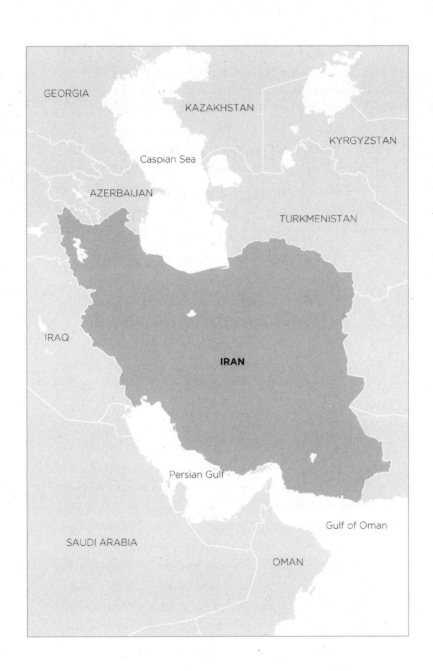

90 Minutes of Escape

In probably no other country does religion shape football as much as in Iran. The arch-conservative clergy fears collective outbursts of emotion and has the stadiums closely guarded by the Revolutionary Guards. The political reformers associate the national team with a symbol of new beginnings, but time and again they are blocked by hardliners, for example on the women's issue.

REZA WAS well known in the police station of his neighbourhood in Tehran. Twice a year he came into custody, sometimes three times. In the mid-1990s, Reza was not yet 20 years old. He attended readings by critical writers, met with left-wing students at his law school. He was seen with alcohol, also with an unmarried woman. So, he had to spend some nights in the police station, and once he received lashes. Reza, the son of a communist, was not brought up religiously. But his everyday life in Iran was determined by religious leaders.

The Iranian economy was in the ground, the national debt was growing. In 1997, 70 per cent of the population was under 25. Like Reza, many of them were considering leaving the country. They were anxious about the upcoming presidential election, in which 238 candidates wanted to take part. The 'Guardian Council', dominated by clerics, examined their

'Islamic fidelity to the constitution' and allowed only four candidates to run. The conservative election favourite Ali Akbar Nateq Nuri had the revolutionary leader Ali Khamenei on his side, the highest spiritual and political authority in the country.

Then came the sensation: on 23 May 1997, the reformist politician Mohammad Chātami won the election. With a high voter turnout of 80 per cent, Chātami received 70 per cent of the votes, mainly from academics, young people and women. 'It was a special atmosphere that we didn't know,' says Reza. 'We thought the country was finally opening up.' Writers, directors and intellectuals who had been persecuted or exiled since the 1979 Islamic Revolution hoped for a second, liberal revolution.

The Iranian national football team had had problems in qualifying for the 1998 World Cup. Coach Mayeli Kohan resisted picking players who played in foreign leagues, calling them traitors. After the 0-2 loss against Qatar, his attitude was discussed in parliament. Kohan's successor, the Brazilian Valdeir Vieira, expanded the roster. And so the Iranian team had a chance in the elimination matches for the World Cup against Australia, even after the 1-1 draw in the first leg in front of more than 100,000 spectators in Tehran.

Reza remembers well the return match on 29 November 1997 in Melbourne, the TV broadcast started at lunchtime in Tehran. Australia led 2-0 at the start of the second half. Reza turned off the TV dejectedly, but soon heard shouts of joy from the neighbourhood. The Iranian team managed to draw the game 2-2 in the last 15 minutes – and thus qualify for the World Cup. 'All the dams broke,' Reza recalls. 'People poured into the streets everywhere, there was even alcohol. Women danced without headscarves. The security forces held back because they couldn't possibly have slowed down these crowds. We were longing for such an outburst.'

Spectators or secret service

In his book *The Turbulent World of Middle East Soccer*, the publicist James M. Dorsey describes how the emotions inspired by the World Cup qualification were transferred to everyday life in Iran. Populations with different traditions, sometimes in conflict, came together through football: Persians, Assyrians, Armenians. Around 20 million people had voted for Mohammad Chātami in the election – and thus for a fundamental change. According to Dorsey, the World Cup qualification gave the voters another demonstration of power. For almost 20 years, large gatherings of people had been almost impossible because of strict controls. And now, protest banners and chants of invective against the regime were mixed in with the celebrations. Could football pose a threat to the powerful clergy?

Reza, born two years before the Islamic Revolution and raised in Tehran, knows the answer. His family's flat was two kilometres from the Azadi Stadium, the most important sports venue in Iran. Since childhood, Reza has been a fan of Persepolis, one of the capital's two major clubs. Reza has seen dozens of games at the Azadi. He liked the collective cheering after a late winning goal, sometimes in front of more than 100,000 fans. What he didn't like: strict controls, aggressive chaperones, honouring war veterans before matches or calls to prayer at half-time. Reza believes that every 50th spectator was working for the secret service: 'Fans had to have banners approved by security forces. Groups needed approval to designate their leaders.' Once, Reza was arrested at the Azadi Stadium for an insult. 'Azadi means freedom,' he says. 'But it has nothing to do with freedom.'

And yet, for Iranians, football is a platform for feelings of freedom. At the 1998 World Cup in France, Iran was due to meet the USA. The two countries have not had diplomatic relations since 1980. During the Islamic Revolution, Iranian students had occupied the US embassy in Tehran and taken 52 diplomats hostage. The 1998 match fell into a phase of détente.

The newly elected President Chātami had spoken out in favour of a 'new relationship' in a CNN interview; he spoke of a 'dialogue of civilisations'. US President Bill Clinton sent friendly greetings to Tehran on Iranian holidays. He had his picture taken at the White House with American wrestlers who had competed in Iran. And in a video message, Clinton called the 1998 World Cup match a sign against alienation.

Many clerics in Iran saw it differently. Religious leader Ali Khamenei spoke out against the Iranian team moving towards the American team while shaking hands before the match, as was protocol. In addition, Iranians were outraged by the rerun of the US film *Not Without My Daughter* on French television. The film deals with the escape of an American mother from her violent Iranian husband.

FIFA wanted to counteract the tensions and declared the explosive match day on 21 June 1998 a 'Fair Play Day'. The referee was Urs Meier from Switzerland. This was also significant: since 1981, Switzerland, which is considered neutral, had officially mediated US interests in Tehran. The players presented each other with flowers and posed for a joint photo, not the usual practice on such occasions. 'This gesture was not only understood in Iran as a sign of international understanding,' says Omid Nouripour, leader of the Green Party in Germany with Iranian roots. 'It was also an expression of the longing for international recognition and for an end to isolation.'

Twenty years on, journalist Keith Duggan recalled in the *Irish Times* newspaper that the match in Lyon was also accompanied by protests. Supporters of the so-called People's Mujahedin displayed banners and photos of opposition figure Maryam Rajavi. In the 1980 Iranian presidential election, shortly after the revolution, her husband Massoud Rajavi had been the People's Mujahedin candidate. Maryam Rajavi has been living in Paris with many comrades-in-arms for almost 40 years. From exile, her movement works against the regime in Tehran. At the stadium in Lyon, a large contingent of security forces was supposed to prevent a possible storming of the pitch. 'I only found out about this later,' says the Iranian football fan Reza. 'On TV, only happy spectators were shown in the stands. The protests went completely under the radar.'

That was also because of the game. The Iranian team, coached by Jalal Talebi, an exile from California with Iranian roots, wrestled down the USA 2-1, their first ever victory at a World Cup finals. Again, hundreds of thousands poured into the streets of Iran. Horns sounded, banned music was played, there were even a few thousand women at the national team's welcome party. 'For 20 years, Iranians in our country and in the diaspora had no common reason to cheer,' said Hamid Estili, scorer of the first goal against the USA. 'Football gave us the chance.'

For decades, reforming forces could, at best, meet in secret in small groups. The mass mobilisation around football showed them how many like-minded people wanted to shed the strict clergy without abandoning religion in the process. Reza says that the positive mood of those days has lingered on for a long time. Students like him became even more committed to social change. 'For those in power, the enthusiasm at football was a shock,' says Iranian filmmaker Ayat Najafi. 'For the government, everything in public life has to have a limit, but in football there is no limit. So it had to control football more strictly.' On the very day of the World Cup match against the USA, the conservative-leaning parliament ousted Interior Minister Abdollah Nouri, one of the most progressive forces in President Chātami's cabinet. Nouri aggressively campaigned for freedom of expression and a 'democratic Islam'. 'I was saddened by this ousting,' says Najafi. 'In the frenzy of football victory, this was unfortunately lost on many reformers as well.'

Fans attacked banks and government buildings

In an interview for this book, analyst and Iran expert David Jalilvand explains how Ali Khamenei's entourage pushed back liberalisation in the late 1990s. The judiciary, military and intelligence services follow the religious leader, not the president. In July 1999, a court order led to the banning of *Salam*, a reform-oriented newspaper from Mohammad Chātami's circle. A student protest against religious leaders grew into the largest demonstrations since the Islamic Revolution.

'There was a series of murders of intellectuals,' says Jalilvand. 'The regime had the protests put down and the Guardian Council blocked reform plans by the Chātami government.' Freedom of expression and assembly were restricted. Hundreds of students, human rights activists and politicians were imprisoned, including former Interior Minister Abdollah Nouri. In contrast, football fan and law student Reza was able to convince the police that he had just happened to pass by the demonstration. So he was released after 48 hours in custody. At the end of 1999, two years after the celebrated World Cup qualification, Reza applied for asylum in Germany. 'It became too dangerous. I wanted to go on living.'

But the reform movement in Iran had not yet died down. The Guardian Council continuously rejected progressive candidates seeking political office. Nevertheless, in the 2000 parliamentary elections, the conservatives lost their majority for the first time in 21 years. Young voters voted for Chātami's fellow campaigners; at that time, only six per cent of the population was older than 60. But it was precisely from this minority that the religious power elite recruited, which Chātami wanted to push back. The judiciary banned more media and silenced critics. Demonstrations were taboo.

The Iranian government viewed the qualifying campaign for the 2002 World Cup in Japan and South Korea with concern. Iran, which sees itself as the centre of Shia Islam, had to compete in a group with arch-rival Saudi Arabia, the supposed protecting power of the Sunnis. In the last group match on 21 October 2001, a victory in Bahrain would have been enough for Iran to qualify directly for the World Cup. In Bahrain, dominated for centuries by Persia, the majority of the population is Shia, but the ruling house is Sunni. Big Iran lost 3-1 to tiny Bahrain, with some of the host nation's players waving flags of Saudi Arabia, a key ally of their government. In Tehran, some fans attacked banks and government buildings.

Saudi Arabia qualified directly for the World Cup, while Iran later failed to beat Ireland in the play-offs. 'In Iran, people claimed that the team failed on purpose due to pressure from the government to prevent new mass gatherings,' says filmmaker Ayat Najafi. 'I don't believe it.' According to Najafi, the liberals' frustration also had to do with the fact that President Chātami's reforms were not going fast enough for them. There was at least a small consolation during the 2002 World Cup: Saudi Arabia lost 0-8 to Germany. Najafi: 'There was great joy in Tehran, sweets were distributed in the markets.'

Football for Western values

The roots for this emotionality and the political significance of football go back about a century. In an essay for the journal *Iranian Studies*, long-time Harvard scholar Houchang Chehabi names a patron: Reza Pahlavi, Shah of Persia between 1925 and 1941. After years of foreign influence by the British and Russians, the monarch wanted to modernise the backward and almost bankrupt Persia: through expansion and reforms in infrastructure, health-care, education and justice. Unlike his contemporary Mustafa Kemal Atatürk in Turkey, Reza Pahlavi failed to transform Iran into a republic; the opposition of the clergy was too powerful.

The German cultural scientist Gerhard Schweizer writes in his book *Understanding Iran* that the Shah oriented himself towards the West by other means. He propagated a European style of dress for men and rejected the face veil for women. He had the ancestral state name Persia, which had been perceived as a foreign designation, replaced by Iran in 1935. The Shah demonstrated his distance from the clergy in various ways. Once he even beat up a mullah in public.

In everyday culture, football was a way 'to bring Western values into the country', writes Iran researcher Houchang Chehabi in his essay *The Political History of Football in Iran*. In the decades before, it had been the British who gradually introduced football: as teachers in missionary schools, soldiers and oil industry workers. The members of the Football Association, founded in 1920, were subjected to hostility because their short sports shorts violated Islamic dress codes. The Shah's appointment as honorary president marked a breakthrough for the association. Reza Pahlavi attended a friendly match between the Iranians and the British, and also sent a squad to a tournament in Baku. Senior officials described the game as an important element for health and cohesion among the population.

Like Reza Pahlavi, his eldest son and successor was not a democrat. As Shah, Mohammad Reza Pahlavi maintained contacts with the USA and Europe from 1941 onwards, but he was not really interested in their welfare-state ideas, reports cultural scientist Gerhard Schweizer. After the nationalisation of the oil industry, only a small elite profited from the upswing in Iran. The ruling family placed a fortune in foreign accounts. Meanwhile, many civil servants, policemen and teachers suffered from malnutrition. In the mid-1950s, Iran had a population of 18 million; by 1970, it was almost 30 million.

More and more people were moving to the cities for work. With an estimated 50,000 employees, the SAVAK secret service was supposed to suppress any resistance.

At the end of the 1960s, when urbanisation and industrialisation were breaking up old milieus, football offered a means of identification, especially with the two big clubs in Tehran. Persepolis, named after the capital of the ancient Persian Empire, gathered many workers around it; the club colour, red. Taj (the Crown), founded by a general, was close to the elites, and its club colour was blue. Taj celebrated the birthdays of the ruling family and distributed publicity photos of its players with actresses. Followers of the Shah had some mosques destroyed to make room for football fields. For the clerics, this was a reason to renew their criticism of the monarchy, according to Iran expert Houchang Chehabi. The accusation: the population is distracted from economic problems by football.

Iranian football reached a new political dimension in 1968, when the national team hosted the Asian Cup in Tehran against Israel. Under Shah Mohammad Reza Pahlavi, Iran was the second Islamic state after Turkey to recognise Israel, and relations were considered stable. After Israel's victory in the 1967 Six-Day War, however, many Iranians sympathised with the defeated Arab states. These tensions were felt at the 1968 tournament. A rumour spread in Tehran that Jewish entrepreneurs had distributed thousands of tickets to Iranians of the Jewish faith as support for Israel. As a result, spectators were allowed into the Amjadeih Stadium free of charge, allegedly because the Shah wanted to demonstrate his pro-Islamic stance.

With a 2-1 win, the Iranian team secured the Asian Championship – and was able to repeat this triumph in 1972 and 1976. National players were now invited on television, and the Shah also appeared with them. Parviz Ghelichkhani, who scored the late winning goal against Israel, stood out as a political voice. 'He criticised the regime and did not want to be instrumentalised by the Shah,' says filmmaker Ayat Najafi, who has studied Iranian football history for a documentary. Because of his criticism, Ghelichkhani was imprisoned for two months in 1972. He moved to the USA in 1978, where he cancelled his participation in the World Cup in Argentina at a press conference in protest against the Shah. Later, Ghelichkhani settled in Paris, where he edited a magazine on politics and culture. 'Ghelichkhani gave us orientation,' says Ayat Najafi. 'I don't think there will be another legend like him in football.'

Pitches turned into places of prayer

In the late 1970s, the economic crisis in Iran came to a head with strikes, demonstrations and riots. Especially in the countryside, the population wanted a ruler who exemplified modesty and religiosity, a ruler like Ruhollah Khomeini. The Shah went into exile in France, a Regency Council took over and, after his own return from exile in 1979, the Ayatollah took power and promised a culture of tolerance, but soon there was little left of it. 'There was an attempt to Islamise everything,' says political consultant David Jalilvand, who travels regularly in Iran. Revolutionary leader Khomeini had constitutional bodies staffed by Shia Muslims. Western-trained lawyers, teachers and economists were replaced by clerics. After the closure of universities, newspapers and banks, Khomeini took increasingly drastic action against dissidents. Politically motivated executions under Ruhollah Khomeini are estimated at up to 30,000.

Leisure culture in the public sphere was on the verge of upheaval. 'Cinemas, bars and theatres were closed,' says Jalilvand. 'There was also an attempt to oust football as un-Islamic.' The municipality from Bushehr in southern Iran commented in a leaflet: 'Wouldn't it be better to spend public funds on building schools and hospitals? Wouldn't it make more sense to help our brothers of Jihad in remote areas instead of engaging in ridiculous games like the US and Britain? Have we solved all social, cultural and economic problems so that we can devote ourselves to sport?' The leaflet appeared in late 1980 during the early stages of the first Gulf War between Iran and Iraq. At the same time, the national team was playing in the Asian Championship in Kuwait.

The clergy soon realised that banning popular football could stir up those groups to whom it owed part of the revolution: the conservative peasants and less educated workers. Instead, the regime established a tight network of control: Taj, the Shah's former club, was placed under the state organisation for education and renamed Esteghlal (Independence). Rival Persepolis came under the care of the Ministry of Industry, but continued to gather critics of the regime. In the Islamic Republic's first presidential election in 1980, Persepolis supported People's Mujahideen candidate Massoud Rajavi, but Ayatollah Khomeini disqualified him.

Religious disputes always ignited along football, Houchang Chehabi discusses. A few examples: The arch-conservatives complained to players about uncovered body parts and Latin lettering on jerseys. They demanded Islamic chanting in stadiums and pushed for some sports fields to be turned into places of prayer. Liberal voices saw football as an ideology-free entertainment that the population deserved in view of high unemployment. The Green politician Omid Nouripour, who has been a follower of Persepolis since childhood, says: 'Football as religion: this slogan may be right in many places, but not in Iran. In a society where religion is supposed to dominate all everyday life by state order, football is the ultimate escape from it. In the stadiums, people live out what they are not allowed to do elsewhere. That's why the atmosphere in the stadiums is always tense.' In education and health programmes, authorities usually left football unmentioned, new pitches and halls were rarely created.

The Revolutionary Guard became the most influential control body in football. After the overthrow of the Shah in 1979, Ruhollah Khomeini set up this paramilitary organisation to 'protect the regime'. Its initial 10,000 members were recruited from Islamist students and supporters of the radical Hezbollah. During the first Gulf War against Iraq, the Revolutionary Guard supported the military and grew to 300,000 members; after the end of the war in 1988, it took over internal security tasks. It only has to accept orders from the revolutionary leader; as a rule, it does not pay taxes and customs duties.

Iran expert Cornelius Adebahr of the German Council on Foreign Relations analyses the enormous importance of the Revolutionary Guard for the Iranian economy: its leading members and sub-groups are involved in thousands of major projects, in the oil industry, in the construction sector, in transport, sometimes worth several billion pounds. In addition, the Revolutionary Guard controls some news agencies, internet services and mobile phone companies. 'In Iran, even in football, nothing works without the Revolutionary Guard,' says Reza, a football fan who lives near Berlin. 'It's a bit like in the GDR. The steel industry and car manufacturing also have their own clubs, and the Revolutionary Guard supervises everything. So football is closely tied to the state.'

For the US broadcaster Radio Free Europe, journalist Kristin Deasy explained the network of the Revolutionary Guard in football: Akbar Ghamkhar was the first commander to take over a top club, as chairman of Persepolis in 2002. Several followers were given leadership positions at other clubs, including the football association and the professional league. Kristin Deasy reports that the Revolutionary Guard ensures tax benefits for clubs and protects their players from problems if, for example, they drink alcohol without permission or break their fast. The recruitment of young players is based within the Revolutionary Guard at the Basiji, a militia of volunteers. Thousands of young people join the Basiji because they hope to get a better place to study or a well-paid civil service job.

Green armbands in support of protesters

Mahmoud Ahmadinejad, the sixth president of the Islamic Republic, in power between 2005 and 2013, had a close relationship with the Revolutionary Guard. For the cultural scientist Gerhard Schweizer, he was a 'radical fundamentalist' in office with little willingness to engage in dialogue. Ahmadinejad wanted to reverse the reforms of his predecessor Mohammad Chātami. He had social housing built, but also cracked down on 'un-Islamic ideas' and demanded an 'Islamic dress code' from women. In his first cabinet, Ahmadinejad filled 13 of the 21 ministerial posts with former commanders of the Revolutionary Guard.

The disclosure platform Wikileaks published information from US diplomats in Tehran in 2010, which read, among other things: 'Ahmadinejad has used a lot of political capital in Iranian football. He is using the popularity of football to reach out to his electorate.' Ahmadinejad attended training sessions of the national team and had his picture taken during penalty shootouts. For a match in North Korea, he provided the team with a government plane. According to Middle East expert James M. Dorsey, he is also said to have made efforts to remove disagreeable voices in football, such as federation president Ali Kafashian. Ahmadinejad countered criticism from FIFA, which forbids interference: 'We will respect FIFA rules, but FIFA is only an agency and it should not be allowed to interfere in Iran's internal affairs.'

Ahmadinejad's football ambitions were conspicuous during his campaign for re-election. On 28 March 2009, two and a half months before the election, the Iranian team lost 2-1 at home to Saudi Arabia in the World Cup qualifiers, and hours later national coach Ali Daei, who had also played for FC Bayern, was sacked. 'Ahmadinejad is said to have instigated the sacking,' says director Ayat Najafi. 'He considered Ali Daei a political opponent and wanted to show strength.'

A total of 475 people applied to stand in the presidential election in 2009, including 42 women. But the Guardian Council, a spiritual control body, only allowed four candidates. In a society marked by unemployment and poverty, the moderate candidate Mir Hossein Mussawi emerged as a beacon of hope: the colour of his movement, green. In the election on 12 June 2009, Mahmoud Ahmadinejad won an absolute majority with 62.6 per cent, and a run-off was not necessary. Iranian and foreign observers provided evidence of election manipulation. Millions of people protested across the country, there were street battles with deaths and injuries.

On 17 June, five days after the election, the Iranian national team played in South Korea for its last chance to qualify for the World Cup. At the Seoul stadium, Iranian fans unfurled a banner reading 'Go to hell, dictator'. Some waved flags with the words 'Free Iran'. In front of millions of TV viewers, six Iranian players wore green armbands in solidarity with the protesters and Mir Hossein Mussawi. 'That was an encouragement for many people,' says Omid Nouripour, who had come to Frankfurt from Tehran with his family in 1988. 'The fact that the wristbands disappeared in the second half mobilised even more people for the street.'

Had government officials exerted pressure in the changing room? In a later interview with the *New York Times*, the national coach at the time, Afshin Ghotbi, professed ignorance. His team drew 1-1 against South Korea and failed to qualify. Afshin Ghotbi believes they were too distracted: 'The players saw the pictures of the demonstrations on CNN and BBC.

They were also in touch with friends and families. The violence on the streets claimed their minds.'

Reza, an Iranian football fan, followed the protests in the media, from his home in Germany, especially on social media. He says: 'No one really cared about football at the time. Maybe it was good that Iran didn't qualify, otherwise Ahmadinejād would have used it for himself.' At times, protesters displayed photos of the players wearing green armbands against South Korea, in addition to green flags and headbands. The protests against the regime, which became known as the Green Movement, continued until autumn 2009. According to the opposition, 72 people were killed and several thousand arrested, many of whom are still missing. The presidential candidate Mir Hossein Mussawi was later placed under house arrest. And Iranian media are still forbidden from publishing photos of or quotes from former President Mohammad Chātami.

During Mahmoud Ahmadinejad's term in office, the divisions between reformers, moderates, conservatives and hardliners, between the young and the older generation, deepened. On the one hand, pictures and videos leaked to the public showing students at forbidden parties with alcohol and western music. On the other hand, the security apparatus wanted to prevent new protests, and the repression reached far into the everyday life of the citizens. In 2011, a memorial service was held for Nasser Hejazi, the acclaimed national goalkeeper of the 1970s, and 10,000 mourners gathered at Tehran's Azadi Stadium, probably because Hejazi had publicly denounced the social divide.

James M. Dorsey writes about the protests during the ceremony in *The Turbulent World of Middle East Soccer*. 'Hejazi, you spoke on behalf of the people,' supporters chanted. 'Nasser, rise up, the people can't take it anymore.' The security forces insisted the coffin was moved more quickly. The Arab Spring had just unfolded in some Middle Eastern countries, with presidents in Egypt and Tunisia toppled. Now Iranian football fans at the cemetery were chanting, 'Mubarak, Ben Ali, now it's your turn, Khamenei!'

Events like these led hardliner Mahmoud Ahmadinejad and the spiritual control bodies to expand repression. 'The stadium is often a space of politico-religious expressions that are in line with the system,' says Christoph Becker, editor of the *Frankfurter Allgemeine Zeitung*, who has been shedding light on the links between sport and religion in Iran for years. Becker recalls a World Cup qualifier against South Korea in October 2016, on the eve of Ashura. On this day, Shia Muslims commemorate the Battle of Karbala, which sealed the division between Shias and Sunnis in the year 680 of our era.

The Iranian Football Association wanted to postpone the match against South Korea, but FIFA forbade religious interference. Members of the Basiji militia and the radical Hezbollah threatened to attack football fans. Clerics instructed stadium-goers to wear black clothing and refrain from clapping. During the match, clerics waved black flags and chanted in memory of the martyr Hussein, a grandson of the Prophet Muhammad, and displayed banners reading, 'Hussein, the eternal voice of justice'. The Iranian federation was fined. 'But the federation accepts this fine, there is always money for that,' says Christoph Becker.

The moderately respected President Ahmadinejād tried a few things to gain a hearing in liberal circles; he even spoke out in favour of female spectators at men's games. After the revolution, the clergy had restricted women's rights. Women had to get used to veiling again, the minimum age for marriage was lowered from 18 to 13 and extramarital sex was made a punishable offence. Men's games in football, basketball and volleyball were closed to women, officially, to protect them from vulgar spectators. Some presidents campaigned for the ban to be lifted, but the clergy always retained the final say.

Breakthrough for the women's team

Maryam Irandoost was born during the revolutionary period, in 1979. In her hometown of Bandar Anzali on the Caspian Sea, her father had been the coach of the professional club Malavan. 'When he was at matches, I used to drive around the stadium in the car. I kind of wanted to be there and take in the atmosphere.' Irandoost enjoyed a privilege many of her friends were denied: she was able to watch the Iranian men's national team play live at the World Cups in Brazil in 2014 and Russia in 2018. 'At the beginning I was crying because it was hard to believe. It was like heaven.'

When Iranian football was reported on in the West, a main topic was the exclusion of female spectators. For years, women's rights activists campaigned for the lifting of this ban in their 'Open Stadiums' initiative. Successive FIFA presidents, Sepp Blatter and Gianni Infantino, visited Tehran and claimed to have exerted pressure, but a breakthrough was not forthcoming. At international matches or in the Asian Champions League, female fans from the visiting nations were sometimes allowed into the Azadi stadium. In contrast, Iranian women had to settle for public viewing during the 2018 World Cup after long negotiations. And so, photos of women who gained entry to men's games with glued-on beards and loose clothing circulated on social networks. The women were often caught and taken into custody.

Maryam Irandoost, however, resists the Western narrative of the always oppressed and hopeless Iranian woman. As a child and teenager, she had played football, but during puberty she experienced hostility and took a break, studying sports science and learning to play the piano. 'The desire for football was just too great,' she says. 'We have so many talented female players, and we want to keep fighting for equality.' In recent years, dozens of women's teams have emerged. The women's national team was founded in 2005. But for a long time, the squad was hardly active, because the Ministry of Sport wanted to keep the attention on women limited.

Irandoost has been making contacts in football for years. This is one of the reasons why she came back into football and was entrusted with rebuilding the national team in 2021. Irandoost, then 41 years old, travelled the country, looking for talented players. She organised friendly matches and campaigned for players to be paid. Gradually, the Iranian Football Association opened up, also due to pressure from FIFA. In January 2022 for the first time, the Iranian women took part in the Asian Championship. In Iran itself, however, the major media apparently did not give this development much coverage. 'We are campaigning for better facilities,' says Irandoost. 'Football teaches women to stand up for their rights.'

Unwanted spectators – ambitious players: football illustrates the complex legal situation for women in Iran. When it comes to divorce, inheritance or testifying, women are at a legal disadvantage compared to men. On the other hand, they have opportunities that women in Saudi Arabia or in some Gulf States do not have. Iranian women can vote and be elected to political office. They can become lawyers, but not judges. They can rise to vice-president but not president. 'We have successful women entrepreneurs, scientists and actresses,' says photographer Maryam Majd, who worked for the women's magazine *Zanan* before it was banned in 2009. In many universities, female students outnumber men.

Majd wanted to document the 2011 Women's World Cup in Germany, but she was prevented from leaving the country and temporarily imprisoned. She doesn't want to talk about it today, not even about the censorship authorities who make it difficult for media professionals to work. Instead, she emphasises the positive in workshops with young women photographers. 'Even within our system, we can portray successful and confident female athletes.' Majd photographed the 2019 World Cup in

France and weeks later was at the festival of the women's rights group Discover Football in Berlin. The renowned organisation World Press Photo nominated her work for a competition.

Maryam Majd and her fellow women were shocked to learn of Sahar Khodayari's death. The young Esteghal supporter had set herself on fire on 2 September 2019 in protest against an impending imprisonment. Masoud Shojaei, captain of Iran's national team, wrote on Instagram: 'The self-immolation of a woman who was charged because she wanted to watch a football match is the result of disgusting thinking and will be completely incomprehensible to future generations.' A stadium will eventually be named after her, said Andranik Teymourian, for a long time the only national player of Christian faith.

The international headlines about Sahar Khodayari's death put further pressure on Iran's football federation. FIFA threatened to exclude the Iranian national team from qualifying for the 2022 World Cup. And so the federation relented: on 10 October 2019, almost 4,000 women were allowed to watch the home match against Cambodia. They were assigned special entrances, female police officers and stadium guides, they had to remain segregated in the fenced stands, and there were no toilets for women. Activist Maryam Shodjaei, sister of the captain, commented: 'This is discrimination. Women are being forced to accept separate ticketing. But women must be given full access everywhere, including the league.' For league matches, women are still not allowed into stadiums on a regular basis, with Covid being used as an official reason for a long time.

Sanctions also damage the sport

The successor of Mahmoud Ahmadinejad did not do much about women's rights in football. On 14 June 2013, Hassan Rohani had received 50.7 per cent of the vote in the presidential election. Four days later, the Iranian team won 1-0 in South

Korea and qualified for the 2014 World Cup in Brazil. Again, Iranians celebrated in the streets, but less euphorically than in 1997.

Hassan Rohani spoke on the phone with US President Barack Obama shortly after his election; it was the first contact between the heads of state of both countries since 1979. After long negotiations with the USA and other nations, in 2015 Iran agreed to a nuclear programme without nuclear weapons. The end of isolation brought investors to Iran. European airlines started flying to Tehran again, and five million tourists came in 2016. But in 2018, Obama's successor Donald Trump terminated the nuclear agreement and tightened sanctions. 'The US wants to cut Iran off from its most important oil buyers and threatens companies involved in business with the Iranian government with penalties,' explains Iran expert Cornelius Adebahr. At the same time, Trump agreed on arms deliveries to Saudi Arabia worth the equivalent of 100 billion euros.

Iran had hoped for investments from abroad of more than £40bn, but in fact less than £5bn flowed. Meanwhile, the average monthly income is only £350, and around 30 per cent of young adults are unemployed. In football, officials complain that it is more difficult to find sponsors. The exclusion of Iranian banks from international financial transactions poses challenges for the federation and its clubs when it comes to payments. On several occasions, national associations cancelled matches against Iran at short notice. 'Nobody wants to play against us,' said Carlos Queiroz, Iran's national coach between 2011 and 2018, shortly before the World Cup in Russia.

Corporations from the US and Europe withdrew their employees from Iran. The US sporting goods company Nike banned Iranian footballers from wearing its shoes at the 2018 World Cup. Some players bought other models from sports shops or borrowed them from club colleagues. After the World

Cup, Adidas also announced that it would not renew its contract beyond 2018. According to the Iranian news agency INSA, the company had not wanted to jeopardise its business in the USA. 'The sanctions give the regime a bit of freedom of movement,' says Green foreign policy expert Omid Nouripour. 'Many people say that if the national team is not successful, it's the Americans' fault and not the mismanagement in the federation.' Quite a few alliances promoted a boycott of Nike products in 2018.

Where is Iran heading more than 40 years after the revolution? The number of students has risen from 2.8 million in 2007 to almost five million. In scientific publications, the share of Iranian researchers has grown massively. On the other hand, Amnesty International published a report in 2016 stating that executions had increased hugely under President Hassan Rohani. Critical voices are sanctioned, in football too. Mehdi Taj, then president of the Iranian Federation, insisted that reporters address only sporting issues. Taj said, 'For irrelevant questions, we will first confiscate the press card. And punish him with a four-year ban if he repeats.' The journalists' protests that followed led to the sports minister intervening.

In this atmosphere, few players comment on political issues. In February 2019, then Iranian Foreign Minister Mohammad Sarif responded to Western criticism of Iranian influence in various conflicts: 'We are proud to be under pressure because we defend the people of Palestine, Lebanon, Yemen and Syria,' Sarif said. In response, Voria Ghafouri, an Iranian international who plays for Esteghlal, posted a message to the foreign minister on Instagram: 'They are not under pressure. It's the ordinary people who are under pressure.'

Revolutionary Leader Ali Khamenei intervened in a speech: 'Some people who benefit from peace and security in the country, and who enjoy their jobs and their favourite sports, are biting the hand that feeds them.' The Ministry of Sport called in Voria Ghafouri and made it clear that footballers should refrain from political comments. At Esteghlal's next home match, fans loudly chanted his name. Ghafouri did not allow his mouth to be shut, but from then on he was less outspoken. In November 2019, tens of thousands of Iranians demonstrated again against economic policies, especially against the increase in petrol prices. The regime retaliated brutally. More than 1,000 people were reportedly killed in the process, and the internet was completely shut down for several days. Voria Ghafouri wrote: 'Life is too short to forget these black days.'

In January 2020, a completely different picture emerged. Like hundreds of thousands of Iranians, national player Mehdi Torabi took part in the funeral march for Qasem Soleimani. The Iranian general had been killed by a US drone in Baghdad. Dozens of professional footballers also expressed solidarity. The state media reported it extensively. First division clubs placed photos of Soleimani on the pitch, players bowed and laid flowers. Whether they did so voluntarily, however, may be doubted.

In 2021, a hardliner was again elected president in Iran: Ebrahim Raisi. During the same period, the Iranian team qualified for the World Cup in Qatar. Women were to be admitted to the stadium for the last home match. However, the match against Lebanon did not take place in Tehran, but in Mashhad in the northeast, a stronghold of the hardliners.

On the day of the match, hundreds of women stood in front of locked gates with their valid tickets and were not allowed in. This led to protests. According to eyewitnesses, the police used pepper spray against the women. It seems that Iranian football is at a standstill. Not in sporting terms, but politically.

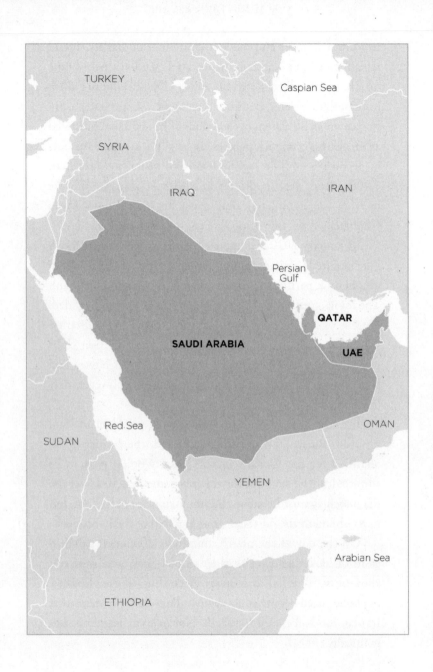

Megaphone For Dispute

Looking towards a post-oil future, the sheikdoms in the Persian Gulf are competing for investors, skilled workers and tourists. In football, Qatar, the United Arab Emirates and Saudi Arabia are all trying to win major events, club shares and sponsorship contracts. Small Qatar in particular is putting down roots in world politics through the 2022 World Cup, but its hostile neighbours look sceptically at any reform. What are the consequences of the power games for the Middle East and the international sports industry?

IN JANUARY 2019, Qatar's national team was on the verge of its greatest success. Without conceding a goal, they had stormed into the semi-finals of the Asian Cup, where they would face the hosts, the United Arab Emirates (UAE). But the Qatari players and coaches were holding back on gestures of triumph, knowing they were not welcome in their neighbouring state. On their journey to the tournament, they had to stop over in Kuwait. One of their officials had initially not been allowed to enter the country. The few journalists reporting for Qatari media from the Asian Cup were of other nationalities. There were almost no Qatari fans in the stadiums, yet their capital Doha is only about 500km away.

Before the semi-final in Abu Dhabi, the capital of the United Arab Emirates, the situation was getting worse. The sports authority distributed tickets almost exclusively to 'loyal fans' of the host nation, free of charge as soon as they identified themselves as citizens. In the quarter-final against South Korea, spectators from Oman cheered Qatar's victory – Abu Dhabi's leadership wanted to prevent a repeat. Reports were circulating that support for Qatar could be legally punished. But the Qatari team played well in the semi-final and won 4-0. Spectators threw bottles and shoes onto the grass, a sign of deep dislike in the Arab world. Three days later, Qatar also won the final against Japan, and officials from the Emirates stayed away from the award ceremony.

Football as a means of expression of political tensions. In 2017, an old conflict in the Gulf came to a head again. At the time, Saudi Arabia imposed an economic blockade on Qatar. The UAE, Bahrain and Egypt joined in and also suspended their diplomatic relations with Doha. Their accusation: Qatar supports terrorist groups and is too close to the Muslim Brotherhood and Iran. Saudi Arabia suspended food imports to Qatar. Families were separated by the disruption of important travel routes. The state airline Qatar Airways was no longer allowed to use Saudi airspace and had to adapt to longer, more expensive routes. Qatar's economic growth received a dent.

'Football is a mirror of the tensions in the Gulf,' says Jassim Matar Kunji, a former goalkeeper in Qatar's professional league and now a journalist for Al Jazeera. Football relations between Qatar and Saudi Arabia and the United Arab Emirates have seen cancellations of sponsorship deals, cancelled player transfers and refused handshakes at junior matches. Saudi players walked out of a press conference when they spotted microphones from Qatari broadcasters.

'Many Qataris thought an invasion by Saudi Arabia was possible,' says Jassim Matar Kunji. Saudi Arabia's army numbers around 200,000 soldiers, Qatar's around 10,000. To compensate for its military inferiority, Qatar is pursuing an elaborate strategy of soft power, with investments worth billions in culture, science and football, including major events, club shares and sponsorship partnerships with Paris Saint-Germain and FC Bayern Munich. Hosting the 2022 World Cup is the most important part of this strategy. It is therefore worth taking a close look at Qatar's sporting and also political rise.

Sporting events as a life insurance

A good 50 years ago, the Arab centres of power were still in Cairo, Baghdad and Damascus. The small sheikdoms on the Arabian Peninsula such as Kuwait, Bahrain and the UAE did not yet play a role. Qatar, for example, which had been under Bahraini, Ottoman and finally British control since the end of the 18th century, had just 100,000 inhabitants in 1971, the year of its independence. Like Bahrain, Qatar refused to join the UAE, encouraged by the discovery of the world's largest natural gas field off the Qatari coast.

Qatar began to modernise in the 1970s, at that time still under the military protection of its large neighbour Saudi Arabia. In 1981, the two states joined forces with Oman, the UAE, Bahrain and Kuwait to form the Gulf Cooperation Council (GCC) as an economic and security network against Iran's ambitions to become a great power. Time and again there were disputes and provocations within the council. In 1990, the all-powerful Iraq under Saddam Hussein invaded small Kuwait, and the USA moved in to liberate it.

The smaller states in the region became aware that they would be clearly outgunned in a similar attack. 'The Qataris want to be perceived so strongly that something like this wouldn't happen to them,' says political scientist Danyel Reiche of Georgetown University in Doha. Saudi Arabia's area is 200 times that of Qatar. Iran's population is 40 times that of Qatar. So, Qatar has one of the most elaborate soft power strategies in the world. 'The Qataris see sporting events as a kind of life insurance,' says Reiche.

How did Qatar, a state with a population of around 2.5 million, become rooted in world politics so quickly? What role does football play? And what conflicts have arisen from it in the Persian Gulf?

Traditionally, the most important decisions in Qatar are made by a handful of people, writes political scientist Mehran Kamrava in his book *Qatar: Small State, Big Politics*. Since the 19th century, the Al Thani dynasty, originally from Saudi Arabia, has been the ruler of Qatar. In 1995, Hamad bin Chalifa Al Thani deposed his own father in a non-violent coup. In Saudi Arabia and the UAE, the monarchies also feared losing power. They wanted to restore the old conditions in Qatar, but a coup backed by them failed in 1996.

The Emir Hamad bin Chalifa Al Thani wanted to free Qatar from Saudi Arabia's grip. From 1996 onwards, he had the news channel Al Jazeera set up in Doha, which was to become one of the most important sources of information in the Arab world, but was reticent to criticise the Al Thanis. The emir opened up the economy to foreign investors and had hundreds of thousands of low-wage workers recruited from South Asia to build new neighbourhoods. With Musa bint Nasser al-Missned, one of his three wives, he pushed ahead with the construction of Education City. Since the beginning of the millennium, a dozen branches of renowned universities have settled on the 14km-square campus in western Doha. They are from the USA, Great Britain and France, three of the five permanent members of the United Nations Security Council. Other new institutions include the Museum of Islamic Art, the Philharmonic Orchestra, the Doha Tribeca Film Festival. Plus, countless promotional videos and advertisements about Qatar in Western media.

With these measures, Qatar secured important contacts in Europe and North America. But the soft power had not yet reached a broad global public. 'Football put Qatar on the world map,' says Matthias Krug, author of the book *Journeys on a Football Carpet* about Qatar's football history. And he emphasises: 'It's not that the country started from scratch for this. Qatar has also had a football culture for a long time. It's just not like in Europe.'

In the 1940s, British oil workers had brought football to the Gulf, with balls made from bundles of socks and pitch markings made from oil. In addition, Qatari exchange students learned to appreciate the game in Egypt and Jordan. Qatar was then a small community of Bedouin tribes and pearl fishermen with a few thousand inhabitants. The first football association was founded in 1960 and joined FIFA in 1972. In 1962, the first stadium with grass in the Gulf region was opened in Doha, writes Krug. In 1971, Muhammad Ali boxed there, two years later Pelé was a guest with FC Santos. In 1981, Qatar reached the final of the U-20 World Cup in Australia. The national team narrowly missed qualifying for the 1990 World Cup and lost in the quarter-finals of the 1992 Olympic Games in Barcelona. At that time, the national league was still in its infancy.

The few successes were not yet based on a systematic approach. The new Emir Hamad bin Chalifa Al Thani wanted to change that from the mid-1990s onwards, with more efficient talent development and by hosting prestigious sporting events, in tennis, basketball, golf and football, especially for young talent. 'A key event was the successful staging of the Asian Games in Doha in 2006,' explains Mahfoud Amara, head of the sports science programme at Qatar University. 'Sport was established as a strategy to make the economy independent of oil and gas exports in the long term.' Soon, dozens of international competitions were being held annually in Doha. The emir took over patronage of local football tournaments, but also camel-riding races and falcon-breeding competitions, ostensibly to strengthen old traditions. However, Qatar's progress only made headlines worldwide in December 2010 after the awarding of the 2022 World Cup, which is still accompanied by allegations of corruption.

In the years surrounding the awarding of the World Cup, the Qatari ruling house sought closer relations with European football. Attempts to take over clubs, such as Manchester United and AS Roma, failed. Soon, the focus was on France, where the ruling Al Thani family owned real estate, company shares and art, and had also built up a resilient and controversial relationship with then-President Nicolas Sarkozy. From 2011 onwards, Qatar secured all the shares in Paris Saint-Germain through the investor group Qatar Sports Investments. Nasser Al-Khelaifi, a confidant of the emir, was installed as chairman of the board and the Qatar Tourism Authority became the main sponsor.

According to some estimates, Qatar has since invested up to £1bn in PSG – and has often been criticised for its financial dealings. After all, the owner and the sponsor could hardly be separated. In 2011, Qatar also became a sponsor of FC Barcelona through the Qatar Foundation. The state-owned airline Qatar Airways became the Catalan club's first ever commercial shirt sponsor. More and more top clubs were spending their winter training camps in Doha, with FC Bayern coming for the tenth time in 2020. Qatar was now a media topic far beyond the Arabian Peninsula.

The Neymar transfer masked Qatar's isolation

Among Middle East experts, the extent to which the football networks have strengthened Qatar's political influence is disputed. The fact is that the ruling family also invested in other sectors during the same period, especially in countries that suffered from the economic crisis from 2008 onwards. And it took a stand during the Arab Spring in 2011 and afterwards: for the Muslim Brotherhood in Egypt, for Islamic forces in Tunisia, for the rebels in Libya against Gaddafi and in Syria against Assad. 'Qatar wants to position itself as a leading regional power,' says Joachim Paul, who has worked intensively on the Gulf region for the German Heinrich Böll Foundation. 'Saudi Arabia and the United Arab Emirates would rather contain political Islam, especially the Muslim Brotherhood.' In March 2014, Saudi Arabia, the UAE and Bahrain withdrew their ambassadors from Doha.

A documentary by the Franco-German broadcaster ARTE from 2019 also attributes the 'new Gulf war' to the generational change among rulers: in 2013, Tamim bin Hamad Al Thani took power from his father in Qatar; at 33, he was the youngest head of state in the Arab world. In Saudi Arabia, Mohammed bin Salman, known as MBS, emerged from the king's shadow as defence minister in 2015 and crown prince in 2017. And in the United Arab Emirates, Mohamed Ben Zayed, called MBZ, positioned himself as the new strongman. MBS and MBZ allied themselves against Qatar.

Qatar competes for investors, tourists and skilled labour primarily with the UAE, especially Abu Dhabi and Dubai, the two most influential of the seven emirates. Within the UAE, the ruling families often take different paths. For example, in the first Gulf War between Iran and Iraq in 1980, Abu Dhabi and Dubai supported different parties. Economically, Abu Dhabi wants to establish itself as a cultural metropolis and had a spectacular offshoot of the Louvre built for this purpose. The larger Dubai is focusing on shopping centres, family-friendly entertainment and major events such as Expo 2021. The airport in Dubai has become one of the leading hubs between Europe, Asia and Oceania.

And football has played a part in this. The state-owned airline Emirates, founded in 1985 and based in Dubai, entered the most important European leagues as a main or co-sponsor from the beginning of the new millennium, doing deals with Arsenal, AC Milan, Real Madrid, Paris Saint-Germain and Hamburger SV. However, Dubai's attempt to take over Liverpool failed. In 2008, Abu Dhabi followed suit and bought into Manchester City, where the state-owned airline Etihad, competing with Emirates and Qatar Airways, acts as the shirt sponsor. According to estimates in the British media, Abu Dhabi is said to have invested more than £1bn in Manchester City's sporting advancement. The City Football Group acquired further club shares in New York, Melbourne, Yokohama, Torque in Uruguay, Girona in Spain and Chengdu in China.

There are many sums in the billions circulating around the football investments of the Gulf states, but they cannot be seriously verified. It is likely that Abu Dhabi has made heavy losses in football, but the ruling house does not seem to be interested in making a quick profit, writes human rights activist Nicholas McGeehan in an essay for German magazine *11 Freunde*: 'Manchester City and New York City allow Abu Dhabi to gain a foothold in centres of power and influence. The clubs are platforms from which to forge new business links and consolidate old ones.'

McGeehan, a long-time expert with Human Rights Watch, describes how Abu Dhabi sought political allies in London, Paris and Washington, among other places, against the Muslim Brotherhood and unpopular human rights organisations. At home, however, democratic structures are lacking, as is a civil society. Activists quickly end up in prison for critical tweets. Football makes the repressive security apparatus in the UAE seem a little more harmless, argues Christopher Davidson, an expert on the Gulf region and author of *Dubai: The*

Vulnerability of Success. 'Football is a secular and easy way to create tribal affiliation. The sheikhs are visible in the stands, it puts them in touch with the population in a non-political way.'

The list of conflicts over territorial claims, terminology and religious interpretations in the Persian Gulf is long and complex, and that became particularly clear in 2017. Qatar no longer wanted to support Saudi Arabia's alliance in the war in Yemen against the Huthi rebels. According to the ARTE documentary, UAE diplomats are said to have persistently lobbied think tanks in Washington to get Donald Trump's support for a blockade against Qatar. The fact that one of the world's largest US military bases has been stationed in Qatar since 2003 did not seem to matter much to the president. Trump had positioned himself early for Saudi Arabia with his first foreign visit as president to Riyadh.

Saudi Arabia and its allies demanded that Qatar close Al Jazeera and the Qatar Foundation, two of the most important institutions for Doha, among other things. In August 2017, the transfer of Brazilian player Neymar from FC Barcelona to Paris Saint-Germain for a record sum of £185m was announced. 'A strategic milestone,' says Danyel Reiche, editor of the book *Sport, Politics and Society in the Middle East*. 'Shortly after the blockade became known, Qatar changed the narrative in the press. Even though the transfer was incredibly expensive, everyone was only talking about football, no longer about isolated Qatar.'

A few weeks later, the UAE cancelled a friendly against Morocco and scheduled a match against Egypt instead. Morocco had refused to support the blockade against Qatar, probably because the country was then a candidate to host the 2026 World Cup, which was later awarded to the US, Canada and Mexico. The blockading states made sure that Qatar was hardly visible in their countries: football teams from Doha were closely escorted by security forces at official international matches. Several shops in Saudi Arabia pasted over the sponsorship lettering of Qatar Airways on the jerseys of FC Barcelona. The display of Qatari symbols was made a punishable offence. There was no thought of a new edition of the Pan Arab Games. The last time the regional event took place was in Doha in 2011, and since then it has not been possible to agree on a host.

A new dimension of piracy

A visit to BeIN Sports in Doha, the TV network with one of the largest sports rights portfolio worldwide, shows how far the hostility between the neighbours can extend. The channel was founded in 2003 as an offshoot of Al Jazeera and has been independent since 2012. Its chairman is Nasser Al Khelaifi, who also heads Paris Saint-Germain, and since 2019 he has been a member of UEFA Executive Committee.

BeIN Sports' control rooms are state-of-the-art. Every week, hundreds of hours of live sport are broadcast from here to 43 countries on five continents, in Arabic, English and French. The broadcaster has marginalised domestic providers in a number of countries, which has repeatedly brought it criticism, for example in France. In 24 countries in the Middle East and north Africa, BeIN reaches almost 400 million people as the leading sports channel. But not everyone likes this Qatari dominance.

After the blockade began in 2017, BeIN Sports was banned from selling subscriptions in Saudi Arabia. Shortly after, a new channel was launched: BeoutQ aired the same content as BeIN, the same matches, commentary, analysis, but with its own logos, graphics and commercial breaks. Soon after, BeoutQ distributed the material from Qatar to numerous channels of its own. 'This is a new dimension of piracy,' says Jonathan Whitehead, one of the executives at BeIN. 'This industrial theft was ordered from the very top.' Research quickly indicated that BeoutQ's organisation and technology originated in Saudi Arabia. However, information was spread from Riyadh that the investors were from Colombia and Cuba, complemented by the recent backlash that Al Jazeera is a mouthpiece for terror groups and destabilises the region.

Several law firms declined to handle a lawsuit by sports federations against BeoutQ. Did they not want to mess with Saudi Arabia? BeIN turned to the World Trade Organisation in 2018. In the same year, the channel was completely banned from operating in Saudi Arabia, and parts of its equipment were confiscated there. 'Selling TV rights is the main source of revenue for many clubs,' says Whitehead. 'But if our end product is stolen, the TV rights lose their value.' In the regions where BeoutQ can be received, subscription numbers to BeIN have declined. BeIN had to lay off a few hundred staff members.

The television market is a platform on which the feud between Qatar and Saudi Arabia can be well studied. With bizarre consequences: as the main rights holder, BeIN was hardly present at the 2019 Asian Cup in the United Arab Emirates. In Saudi media, even more well-known personalities made fun of it, accompanied by misinformation about Qatar on social media. On BeIN's Arabic programmes, commentators sometimes expressed anger against the blockade states. BeoutQ broadcasted with a time delay and was able to filter out the criticism or insert advertisements. BeIN also called for more solidarity from its rights partners in Europe. For example, from the Italian Football Federation, which has been hosting its Super Cup in Saudi Arabia.

Opposition athletes in Bahrain were tortured

The Royal House in Riyadh entered the sporting arms race in the Persian Gulf comparatively late, in 2016. First with smaller events: in wrestling, chess and in the Formula E racing series. Then with larger ones: in handball with the Club World Cup, in tennis and in heavyweight boxing. And in football? In October 2018, a friendly match between Brazil and Argentina took place in Riyadh. For more than £100m each, Saudi Arabia secured the Italian and Spanish Super Cups. 'In the past, there was no entertainment sector in Saudi Arabia, but slowly the country is opening up,' says reporter Wasim Algabril, who works for British broadcaster SNTV and has roots in Saudi Arabia. 'There is a realisation: The country can be conservative, but it can also be cosmopolitan. Sport has a role to play.' That some concerts, theatres and cinemas are now open was long unthinkable.

'Saudi Crown Prince Mohammed bin Salman's reforms have economic reasons,' explains Mahfoud Amara of Qatar University. 'Sport is an important part of nation branding.' It's a term you come across again and again in the Gulf. For a long time, the Saudi national budget was more than 80 per cent dependent on oil revenues, but resources are finite and more than two-thirds of the growing population is under 30. The regime is developing new economic sectors, reforming its education system and opening up, at least tentatively, to tourism. Since 2019, visitors from 49 countries have been able to apply for a visa. Allegedly, more than £2bn is also to be invested in sport and culture.

Turki Al Sheikh, confidant of the crown prince and chairman of the Saudi Entertainment Authority, is seen as a key figure for the change. In 2018, Al Sheikh took over a club in Asyut, Egypt, moved it to Cairo and renamed it Pyramids FC. After repeated abuse from rival ultras, he sold the club. Instead, Al Sheikh joined Spanish second-division club UD Almería as owner. Can he go the way of Abdullah bin Mosaad bin Abdulaziz Al Saud? The billionaire prince bought 50 per cent of English club Sheffield United in 2013. After long negotiations in 2021, the Public Investment Fund from Saudi

Arabia secured Newcastle United for more than £300m. This makes the club one of the richest in the world. However, this does not come close to the successes of Paris Saint-Germain or Manchester City.

Nevertheless, Human Rights Watch argues in a report that when it comes to emotional debates in football, human rights violations in Saudi Arabia fade into the background. Although women are now allowed to drive, visit stadiums or go to the gym for health promotion, women's rights activists are still being held in custody. 'Social and economic reforms are in the foreground, while political freedoms are more restricted than before,' says Ahmed Al Omran, a Saudi journalist and former correspondent for the *Financial Times*. 'With the arrests, the crown prince and his father are making it unmistakably clear that civil society actors are not allowed to claim success.'

Mohammed bin Salman had dozens of intellectuals and religious scholars arrested in 2017 for not unconditionally supporting his course against Qatar. The repression hits prominent members of the Shia minority particularly hard. But exiles are also in danger, as the gruesome murder of journalist Jamal Khashoggi in the Istanbul consulate in 2018 shows. On a single March day in 2022, 81 people were executed in Saudi Arabia.

The monarchies fear for their power, as has become clear in Bahrain, an island state the size of Hamburg, 40km west of Qatar. Bahrain was a pioneer in cultivating its reputation through sporting events. Since 2004, Formula 1 has been hosted near the capital Manama, at an annual cost of £30m. In 2011, the Formula 1 race in Bahrain was cancelled, the Arab Spring had reached the island. Hundreds of thousands of people demonstrated for weeks for free elections and more participation. Many demanded the overthrow of Chalifa bin Salman Al Chalifa. The world's longest-serving prime minister has been in office since 1971. Bahrain's distinctive feature in the Gulf region is that the royal family belongs to the Sunni interpretation of Islam. However, almost three-quarters of the citizens are Shias, and jobs in ministries, the army or education are usually closed to them. The Bahraini regime repressed protests, also with forces from the Sunni protector Saudi Arabia. According to an international commission of enquiry, 40 people died during demonstrations in 2011, almost 3,000 were imprisoned, many of them tortured. Al Jazeera hardly reported on this, because Qatar was also against regime change in its immediate neighbourhood.

About 150 athletes and coaches are said to have been among the demonstrators in Bahrain, among them national football players like Sayed Mohamed Adnan and the brothers Mohamed and A'ala Hubail. They were considered popular heroes for narrowly missing the 2006 World Cup, but during the Arab Spring they were arrested and ridiculed in the state media. Under international pressure, they and other athletes were released and left the country for Oman, Qatar or Australia. Some returned to Bahrain, others remained under surveillance: the footballer Hakeem al-Araibi, who openly criticised the regime, fled to Australia after being detained, but was arrested again on his honeymoon in Thailand because of an extradition request. He was only allowed to return to Australia in 2019 after several media reports. Quite a few sports officials are said to be involved in state surveillance. Sheikh Salman bin Ibrahim Al Khalifa, a member of Bahrain's ruling family and president of the Asian Football Confederation (AFC) since 2013 and a member of the FIFA board, has kept a low profile.

Thousands of workers became ill or died

The region of the Persian Gulf is marked by tensions and conflicts. Is rapprochement possible at all? One example: in November 2019, the 24th Gulf Cup was to take place in Qatar, this time with five teams instead of eight, because Saudi

Arabia, the UAE and Bahrain were planning a boycott. The economic blockade against Qatar was still in place. Then, two weeks before the tournament, the blockading states surprisingly announced their participation, interrupting their national leagues at short notice to do so. Saudi Arabia's national team travelled to Qatar by domestic airline without any diversions, although direct air traffic had actually been suspended. They were travelling to Doha in a bus with their national colours, and flags with Saudi symbols were also flying in the streets. Qatari media carried comments from the blockade states that indicated a rapprochement. For the Gulf Cup, buses carrying Saudi citizens crossed the border into Qatar for the first time in more than two years. They did not seem to face any hostility in the Doha stadiums.

'There has been a realisation among the Saudis that Qatar is not going to go down on its knees over the blockade,' says Middle East expert Mehran Kamrava of Georgetown University in Doha. 'There had already been several months of diplomatic-level talks between Qatar and Saudi Arabia. The Gulf Cup offered another opportunity. Football creates a wider context where politicians can approach each other more easily. A kind of football diplomacy.'

After the initial months of shock, Qatar had gradually adjusted to the deadlock in 2017. The government diverted tens of billions from sovereign wealth funds into domestic banks. Food imports now came increasingly from Turkey and Iran rather than neighbouring countries. 'The Qataris focused more on their own agriculture and industry,' Mehran Kamrava reports. New ports, greenhouses and desalination plants for seawater were built. Large images of the emir, the Qatari ruler, were projected on building walls in Doha, not only during the 2019 Gulf Cup.

From spring 2020, the Gulf region was also hit hard by Coronavirus. The already low price of oil collapsed, foreign investment declined, and the fledgling tourism sector lost tens of thousands of jobs. At the beginning of January 2021, Saudi Arabia ended its blockade against Qatar after three and a half years. 'It is a fragile peace,' says Middle East expert Kristian Ulrichsen, who has written a book on the Gulf crisis. 'The Gulf states have realised that they need to cooperate during this difficult time.' There are talks about joint technology platforms and a strategy to combat the high rates of diabetes in the region in order to relieve the burden on the health system in the long term.

Riyadh and Dubai also wanted to profit from the 2022 World Cup. If not with tournament matches, then with training camps, sponsorship events or accommodation for fans. Political leaders have declared the crisis over. But that does not mean it is also over at the social level. The blockade has damaged the social structure of the region. Several families with members in Qatar and Saudi Arabia broke up. It will take time for these wounds to heal. Sport will also continue to mirror the decades-long rivalry between Qatar and Saudi Arabia. Doha and Riyadh bid to host the 2030 Asian Games. Doha won the bid, with Riyadh's turn coming four years later. On other issues, compromises will probably not be so easy.

None of the six states in the Gulf Cooperation Council is governed democratically; there is no separation of powers. In *Reporters Without Borders*' press freedom rankings for 2021, Qatar was ranked 128 out of 180 states, the UAE 131, Saudi Arabia 170. LGBTIQ+ communities face persecution. The few civil society organisations are strictly controlled. Large political foundations from the West that are active worldwide are not welcome in the Persian Gulf.

Protests like those in 2011 during the Arab Spring or as recently as 2019 in Algeria, Iran and Lebanon are unlikely in Qatar. The ruling family lets the 250,000 official citizens share in its prosperity. They enjoy enormous privileges in education, health care and job allocation; water and electricity are free of charge for them. Their per capita income is one of the highest in the world – but so is their energy and CO_2 consumption. Although there are sometimes disagreements between influential families, writes political scientist Mehran Kamrava in *Qatar: Small State, Big Politics*, Qatar is basically the only state in the Gulf region without a significant backlash. The emir has built up a dense network of family members and friends in the state, many of them holding several offices, which is quite common in the Gulf. The Shia minority, about 15 per cent of Qatari Muslims, is also considered well integrated.

In the early building phase of the Qatari state, in the 1960s and 1970s, the ruling house feared more resistance. Guest workers came mainly from Egypt, Palestine and Yemen, they spoke the same language as the locals, but many of them had anti-monarchist attitudes. Later, after Iraq's invasion of Kuwait in 1990, the Qatari government sought migrant workers from South Asia, whom it could more easily segregate from society linguistically and culturally. These workers from India, Bangladesh and Pakistan were given a Kafala, a guarantor who could withhold their passports, make it difficult for them to leave the country and prevent them from changing jobs – officially to fight crime, because their home countries had no extradition treaties with Qatar. The migrant workers made the rapid development of Doha possible, they sent a large part of their wages home, thousands of them became ill or died, especially in the high summer temperatures.

The general public in the West only learned about this system, which is also practised in other Gulf states, after the awarding of the World Cup in 2010. Especially in Great Britain and Germany, the media made the inhumane conditions of the workers public. A years-long debate began about the causes and cover-ups of deaths on construction sites. Many estimates for the possible number of victims circulate; some are in four figures; they cannot be verified exactly.

Concessions to conservative circles

It's a question of perspective: by the standards of Europe, whose unions have evolved over decades, Qatar is backward. By the standards of the Gulf region, which does not know workers' movements, Qatar is a model for the future. 'It is very important that football clubs and federations look in detail at labour law issues in Qatar before engaging in Qatar,' says Max Tuñón, head of the Doha office of the ILO, the International Labour Organisation, a UN agency that protects labour rights. 'Whether it's hotels, security services or transport: companies have a duty of care to their workers.' In 2017, the ILO office opened in Doha with 14 staff, and other international organisations are also on the ground.

Qatar introduced the region's first minimum wage. There is now an arbitration board for disputes between employers and workers, as well as a compensation fund in case of unpaid wages. From 2020, workers no longer need an exit permit and are able to change their contracts more easily. With this, the Kafala system seems to be history, but will there be sufficient controls for the implementation of the new laws even after the World Cup? Max Tuñón appeals to Qatari officials and entrepreneurs: 'If migrants have fewer restrictions, it will attract more skilled workers and investors to the country. But we need to do more to make workers feel needed and welcome.'

Of the approximately 2.5 million inhabitants, only ten per cent have a Qatari passport. In no other country is the proportion of immigrants so high, and it is expected to rise further. 'Some business people are worried that the World Cup will open Qatar up too much,' says political scientist Mehran Kamrava. For them, Sharia law is the basis for everything; they fear that in 2022 alcohol will be drunk in public and that gays will not hide their sexuality. In 2018, the emir massively increased alcohol prices through taxes and replaced English with Arabic as the main language at Qatar University. Both are concessions to conservative circles, because soft power in foreign policy can only be pursued with internal political stability. Mehran Kamrava says: 'The World Cup allows politicians to move faster on reforms that parts of the economy don't really want.' However, more conservative ruling houses, such as in Saudi Arabia and the UAE, could see major reforms as a provocation. Particularly as they had tried several times to get involved in the World Cup.

If there is one place the government in Doha wants to show off as a symbol of change, it is the Aspire Academy, the national sports academy, opened in 2004 for the Asian Games two years later. Medicine, science, training and teaching: the academy is one of the world's leading sites for talent development. 'Given the small population, we need to organise our scouting effectively,' says Markus Egger, Aspire's director of sport and strategy. 'We want to go through a development that has taken European countries much more time.' The Aspire Academy focuses on Olympic sports, and most of its attention is on football.

The academy is the centre for perhaps the greatest scouting operation in football history. Hundreds of thousands of youngsters have been observed in dozens of countries on three continents. The awarding of the 2022 World Cup intensified their exchange programme with academics from 50 countries. European youth teams travel to Qatar almost weekly for matches and training camps. KAS Eupen became probably the most important partner institution. Qatari investors bought the club in 2012. 'Qatari players go there to get familiar with European football,' says Ali Al Salat, spokesman for the Qatar Football Federation. 'We want that to continue in the future.'

One of the formative heads of the Aspire Academy is Félix Sánchez Bas, who began his career in his early 20s as a youth coach at FC Barcelona. He moved to the Aspire Academy in 2006. In 2013, he took over Qatar's Under-19 team and led them to win the Asian Championship a year later. He promoted many of his players at that time to the senior national team, which he has coached since 2017. In 2019, they won the Asian Cup in Abu Dhabi, the biggest success in Qatari sporting history. Several of the top performers have roots in other countries because of their ancestors, but only four of the 2019 Asian champions were not born in Qatar. This is in contrast to the Qatari handball team, for example, which surprisingly won silver at the 2015 World Championship at home with mostly naturalised players. Immigrants without sporting credentials generally have to have lived in Qatar for 25 years before they can apply for citizenship.

'If Qatar wants to be successful in the long term after the World Cup, it needs a sports culture,' says political scientist Danyel Reiche. Local clubs, grassroots sports groups or informal street games rarely exist. Even the annual holiday for sport could do little to change that. As in Saudi Arabia and the UAE, the obesity rate in Qatar is far higher than in Europe, resulting in enormous costs for health and care systems. According to a study by the National Olympic Committee, only 15 per cent of Qatari women are active in sports, but hardly ever in team sports, not even football.

Parents often prevent their daughters from training

One can have a good discussion about the causes with Fatma. In a shopping mall in the centre of Doha, she runs a studio for martial arts. The mirrors on the wall are freshly cleaned, the mats on the floor still smell new. Fatma wipes the sweat from her forehead. She has just pushed three friends to top performance in a class. 'I don't do sport just to feel better,' Fatma says. 'I have learned how to withstand pressure in competitions. These lessons also help me in university, my grades have improved. Sport has built my character; it gives me confidence in all areas of life."

Fatma is in her early 20s, she does not want to give her real and full name. She likes to talk about her sports. She sits bolt upright on the chair, using her hands to describe her fighting techniques. But her passion can quickly turn into frustration, sometimes into resignation. Fatma is the head of the sports studio, unofficially. A photo of her is not allowed to appear, not in the entrance area, not on the internet. Her father and brothers want it that way. Fatma has been asked to play for the national football team several times. But her father does not want her to be filmed playing sports. He thinks it would put her on display.

In Fatma's home country, Qatar, Wahhabism shapes the society of the locals. It is a traditionalist interpretation of Sunni Islam. Fatma already felt this in her childhood. She felt oppressed by her brothers. For years she was not allowed to use a mobile phone, and when she was, it was only to make phone calls. The apps were blocked. Only cartoons were shown on the television at home, and her brothers decided on her clothes and friends. These restrictions had serious consequences for Fatma. She developed eating disorders and suffered from depression.

But then she began her studies at an American university, which has a large branch in Doha. In the cafeteria, she got into conversations with students from all continents. Many Qatari women there did not wear the abaya, the traditional black garment that also covers the hair. Fatma took advantage of the university's sports programme. She is one of the greatest talents in basketball and football. But a career as a professional athlete remained blocked for her. 'No men are allowed to watch the games in our football league,' she says. 'It's like an airport.

Cameras and mobile phones are not allowed. Most of the time, parents prevent their daughters from training regularly from a very early age.'

Sport in Qatar is emblematic of the status of women. They often have to get permission from a male guardian, for example, if they want to marry or work in a public job. These are state laws that meet with approval in large parts of Qatari society, says Anna Reuß, who conducts research on the foreign policy of the Gulf states at the Bundeswehr University in Munich. 'These cultures are very patriarchal. In this context, the family is propagated as the smallest social unit in society. The woman is supposed to take care of the family first and foremost.'

Sports activities for women do not have the same status in the Gulf states as in Western societies. For decades, there were hardly any places where Qatari women could exercise without traditional clothing. This is another reason why they often suffer from obesity and diabetes. Studies show that female athletes are interpreted as strong women in a negative sense. And so they are sometimes afraid of being perceived as masculine or even lesbian because of sport.

The Qatari government wants to counter this perception, for political reasons. In the competition with its neighbours Saudi Arabia and the United Arab Emirates, Qatar depends on networks with the USA and Europe. Therefore, the regime cultivates the Western narrative of the 'strong woman' and refers to female leaders in administration and culture. And also to 'inspiring female athletes'. 'Images of female footballers can be used to good effect,' says Anna Reuß. 'You don't see sweaty women in the black abaya, but in jerseys. It's a much more positive image.'

Positive images that go around the world. This is another reason why Qatar organises one sporting event after another. For example, the World Athletics Championships in Doha in 2019, when Qatari hurdler Mariam Farid took part. She says:

'After my race, 20 journalists approached me, most of them from the West. I was surprised that they didn't want to talk to the other runners. After all, some of them were among the world's best, they had already set records. I also beat my best at this World Championships. Nevertheless, the reporters were only interested in my clothes. "Covered from head to toe" was their headline.'

Farid is an articulate woman in her mid-20s. She gives the interview for this chapter in a prestigious Doha hospital. After studying communications, she works here in the press department. Her passion belongs to sports. Mariam Farid played football, swam and finally decided to take up athletics. She speaks four languages, and so she was appointed an official ambassador for the 2019 World Championships. 'Many people in the West hold it against us that the Middle East is closed and [say] that we should open up,' she says. 'But the same people don't want to acknowledge signals of progress, and they will continue to put a stamp on us. But I will continue to work to break stereotypes.'

Many people in the West perceive the Middle East as a culturally uniform region. With Qatar, they associate desert, camels, wealth through oil. And women who only make it to the top against all odds. Mariam Farid emphasises one message again and again: reality is diverse, complex. And it is important to name historical causes.

The Qatar Athletics Federation did not organise a major competition for women for the first time until 1998. At that time, there were no recreational sports for girls and women. At the beginning of the millennium, Musa bint Nasser al-Missned, the second wife of the then-emir, initiated the foundation of the Women's Sports Committee. This organisation was to work 'for gender equality in sport'.

Even then, Qatar's big goal was to host the men's World Cup in football. But in order to win the bid from FIFA, applicants also had to prove that they were promoting girls and women. And so a women's football team was founded in Qatar in 2009. In October 2010, it played its first international match against Bahrain. One and a half months later, the 2022 men's World Cup was awarded to Qatar.

But how serious is the promotion of women footballers? For a long time, the national team was hardly active and was not listed in FIFA's world rankings. In Qatar, the women's league is not part of the Football Association, but is run by the Women's Sports Committee. An unusual set-up. 'Our female footballers have not yet had much experience at international level,' says Amna Al Qassimi, the executive director of the Women's Sports Committee. 'It is important for us that the FC Bayern Munich women's team, for example, comes to Doha regularly for training camps. We then organise joint training sessions. That way, our female players can continue to develop.'

Qatar is acting as a mediator beyond the Gulf

Sport illustrates a field of tension in Qatar: between the official political claim to 'modernity' and the conservative norms in society. The Qatari government repeatedly involves female athletes in its political communication. In November 2021, for example, the Qatari national team played a friendly match against a team from Afghanistan in Doha. In a press release, Qatari decision-makers emphasised their role in the 'safe evacuation of more than 70,000 people from Afghanistan' after the Taliban took power there. Hassan Al Thawadi, Secretary General of the 2022 World Cup organising committee, was quoted: 'We hope we can continue to support these inspiring young women.'

How credible is the commitment to equality, really? Qatar has no tradition of voluntary associations in grassroots sport. The Aspire Academy, one of the largest sports centres in the world, focuses on developing male talent. The Women's Sports

Committee is housed in a former school and is much less well equipped. This makes the Education City, the campus with branches of western universities, more important. 'In the Qatari community, it is not considered acceptable for women to go abroad to study. That would only be possible if they were accompanied by a male family member,' reports communications scholar Susan Dun from Northwestern University in Doha, who moved to Qatar in 2008. 'So the government has expanded the education system in their own country.'

More than 70 per cent of the students at Education City are women. But outside, the situation is different. Seventy per cent of Qatari men are employed, only 37 per cent of women. According to the World Economic Forum's Gender Gap Index, out of 153 countries evaluated, Qatar ranks 83rd in women's education. In female health, Qatar ranks 142nd. In political empowerment, 143rd. Studies from other Middle Eastern countries show regular sport can lead to greater self-confidence and social participation among women.

In business, culture and science, there are now quite a few women in high positions, but this is not the case in sport. And even among men, football is far less glorified than in Europe or Latin America, says Jassim Matar Kunji, formerly a professional goalkeeper and now a journalist for Al Jazeera: 'In many countries, football offers the opportunity for social and economic success. In Qatar, football is one industry among many, but maybe that will change during the World Cup.' The national league has long been seen as a retreat for retirees like Pep Guardiola, Gabriel Batistuta and Marcel Desailly. But the ruling house wants success in Asian competitions and has had several clubs merged into stronger units for this purpose.

The Gulf region is constantly changing, and football has become an important driving force in recent years. From a European perspective, a common narrative seems to be gradually changing: wealthy Qatar, which does not take Human rights seriously, may become the victim of envious neighbours like Saudi Arabia, who view every reform as critical. Qatar can also step in as a gas supplier in the Ukraine-Russia crisis.

Doha is creating its own network and acting as a mediator far beyond the Gulf, with contacts in the West, but also with political Islam in Egypt, Lebanon and Iran. Moreover, Qatar is also expanding its influence in democratic states, with the promotion of mosques and Islamic cultural centres. As early as 2004, the Qatar Olympic Committee donated £4.5m for the new stadium in Sakhnin, an Israeli city where more than 90 per cent of the 30,000 inhabitants are Muslim Arabs. It was apparently the first investment by a Gulf state in an Israeli city. In 2004, FC Bnei Sakhnin won the Israeli Cup. To this day, Qatar does not maintain diplomatic relations with Israel. But the stadium in Sakhnin bears the name of the Qatari capital.

The Emperor's New Game

*The Chinese Communist Party uses football
as a showcase for its global expansion: in the
domestic entertainment industry, professional
clubs promote private consumption among
the population. In Europe, Chinese club
investors expand the economic influence of
their government. In Africa, their construction
companies secure access to raw materials with
new stadiums. The European leagues also want
to profit from this network – and hold back on
criticism of human rights violations.*

IN FEBRUARY 2012, Xi Jinping travelled to Ireland on a
state visit as vice president. The photos showing him in a dark
suit kicking a ball in Dublin went viral internationally. Two
years later, almost 800 million Chinese watched the World
Cup in Brazil on TV. In the official Chinese narrative, the
football boom is closely linked to the rise to power of the
central leadership figure. Already as vice president of the
People's Republic, Xi Jinping was said to have expressed three
wishes for the Chinese national team in 2011: to participate in
a World Cup soon, to host a World Cup and to win a World
Cup by 2050.

The political leadership had state institutions draw up
a joint programme to 'revitalise Chinese football'. In 2015,

details became known: among them the timely construction of 20,000 training centres and 60,000 sports fields, the training of 6,000 coaches and the planning of 20,000 football schools. The state news agency Xinhua described the national team at the time as 'broken', 'humiliating' and a 'national disgrace'. A quote from Xi Jinping: 'My greatest hope for Chinese football is that our teams will soon be among the best in the world.' By 2025, a Chinese sports industry worth £600bn is set to be created with the help of football. That would probably be the largest sports market in the world.

These are seemingly unreal figures that cannot be verified, but they create an impression. One of the recurring motifs for Xi Jinping is the 'Chinese Dream'. According to Xinhua, the renewal of the nation is, for him, 'the greatest dream in modern history'. In other words, Xi wants to make China what it had been in previous centuries: a political, economic and cultural world power.

The German author Stefan Baron writes in his book *The Chinese: Psychogram of a World Power* that Xi has long historical lines in mind. Until the middle of the second millennium of our era, the Chinese empire had a powerful naval fleet and perhaps the greatest inventiveness in the world. Tensions within dynasties, self-isolation and conflicts caused China to miss out on scientific and industrial revolutions. The 19th and 20th centuries are considered ignominious. China had to bow to the influences and occupations of the British, French and Japanese.

In many countries, immigrant Chinese were regarded as cheap labour. In some US cities, they were not allowed to buy property outside their Chinatowns for a long time, and certain professions and schools were closed to them. In China itself, dictator Mao Zedong's totalitarian programmes led to tens of millions of deaths and lasting damage to the economy. In the 1960s, communist China was an internationally isolated agrarian society with low average education.

Measured against this history, writes Baron, the Chinese have achieved something unique. Within three decades, they have transformed one of the poorest countries into one of the largest economies. No country has brought so many people out of poverty so quickly. Although annual growth rates are now no longer in double digits, China accounts for more than a third of global economic growth. By 2049, the centenary of the People's Republic, the 'Chinese Dream' is supposed to have come true. By then, the country will be one of the most modern industrial nations, with average incomes on a par with the USA and the European Union.

Clubs secure sympathy and contacts in politics

Football has never reflected this development – on the contrary. In 1994, the professional league Jia-A was founded at the behest of politicians, and the clubs were dependent on state-owned companies. Bribery, match-fixing and manipulation were part of everyday life. 'China's football was born as a deformed foetus,' wrote a newspaper in Beijing. The league was dissolved in 2003 and re-founded as the Chinese Super League. More scandals followed. The Chinese magazine *Titan* investigated the theory that people could buy their way into the national team for 30,000 euros. Fans, supporters and young players turned away from the game.

Football highlighted a core problem: corruption. In communist China, politics is the control centre of the economy. There is no free market, the state still owns half of the nation's wealth. Despite rapid growth, the wage gap has grown. Around 80 million people in the countryside have to get by on the equivalent of less than £1 a day. 'Poorly paid officials can earn a lot extra through corruption,' writes Stefan Baron. With the right allies, they had little to fear.

That changed with Xi Jinping's rise to power. More than a million party cadres are said to have been punished in the

2010s, most at the local level. In his first term as president, which started in March 2013, 18 of 205 Communist Party Central Committee members were arrested for corruption. The extent to which this was justified remains to be seen; an independent judiciary is non-existent. Xi had important posts filled by confidants. In football, more than 50 officials, referees and players were convicted.

Gradually, well-connected entrepreneurs recognised the political and economic potential of sport. 'When the boss sets the direction, the whole country runs after it,' says journalist Kai Strittmatter, who reported from China for 14 years for the German paper *Süddeutsche Zeitung*. 'The entrepreneurs listen carefully to the signals from Beijing. And when football is proclaimed as a political goal, it also means football is the next big business. And already all the money is pouncing on it.'

In 2010, the Chinese real estate group Evergrande took over a club in the south-eastern metropolis of Guangzhou that had been relegated to the second division because of match-fixing. The club hired well-known coaches such as Marcello Lippi and Luiz Felipe Scolari, and lured star players such as Lucas Barrios, Robinho and Paulinho. In 2014, an offshoot of the Chinese internet giant Alibaba acquired 50 per cent of the club's shares for £150m. This is how Guangzhou Evergrande has risen to become a serial winner in the past decade, with seven national championships and two triumphs in the Asian Champions League.

China's most successful club is shaped by two of the richest men: Xu Jiayin, founder of the Evergrande Group, which specialises in upscale real estate; and Jack Ma, founder of the conglomerate Alibaba, which dominates the Chinese online market. 'Entrepreneurs pursue business interests with their clubs,' says Tariq Panja, a sports policy expert for the *New York Times*. 'It's how they secure sympathy and contacts in politics. And maybe they get privileges like building permits.' In China, the construction sector secured 20 per cent of the gross domestic product. Panja says: 'In football, the private and public sectors come closer together.'

In a statement, the Communist Party rated patriotism for domestic entrepreneurs as the 'highest obligation'. Here, too, Xi Jinping draws his determination from history, writes Baron. After the disasters under Mao Zedong, Deng Xiaoping initiated an economic opening and infrastructure modernisation in the 1980s. Zhu Rongji then led China as prime minister into the World Trade Organisation (WTO) in 2001, and he also wanted to push back state influence in the economy. Xi Jinping is responsible for the next wave of reforms. Instead of exporting cheap and copied mass-produced goods abroad, high-quality products and home-grown innovations have been boosting the domestic economy. 'One of the government's goals is growth through increased consumption,' says Ilker Gündoğan, an East Asian scholar at the Ruhr University in Bochum. 'Football also provides an incentive for the population to spend money on the domestic market, on tickets, TV subscriptions or merchandising.'

With the blessing of the state president, a trial of strength began in the Chinese Super League, helped by growing marketing. After a bidding war, the state-backed China Media Capital group of companies paid eight billion yuan, almost £1bn, for the broadcasting rights from 2016 to 2020. The clubs signed players from Europe and South America who had passed their sporting zenith for sums in the tens of millions. Some of these players received salaries in the tens of millions. One club reportedly offered Real Madrid a transfer fee of £250m for Cristiano Ronaldo. In 2016 alone, according to FIFA's Transfer Matching System, transfer spending by Chinese clubs amounted to around £340m, almost three and a half times as much as all other clubs in Asia combined.

THE EMPEROR'S NEW GAME

'For years, Chinese football fans looked to Europe,' says journalist Nan Xiao of the state-affiliated *Beijing Youth Daily* newspaper. 'Now they were proud that a football culture of their own was emerging in China. Fans crave big-name players, and they put up with the high salaries.' On the one hand, the investments paid off: merchandising revenues and club owners' share prices rose. The average number of spectators per league match grew, and new players were added to the youth teams.

The number of investors in Europe has halved

'But the investments also aroused scepticism among politicians,' says Ilker Gündoğan, who wrote a PhD on football in the Xi Jinping era. 'Transfer spending was described as irrational.' Was the Communist Party worried that entrepreneurs were moving capital abroad? Did the party fear popular envy? In 2016, the average annual income was £6,000; in Shanghai Argentinian player Carlos Tévez earned £450,000 – per week. Or did the government believe that it would be perceived even more as an expansionist threat in Europe? Antonio Conte, then coach at Chelsea, spoke out about what many thought: 'The Chinese market is a threat for everyone. For all the clubs in the world, not just Chelsea.'

The Chinese Football Association reacted in 2017 with new rules without much notice. When they sign a foreign player, a club has to pay a special tax, which is supposed to go into youth development. 'There can now only be four foreigners in a club's squad, with a maximum of three on the field,' says Ai Ting Ting, who works for Chinese state television CCTV. 'In addition, there must be at least one Chinese under the age of 23 on the field.' Fewer stars moved to China after the rules were introduced. Some sponsors saw the advertising value diminish and pulled out.

The companies could not cover their expenses with TV rights, ticket sales and merchandising. Covid made the situation more difficult. After several warnings, the politically controlled football association took action in early 2021: 11 clubs from the first three leagues did not receive a new licence because of financial problems, five clubs dissolved. Shandong Taishan were excluded from the Asian Champions League because of unpaid salaries. In Nanjing, in the east of China, the company Suning had accumulated debts of more than £65m with their club. The group was unable to find a buyer and had to stop operating the football champions. The Evergrande group got into serious financial difficulties, and so football in Guangzhou was also on the brink of extinction.

In the economy under Xi Jinping, it is a fine line between state control and opening up the market. Traditionally, politics and entrepreneurship are blurred. According to 2018 research by the US magazine *Forbes*, China had 373 billionaires. More than 100 of them were members of the National People's Congress, the not-freely-elected parliament. In 2000, according to *Forbes*, none of the world's 500 largest companies by revenue came from China. Now there more than 100 – half owned by the state.

The Communist Party has learned important lessons from the decline of the Soviet Union, according to China expert Stefan Baron. Instead of radically privatising state-owned enterprises, it is working on a slow transition and 80 of the 100 largest state-owned enterprises are to remain in the long term. The banking sector, for example, still lacks significant international competition in China. Does a lack of competition lead to convenience? According to the government, it wants to make the companies more efficient. The goal: global competitiveness and the development of foreign markets.

In this internationalisation, football took on a public relations function. Scholars analyse the background to this in the e-book *China's Football Dream*, edited by Jonathan Sullivan, director of the China Policy Institute at the

University of Nottingham. Since 2014, Chinese companies had invested around £2bn in stakes and acquisitions in about 20 European clubs. Some investors wanted to become better known in important European markets. Others wanted to transfer the knowledge they had acquired over decades from Europe to China and secure the support of the Communist Party. Whether hotel chains or the packaging industry, lamp manufacturers or tourism service providers, the corporations were often interested in clubs that were struggling financially and waiting for sporting success: in England West Bromwich Albion and Wolverhampton Wanderers, in Spain Espanyol, Barcelona and Granada, in France AJ Auxerre and OGC Nice.

But the plan didn't really work out. 'Football was always a loss-making business in China, but this spending went too far for the authorities,' says Tobias Zuser, an Austrian sports sociologist who teaches in Hong Kong. 'The state tightened its control of capital flows abroad.' First, the real estate group Wanda sold shares in Atlético Madrid; Chinese entrepreneurs also withdrew from Aston Villa, Slavia Prague and ADO Den Haag. According to the Communist Party, the clubs had abused China's generosity without reciprocation. The number of investors in Europe has halved to ten and it could fall further. In Italy, ailing trading giant Suning wants to get rid of its majority stake in Inter Milan. The club won its first Serie A championship since 2010 in 2021.

A link in a global entertainment industry

To outsiders, the football offensive sometimes seems contradictory and illogical. For years, investors in Europe were supposed to strengthen Chinese influence. Meanwhile, well-known businessmen have had to take a back seat. Even in China's highest division, many clubs are no longer allowed to have their owners in their names. 'The government wants to limit the social influence of entrepreneurs,' says Simon

Chadwick, founder of the Centre for Eurasian Sports Industry. 'Every now and then, billionaires like Jack Ma of Alibaba disappear from the scene for some time.'

It looks like the People's Republic is targeting its investment more. In the Swiss newspaper *Neue Zürcher Zeitung*, Beijing correspondent Matthias Müller stated that Chinese companies were hardly significant in major sporting events a good one and a half decades ago. That changed with the 2008 Olympic Games in Beijing. In 2016, the electronics manufacturer Hisense sponsored the European Football Championship in France. Due to numerous corruption scandals, many Western sponsors turned their backs on FIFA. According to the market research company Nielsen, FIFA took in around £1.2bn from its advertising partners in the four-year cycle from 2011 to 2014; but between 2015 and 2018, the figure was 11 per cent lower. Chinese companies such as Hisense, the mobile phone company Vivo or the electric scooter manufacturer Yadea filled the gaps. *NZZ* reporter Matthias Müller highlighted the consequence: 'If you break the figures down to the country level, the financiers from China take first place in the ranking.'

The US industry service Front Office Sports documents that Chinese investments are also becoming more important at other interfaces, for example at the Portuguese player agency Gestifute, among others. Likewise with a few national football associations. The online payment platform Alipay has joined the European association UEFA as a sponsor until 2026. And beyond football, the International Olympic Committee (IOC) signed contracts with the IT group Alibaba and the milk producer Mengniu Dairy. Hisense is a partner for the World Cup 2022.

In the global marketing of China, sport is one element among many. Sinologist Philippe Le Corre of the US think tank Brookings spoke about the background in a dossier published by the German daily *Die Welt*: 'Many people in

Europe and America see China as an authoritarian one-party regime that violates human rights and knows neither freedom of the press nor freedom of opinion – this is an obstacle to China's success. To improve China's image, the leadership has systematically analysed what counts in the cultural consciousness of Europeans and Americans.'

Soft power: with this term, the US political scientist Joseph Nye coined the idea of power which relies on cultural attraction, not on economic incentives or military threats. In the 20th century, the USA shaped an everyday culture in many industrialised countries that was overwritten as Western through Hollywood, pop music and fast-food chains. In the 21st century, the Chinese government wants to counteract this: through the several hundred Confucius Institutes worldwide with their Chinese language courses, but also through massive investments in entertainment, culture and tourism. Style-defining institutions which are now partly or completely owned by Chinese investors include the Canadian show provider Cirque du Soleil and the British auction house Sotheby's.

'The marketing possibilities of football serve as a link in a global entertainment industry,' says researcher Jonathan Sullivan, co-founder of the China Soccer Observatory institute. Since 2016, China has had the most lucrative e-sports market. Sullivan adds: 'In China, footballers are not only perceived as athletes, but above all as entertainment figures.'

There are political and economic interests behind the cultural offensive. For decades, China had been a cheap production location for industrialised countries, later a huge sales market for higher-quality products: a German global player like BMW made almost 30 per cent of its profits in China, Volkswagen more than 40. The Communist Party put forward a long-term plan: the country should be a 'world power' by 2049. Xi Jinping put it this way: 'Modern technology is the sharp weapon of a modern state. Our technology lags behind that of developed states. We must adopt an asymmetric strategy to catch up.'

Dependencies through stadium diplomacy

The Communist Party wants to make itself indispensable. This applies to Western industrialised countries, but also to so-called developing countries. This became clear at the beginning of 2022 at the Africa Cup of Nations in Cameroon, a country at war. The Francophone government is fighting against Anglophone separatists in the west of the country. Around 4,000 people are said to have been killed, 700,000 are on the run. For 40 years, Cameroon has been led autocratically by Paul Biya, who has powerful friends in the Far East.

Two of the six stadiums for the Africa Cup of Nations 2022 were built by Chinese companies, in Bafoussam and in Limbe; they are functional buildings for 20,000 spectators each. Local media report that step by step smaller businesses will set up shops nearby, which could create 5,000 jobs. China's state news agency Xinhua also devoted a report to the stadiums, in which Cameroonian regional politician Augustine Awa Fonka also had his say: 'Trade relations between China and Cameroon have a great future.' Cameroon has considerable reserves of oil, iron ore and gold, but the infrastructure to develop them needs to be upgraded. China could help with development.

Cameroon is just one example. China has built more than 100 arenas in developing countries, two-thirds of which are in Africa. Whether Ghana or Angola, Gabon or Equatorial Guinea: Beijing gave cheap and long-term loans to hosts of past African championships. And in return, it secured access to rare resources and raw materials such as oil, copper or cobalt. In the meantime, the People's Republic has become one of the most important trading partners in the countries mentioned. 'China wants to create structural dependencies,' says Simon

Chadwick. 'In Africa, Beijing encounters fewer restrictions than in Europe. And local regimes can present themselves as generous and popular with new stadiums.' These are regimes that have come under criticism for corruption and human rights abuses.

Chinese networks on the African continent have been established for decades. During the Cold War in the 1950s, China under Mao Zedong had drawn economic aid from the Soviet Union. For the common cause, Beijing supported socialist governments and rebels in Africa, also sending construction workers and materials for cheap infrastructure, including sports facilities. In 1964, Premier Zhou Enlai visited ten African states that had become independent. Some ceremonies took place in stadiums. In 1971, the People's Republic joined the United Nations instead of Taiwan – also with support from Africa.

But one can only speak of a construction boom in the 21st century. During his state visit to the Senegalese capital Dakar in 2018, head of state Xi Jinping also visited the new national wrestling stadium, built in 28 months by Chinese companies. 'For many states, stadiums are important landmarks. Shops and neighbourhoods can be built around them,' says Ding Guanghui from the University of Engineering and Architecture in Beijing. 'But the Chinese government also pursues political goals with such buildings.'

Senegal had maintained diplomatic relations with Taiwan since 1995, and the island nation is considered a breakaway region by the People's Republic. Beijing increased the pressure and held out the prospect of investments, including in sports. In 2005, Senegal broke away from Taiwan and established relations with Beijing. Since then, the trade volume between the two states has grown massively. Due to Xi Jinping's visit, Dakar is seen as a symbol for a development that researchers like Ding Guanghui call 'stadium diplomacy'.

Chinese companies built new stadiums not only in Africa, but also in Cambodia, Laos, Haiti and El Salvador; in countries that have suffered destruction through conflicts or disasters. And Beijing also wants to exert influence beyond building. In 2019, the Chinese corporation Huawei introduced the faster mobile phone standard 5G in Egypt, shortly before the start of the Africa Cup of Nations there. The Suez Canal east of Cairo is considered essential for the 'New Silk Road'. By the middle of the 21st century, China wants to connect dozens of countries in Europe, Asia and Africa, through railway lines, highways, pipelines and ports.

Sports facilities are also to be built along the trade route: a stadium in Rijeka, Croatia, an indoor swimming pool in Minsk, Belarus, and a project is also being discussed in Trieste, Italy. 'It is obvious that China is not invading by force of arms, as some states from Europe did in previous centuries,' says Matt Ferchen of Leiden University. 'But some structures are reminiscent of the colonial past.' In Africa, states often commit to importing Chinese goods, which hurts domestic production. Chinese companies often have employees flown in and do without local workers. Often, the stadiums are in a desolate condition after only a few years. The African championships are then long gone, but the sources of raw materials continue to bubble up.

Prominent athletes committed suicide

Xi Jinping is likely to personally push the political football strategy in the future. The US magazine *Foreign Policy* called him the 'most powerful football coach in the world'. Even before his presidency, his foreign trips were punctuated by camera-ready appointments: in 2009, Xi was presented with a jersey of the Leverkusen club of the same name by the German pharmaceutical company Bayer. In 2012, he met the English professional David Beckham in Los Angeles. In 2014, he posed with Wolfsburg youth players equipped by Volkswagen. In the same year, Argentinian politicians presented him with a national jersey of their country with his name on it. And in 2015, he smiled in a stadium photo alongside British Prime Minister David Cameron and Sergio Agüero. The Argentine Manchester City player posted it on social media: 'Thanks for the selfie, President Xi!'

On the same 2015 trip, Xi Jinping presented the National Football Museum in Manchester with memorabilia from the game of Cuju, which the Chinese consider the original form of football. More than 2,000 years ago, soldiers are said to have played with leather balls, presumably filled with hair and feathers. There is a painting of Taizu, the founding emperor of the Song dynasty in the tenth century, showing him kicking a ball with advisors. The fact that Xi Jinping commemorated Cuju in Manchester, of all places, in the so-called motherland of football, can be interpreted in a wider context. Many representatives of the People's Republic feel unappreciated today for numerous achievements that originated in China centuries ago: for example, for printing, gunpowder, the compass – and for the roots of football.

Modern football, however, came to China in the 1870s through the British. Early football centres were commercial metropolises such as Shanghai, Hong Kong and the port city of Tianjin east of Beijing. The Chinese Football Association, founded in 1924, joined FIFA in 1931. The Chinese Civil War and the parallel escalating conflict with Japan almost brought the game to a standstill from the late 1930s onwards. Under Mao Zedong, mass gymnastic exercises outshone the talented national football team. According to an official biography, the 'Great Chairman' himself was an 'outstanding' goalkeeper as a schoolboy.

Mao's revolutionary campaigns, the Great Leap Forward and the Cultural Revolution, claimed tens of millions of victims and destroyed many everyday cultures. Domestic elite sport was demonised as 'bourgeois ideology' and 'capitalist practice'. Red guards attacked prominent athletes, coaches, officials. They destroyed trophies and medals. Several table tennis players who had been revered as heroes in the fifties and sixties committed suicide.

The British journalist Jonathan White explains in *Foreign Policy* the ban on football from 1966 onwards: many communists had no love for competition from the West; moreover, even meetings of smaller groups could be considered a conspiracy against the regime. Under Mao, the People's Republic closed itself off to foreign countries. In international organisations, the representative of the 'Chinese people' was mostly Taiwan, officially the Republic of China, also in the United Nations and in FIFA. The background to this is that after the civil war, the defeated nationalist Kuomintang had withdrawn to the island of Taiwan in 1949, but continued to claim sole representation of China.

Only with the economic opening from the 1970s onwards did the People's Republic return to the world community, in 1979 re-joining FIFA. Under pressure from Beijing, Taiwan was sidelined. The island state was allowed to participate in the Olympics and international football competitions as Chinese Taipei. This was made possible by the ambiguity of the name. The People's Republic considers Taipei to be a city of China. Taiwan, on the other hand, ascribes the adjective 'Chinese' a cultural rather than a governmental meaning. Democratic Taiwan competes with a neutral flag and anthem.

In Beijing, the reformist politician Deng Xiaoping, who had learned to appreciate football as an exchange worker in the 1920s, introduced a managed capitalism. The rapprochement with the USA included a visit to Beijing by New York Cosmos with Pelé and Franz Beckenbauer. Millions of Chinese from the provinces were allowed to seek work in the metropolises from 1985, soon with a five-day week. Thus, it was the urban middle class that established football as a leisure pastime. But the breakthrough of the Chinese professional league only came decades later.

FC Bayern travel to Asia with large delegations

In the 21st century, football is increasingly becoming a reflection of Chinese expansion. A few weeks after Xi Jinping's visit to Manchester in 2015, a Chinese investment group acquired 14 per cent of Manchester City for £320m. The seller of the shares was Khaldoon Al Mubarak. The entrepreneur from the Gulf emirate of Abu Dhabi has been the club's main owner and chairman since 2008. Earlier in 2019, his City Football Group acquired Chinese third division club Sichuan Jiuniu in the city of Chengdu. Etihad, the Abu Dhabi state-owned airline and Manchester City's main sponsor, announced plans to establish a hub for south-west China in Chengdu. A few weeks later, the Beijing and Abu Dhabi governments signed further trade agreements. 'China and the Emirates are two growing centres for the football industry of the future,' says China researcher Simon Chadwick. 'China wants to win not only on the pitch, but especially off it.'

Besides Manchester City, numerous top European clubs are establishing relations with China, often with their own branches. FC Bayern, from Germany, are particularly active. Since 2012, the Munich team has usually spent a summer tour in China every two years, with matches, press rounds, advertising appointments and contract signings. The FC Bayern office in Shanghai has been laying the foundations since 2016.

'If you are serious about China, you have to be on the ground all year round,' says Martin Hägele. 'And with employees who speak Chinese. That way we avoid cultural misunderstandings.' Hägele worked as a sports reporter for 30 years. In the 1990s, he established contacts with East Asian media and wrote columns for Japanese newspapers. Word got around at FC Bayern, where he set up the International Relations Department from 2005. Hägele worked to get more foreign journalists interviews with Bayern players. And he relied on experts from the target markets.

One priority was China. In our interview, Hägele describes how a stable relationship in a faraway country that sometimes seems very different to us depends on small steps. Hägele attended receptions hosted by the Chinese Consul General in Munich. With a colleague from China with media experience, he aroused greater interest in FC Bayern at the state television station CCTV.

FC Bayern try to cultivate contacts, which in Confucianist-influenced China can be captured by the term 'guanxi'. According to the journalist Stefan Baron, the status of a Chinese also depends on the quality and reach of his networks. Contacts are cultivated ceremonially with invitations or gifts. This can lead to new relationships, which often seem more important to many Chinese than contracts. In this network, people who are higher up in particular do not want to lose their authority. And so, Li Keqiang was probably also concerned with saving face in 2015. The then Prime Minister of the People's Republic told FC Bayern that he would like to attend their planned match in Beijing's Olympic Stadium. However, he was reluctant for them to play against a Chinese team, as this would probably result in a defeat for the host team. FC Bayern played against FC Valencia instead.

The Harvard Business School study on FC Bayern's China strategy also elaborates on long-term brand building. The Munich team opened an online shop on Alibaba in 2015. Four employees publish content in dense cycles on social networks such as Sina Weibo, WeChat and Youku, which are the most important sources of information for hundreds of millions of

Chinese. US portals like Google, Facebook and YouTube are blocked in China. FC Bayern's online editors effectively put the most famous players like Thomas Müller and Manuel Neuer in the centre. Surveys had shown that the majority of Chinese fans are interested in stars. In addition, the Munich jersey colour red evokes associations with the Chinese flag.

FC Bayern's preparations for a summer tour of China take longer than half a year, the programme fills hundreds of pages for dozens of appointments. The players give interviews in China, shoot commercials, meet sponsors, sign autographs. They visit shopping centres, car manufacturers, golf tournaments, breweries. Former CEO Karl-Heinz Rummenigge held a discussion with students at the Tongji University in Shanghai, which was founded by German scientists in 1907. FC Bayern travel to Asia with large delegations, so the club's shareholders and sponsors can also arrange investments. Audi now sells more cars in China than in Germany. In China, Adidas can keep up with world market leader Nike with annual growth rates of up to 30 per cent. Whether this trend will continue after the pandemic remains to be seen.

A vehicle for a new nationalism

So, football is making relations between Western Europe and China more commonplace. Does this also lead to less questioning of the Communist Party's policies? The list of human rights violations documented by non-governmental organisations is long. Because of strict censorship and the imprisonment of more than 100 journalists and bloggers, China ranks 177th out of 180 in Reporters Without Borders' press freedom ranking.

In his book *The Reinvention of Dictatorship*, long-time correspondent Kai Strittmatter provides information about the massive expansion of the surveillance apparatus: millions of cameras for facial recognition in public spaces, 30,000 internet sensors and a the new social credit system, under which the government wants to rate citizens in a points system according to performance, behaviour and finances. As a result, buying a house, finding a job or getting into school can be made easier or more difficult. Another consequence of rapid economic growth is the pollution of air, water and soil.

Civil rights and environmental damage almost never come up in the engagement of European clubs in China. It was different when Chinese football came to Germany. On the initiative of the Chancellery, Angela Merkel and Xi Jinping visited a youth game in Berlin in July 2017. They also discussed the agreed exchange in coach, youth and referee training between the German and the Chinese football associations. In addition, a Chinese Under-20 team was to take part in a regional German league, in return for a fee for the German fourth-division teams.

At the first match of the Chinese U20 team in Mainz in November 2017, some spectators showed flags of Tibet, which had been annexed by the People's Republic in 1951. The visiting team considered this a provocation and prematurely ended the match, which was being broadcast on Chinese television. Subsequently, the Chinese government called on the German football federation (DFB) to ban political statements from grounds. The foreign ministry spoke of 'anti-Chinese activities'. The party-affiliated English-language daily *Global Times* commented: 'The Germans should be ashamed of themselves for not being in control of the stadium.' Further guest appearances by the Chinese juniors were cancelled. According to the German daily *Handelsblatt*, representatives of the DFB reportedly apologised to China for the Tibet flags, allegedly at the insistence of some Bundesliga clubs who feared for the loss of their Chinese sponsors. In addition, many of their German advertising partners have branches in China. The People's Republic is still an important production location.

The Communist Party often reacts to criticism from the West with similar arguments: The People's Republic has its own view of human rights; the first priority is social security and increasing the prosperity of the population. The party reacts with defensive reflexes when it perceives arrogance or paternalism towards Chinese culture, for example in July 2019. The official Xinhua news agency commented in English on Manchester City's trip to China. It said coach Pep Guardiola had consistently ignored Chinese fans and journalists. Only fans with expensive special tickets had been able to get near the players. Xinhua complained of 'second-class treatment', wrote of 'arrogance' and 'discrimination'. Guardiola contradicted the account.

Experts report growing nationalism under Xi Jinping. In 2015, the Ministry of Education introduced Chinese culture textbooks, Western children's books are being pushed back. Simon Lang, who researched for the Mercator Institute for China Studies in Berlin, says: 'Football serves the government to fill the legitimising void. It has fed itself for decades on class struggle and most recently on strong economic growth. With that now gone, football offers itself as a vehicle for a new nationalism.'

The Chinese Football Association has undergone some restructuring. 'But it has never been truly independent,' says British reporter John Duerden, who covers football in Asia for *The Guardian* and the BBC, among others. 'The federation has been influenced and controlled by politics.' Football is also supposed to instil discipline, determination and resilience.

Some popular players received bans for not covering their tattoos or grabbing their faces during the national anthem. In October 2018, the federation gathered 50 young professionals at a military camp without regard to league operations. Photos showed them bare-chested in the snow. In 2019, Chinese female footballers received lessons entitled 'Motherland in my heart' ahead of the World Cup in France. This involved 'deepening their understanding of patriotic rules at the moral, legal and political levels'. In 2020, the Ministry of Education required schools to hire retired athletes to, 'cultivate masculinity in students'.

Time and again, Chinese politicians criticise the cultural influence from outside: films from Hollywood and pop music from South Korea. In football, there are hardly any efforts to place Chinese talents with European clubs. Wang Shuang moved to Paris Saint-Germain in 2018 as one of the best national players. Chinese officials and fans soon formulated the expectation that she should focus on the national team, and since 2019 she has been playing again in her native city of Wuhan.

Competition in China is tough – teamwork suffers

China still lacks the strongest medium for identity-building in football: a competitive men's national team. That is why the Communist Party's reform programme attaches great importance to young talent. In the medium term, 30 million young people are to learn the game of football in their schools, and the best of them are to be promoted. Numerous European clubs send coaches, medical staff and equipment to China. Real Madrid cooperates with the Guangzhou Evergrande Academy, one of the world's largest sports complexes with 50 football pitches, 500 employees and 3,000 players. These official figures and the actual implementation cannot be verified by outsiders, but potential is there: China has 160 million children of primary and middle school age.

Nevertheless, there are cultural obstacles. To limit population growth, Chinese families were generally only allowed to have one child between 1979 and 2015. 'Most parents didn't want to risk their only children getting injured playing a sport,' says Tariq Panja, who researched China several times, first for Bloomberg and later for the *New York Times*. Martial arts were frowned upon, rough team games like basketball or football remained in the background.

Education is traditionally seen as the most likely path to prosperity. Parents spend at least a third of their income on school, tuition and universities. In primary school classes with up to 50 children, there is no room for individual attention, says Panja: 'Competition in China is tough. For years, it's all about getting into the best universities for young people. As a result, teamwork suffers – even in sports.' Chinese teams are less successful at the Olympics than individual athletes. Bernd Schuster, who coached the Chinese first division team Dalian Yifang, said in the newspaper *Die Welt*: 'When I ask a player for advice or ask him for his opinion, he says: "My opinion doesn't count. You are the coach, you know what to do." They don't make decisions, because they are worried about making the wrong ones and being punished for it.'

So far, the Chinese national team has only qualified for the 2002 World Cup in Japan and South Korea, failing in the preliminary round without a point or a goal. A successful team could accelerate cultural change enormously. In research by East Asian scholar Ilker Gündoğan, it was found that Chinese fans take their national team far more seriously than supporters in other countries. In the 16-20 age group, two-thirds of respondents link football with the realisation of the 'Chinese Dream', the renewal of the country under Xi Jinping. Among the 31- to 40-year-olds, the figure was 44 per cent, about 20 per cent less. Among the young generation growing up under Xi Jinping, nationalism seems to be more likely to catch on.

But football can also let patriotism get out of hand, as historical events show: In 1984, Beijing and London agreed to return the British Crown Colony of Hong Kong to China in 1997, after which, according to the plan, the city would retain a free-market economy for 50 years: 'One country, two systems.' Six months after this historic agreement, the national football teams of the People's Republic and Hong Kong met in Beijing. With a win, the Chinese could almost have secured qualification for the 1986 World Cup, which would have been their first. But they lost 1-2 against the underdogs and failed. After the match, fans set cars on fire and surrounded the players' quarters, and the police took 120 people into custody.

China and Hong Kong met again in the qualifiers for the 2018 World Cup. Hong Kong has been a special administrative region of China since 1997, but with a free-market economy and a high degree of self-determination. People in Hong Kong have repeatedly protested against Beijing, and in autumn 2014 they occupied financial and government districts, which became known as the 'Umbrella Revolution'. Before the qualifying matches for 2018, the Chinese Football Association referred to their opponents on a poster as 'Hong Kong, China', accompanied by the comment: 'This team has players with black, yellow and white skin. It is important to be vigilant against such a diverse team!' Many Hong Kong fans saw this as racism.

Since 1997, Hong Kong has been using the Chinese anthem, rather than the British one. Before the qualifying second leg in Hong Kong, home fans turned their backs to the pitch and booed the Chinese anthem. According to the BBC, the 500 Chinese travelling with the team waved red flags and sang communist songs. The Hong Kong Football Association was fined by FIFA for the booing, but spectators have also rioted against their own anthem at subsequent home matches, such as the September 2019 clash against Iran. Fans booed, stuck out their middle fingers and chanted: 'Glory to Hong Kong.'

'Especially the national team has become an icon for many Hong Kong people. At the home games, they could live out their local identity,' says Hong Kong sociologist and blogger Lee Chun Wing. 'Many fans were born in the nineties, or even later. This younger generation no longer wants to identify with Chinese culture, not with pop singers and not even with athletes. For them, if you love Hong Kong, you can't love China.'

This younger generation was shaping the biggest demonstrations against Beijing in decades from 2019, often with hundreds of thousands of participants. Some Hong Kong footballers were showing solidarity with the movement. There were blockades and riots with hundreds injured. The Communist Party called in the military, bringing back memories of the 1989 crackdown on the Tiananmen Square protests, when 2,600 people died.

After the uprising, new laws were passed. If Hong Kong fans were to boo the Chinese anthem now, they could be arrested, says Lee Chun Wing: 'On the other hand, this dislike could also help the Communist Party: Its nationalism is based on a clear demarcation from internal and external enemies.' For China, it is an advantage that Hong Kong has its own, separate memberships in international organisations like FIFA. So Beijing effectively has two voices in important decisions.

Planned economy without a plan

In the West, criticism against Chinese dominance remains muted. But there are exceptions. On 4 October 2019, a spiral began that is likely to haunt professional sports for a long time to come. Daryl Morey, manager of the Houston Rockets basketball club, sent out a tweet: 'Fight for freedom. Stand with Hong Kong.' As a result, the Chinese Basketball Association broke off relations with the Rockets. A bank from Shanghai cancelled its sponsorship contract, Chinese state television removed preparation games for the NBA season from its programme, online retailers removed their products from the range. Daryl Morey and other NBA officials backed down and only made friendly comments about China. The US television station ESPN even showed a map of the People's Republic, which also marked Taiwan as its national territory.

A few weeks later, Mesut Özil, then of Arsenal, criticised the oppression of the Uyghurs in China in a tweet. According to the UN, more than one million people are being held in the western province of Xinjiang for renouncing Islam. Professional players Erfan Hezim and Erpat Ablekrem are also said to have been detained. Mesut Özil wrote that 'Western states' are drawing attention to this. But: 'Why not the Muslim world?'

The Communist Party hit back. CCTV took the Arsenal broadcast off the air. The online forum Tieba closed down an Özil fan club, an electronics company deleted his character from a computer game. Even his own club did not support him. And thus followed airlines, hotel chains and film studios that now exclude sensitive topics such as Taiwan, Tibet or Hong Kong under pressure from Beijing. Simon Chadwick, an expert on geopolitics in sport, concludes: 'European football clubs will also have to weigh things up carefully: If they are critical of Beijing, they may lose high revenues. If they are uncritical, they come into conflict with domestic fans and international human rights activists.'

In mainland China, the state-controlled media hardly reports on protests like those in Hong Kong anyway. And when they do, they stir up outrage against foreign countries, backed by statements from patriotic artists, actors and academics. In 2017, broadcasters were instructed to promote 'Chinese culture' and refrain from 'foreign content' during prime time. Victories of the Chinese national football team are a popular topic. This one-sided reporting led to the fact that, according to Stefan Baron, many Chinese would even approve of a violent conquest of Taiwan.

China wants to host a World Cup for the first time in the 2030s. Xi Jinping needs high-profile stages for his nationalism. Especially for his own people. As economic growth slowed, the Communist Party grew sceptical about Chinese investment abroad. After expensive signings of Brazilian players and stakes in European clubs, the Party wanted football with 'Chinese characteristics'. The billionaires heard the signals and focused more on the domestic market. The 2023 Asian Cup could have been an important stepping stone. But then Covid brought a large part of the Chinese economy to a standstill. China cancelled the Asian Cup. This does not stop the breakthrough in football, but at most postpones it.

A Team Photo as Life Insurance

*In African countries like Rwanda, football is
a driver of social divisions, but also of unity.
For the genocide against the Tutsi, the militias
recruited their fighters on football fields and
in stands. The rebel army, on the other hand,
founded a club to keep its soldiers happy. After
the genocide, memorial tournaments brought
people together again. Now, Rwanda is regarded
as a model state – and sport illustrates the
ambiguity of development aid.*

IN MARCH 1994, the catastrophe in Rwanda was already
looming, but for one afternoon the hatred remained hidden.
In the African Cup Winners' competition, Rayon Sports, the
most popular club in the country, hosted the Sudanese club Al
Hilal. Rayon had lost the first leg 1-0, but now in the return
match in the capital Kigali, one goal after another was scored.
Rayon won 4-1 and advanced to the third round, the biggest
success in Rwanda's football history so far. More than 30,000
people cheered in the Amahoro stadium. Hutu and Tutsi sang
and danced together.

'Rwanda broke apart, but we experienced a moment of
unity,' says Eric Eugène Murangwa, then goalkeeper for
Rayon Sports and one of three Tutsi in the team. After the
victory against Al Hilal, fans celebrated late into the night.

Hutu also patted Murangwa on the back, bought him beer, gave him money. Radio stations' reports were full of praise, soldiers waved white and blue Rayon flags, even the state president wanted to appear on television with the players. Murangwa didn't really feel like it, because he knew that this affection was not genuine. Everyday life looked different for Tutsi in the early 1990s – and the reasons for this go back many generations.

It was not language, religion or culture that separated the two groups in Rwanda, but social status. In the 19th century, the Tutsi minority was mainly involved in cattle breeding. They gained more and more power over the Hutu majority, who were engaged in agriculture. In their colonial rule, first the Germans and later the Belgians loaded this hierarchy with biological pseudo-characteristics. The Tutsi were considered the dominant, superior race. There was repeated violence between the two groups, especially after Rwanda's independence in 1962. Hundreds of thousands of Tutsi fled to neighbouring countries in fear of the new Hutu rule. Thousands of Tutsi who stayed behind were killed.

Murder lists and arms caches

Football, brought into the country by the colonial powers, was integral to this history. The Rwandan king, tolerated by Belgium, had kept a team in order to be more in touch with the population, says former journalist Jules Karangwa, who works for the Rwanda Football Association and has studied the history. 'Football was the ideal tool for communication. And many groups took advantage of it.' After Rwanda's independence, many of the now oppressed Tutsi joined together in teams. They had few other opportunities to meet in public; higher education and jobs were closed to them. This is how, for example, Kiyovu Sports was founded, still active in the first division today.

From the 1970s onwards, the situation in east Africa radicalised, including in small Rwanda. The football association, founded in 1972, and the clubs that played in the first division were determined by members of the MRND, the only legal party. 'The Tutsi were marginalised everywhere,' says Jules Karangwa. 'The coach of the national team was ordered by the government to let only Hutu play.' An economic crisis in the 1980s deepened the divisions. To the public, the Rwandan government pretended to want to reintegrate Tutsi who had fled to exile. But in the background, genocide was being prepared, with arms caches, kill lists and combat training.

One of the driving forces behind the increasing violence was the Interahamwe, a paramilitary organisation of the Hutu state party. The Interahamwe recruited young fighters on football pitches and in grandstands, Jules Karangwa reports: 'Many of their propaganda events took place near stadiums, there were long speeches with music and drums.' Meanwhile, the Tutsi who were in exile formed a rebel army, the Rwandan Patriotic Front (RPF). In 1990, it invaded Rwanda for the first time, the beginning of the civil war. Tutsi in the capital Kigali were now watched even more closely, including celebrities.

Goalkeeper Eric Murangwa had grown up knowing he was different. At school, at the doctor's, in a queue: as a Tutsi, he felt disadvantaged. 'I asked my parents about the reasons, but I didn't get any real answers. It was like that in many families.' But Murangwa found that this inferiority was not so strongly expressed in football: 'Everywhere I was asked about my ethnicity, but on the pitch it mattered less. The colleagues were all about sport.'

Things came to a head during the civil war, says journalist Paul Doyle, writing in *The Guardian* about Murangwa's life. Several times the bus of his club Rayon Sports was stopped by militias, several times the Tutsi from the team were searched and threatened. 'The stadiums were very crowded,' Murangwa recounts. 'I stood in the goal and felt the hatred of the fans behind me. They called me a cockroach and a snake.' At one point, Murangwa refused to play in Gisenyi, the birthplace of President Juvénal Habyarimana; the stronghold of the radical Hutu seemed too dangerous to him. Some officials of his own club took offence.

Footballers kill team-mates

Eric Murangwa, born in 1976, is a gently articulate man. My interview with him takes place in January 2020 in his adopted home of London. He has just spent almost three hours discussing Rwanda with young people at a school. Murangwa leans forward in the restaurant, rests his arms on the table, his eyes look tired, but he speaks with concentration. And so, one encounters an admonisher who does not seem to tire, no matter how often he has to mentally return to the weeks of the unimaginable.

On the evening of 6 April 1994, Rwandan President Habyarimana's plane was shot down on approach to Kigali, killing all passengers. To this day, the exact causes are not clear. One assumption is that the president's stance was not radical enough for many extremist Hutu. Barely 30 minutes later, the first murders of influential Tutsi and critical Hutu began in Kigali. The perpetrators worked through murder lists step by step.

In the early hours of the morning, Murangwa was roused from his sleep. He had become accustomed to the sounds of grenades during the civil war, but now the gunshots and death screams are getting closer. Five or six soldiers stormed his flat, he reports, pushing him face down on the floor, laying waste to the furnishings. 'I thought I was going to die,' he says. At one point, one of the fighters caught sight of a picture of Rayon Sports in a fallen photo album. 'Are you Toto?' the soldier asked. Toto, the Swahili translation for 'the boy', is Murangwa's nickname, as he made his first division debut at 16.

The aggressive soldier was suddenly calm. He had been a fan of Rayon Sports for a long time, he told Murangwa, and thanked the goalkeeper for the great victory against the Sudanese team of Al Hilal, only a month ago. Then the soldier gave him some advice: Murangwa should leave the doors and window curtains open, he said, so the house would look empty to other militias. And indeed, Murangwa was left alone for the next few hours.

It was the first of nearly 100 days, at the end of which at least 800,000 people were dead, about 75 per cent of the Tutsi as well as moderate Hutu. The perpetrators came from the army, the presidential guard, the police, but the general population also took part in the mass murder: teachers killed their pupils, children their uncles, footballers their team-mates. 'You were often in more danger from people you knew than from people you didn't know,' says Murangwa. 'My team-mates knew my political stance, they could have betrayed me. But they chose sanity over madness.'

When Murangwa talks about the genocide, he also focuses on the last sparks of humanity. He mentions his Hutu colleagues who organised hiding places for him, bribed policemen, got him food. Several times Murangwa freed himself from threatening situations because the killers saw in him a role model from football. For a few days he stayed with Jean-Marie Vianney Mudahinyuka, known as Zuzu, a former Rayon Sports official. They ate together, played cards and talked about football. Later, Murangwa learned that Zuzu had been sent to prison for life for the murders of several hundred Tutsi. 'The world was not black and white,' Murangwa says. 'There were people who tortured and killed others. But the same people saved others' lives the next day. It was a time of madness.'

Ambassadors of a new society

In July 1994, the liberation of Rwanda by the rebel army RPF was almost complete. Hundreds of thousands of Hutu fled abroad, mainly to Zaire, now the Democratic Republic of Congo. In Rwanda, around 400,000 girls and women had become victims of rape; 300,000 children were living without parents. Trust in institutions had been shaken, especially in the Catholic Church, which in many cases had tolerated and enabled the killings.

There was not much for Rwandans to hold on to. Thirty people from Eric Murangwa's extended family circle were dead. But he forced himself to look forward and went in search of old team-mates. In those days, survivors talked about mass graves, epidemics and worries about a flare-up of civil war. Murangwa walked the streets incessantly and eventually found five old team-mates – out of a total of 30. They arranged to train with other players, and just four months after the genocide, Rayon Sports met Kiyovu Sports in a match. 'There were more than 15,000 people in the stadium. The match was the first big event where people felt something like joy again.'

After the game, several family members approached him. They had thought he was dead. Soon after, memorial tournaments and friendly matches were held. Murangwa was named captain of the new national team. 'We were ambassadors of a new society. Especially at matches in other countries, we promoted to exiles to rebuild the country. Most of them thought there was no life left in Rwanda at all.' As if the situation wasn't complicated enough, some national players complained about low bonuses and bad hotels. They felt unrepresented by their captain, because Murangwa emphasised above all the socio-political importance of the team. And so he resigned as captain.

The political situation was far from stable. In neighbouring countries, Hutu extremists were gearing up for a re-invasion of

Rwanda. In February 1995, Rwanda's national team was pelted with stones at a tournament in neighbouring Uganda to the north. In Kigali itself, prominent Tutsi were murdered. Eric Murangwa also received threats and felt he was being watched. In June 1996, he was on his way back from Tunisia with the national team. During a stopover in Paris, he broke away and fled to Belgium. But he didn't want to stay there either. Again and again he met Hutu who had fled and were involved in the genocide. In 1997, he applied for asylum in London. Soon after, he travelled to Rwanda and explained the circumstances of his escape to the Minister of Sport. Several fans had called him a traitor. Murangwa founded several projects and visited schools, youth institutions and universities with other survivors.

Kigali as a conference centre

Eric Murangwa's biography is comparatively unknown in Europe. As a book that looks at politics and history with the help of football, it could – in theory – describe the lives of millions of Africans. The continent, three times the size of Europe, is home to more than 3,000 ethnic groups and 2,000 languages. The 55 countries with their 1.3 billion mostly young people are diverse and contrasting. Yet Africa is still often perceived as a large entity, even in Western Europe. These patterns of thought are centuries old and were consolidated above all at the end of the 19th century, when European states divided the continent into colonies among themselves.

Reports about Africa in Britain are usually about crises and conflicts. One fifth of the people living in Africa are undernourished. Half a billion people have no electricity. In the World Bank's Business Climate Index, 18 of the 25 countries with the worst conditions are in Africa. Several states are rich in oil, copper, cobalt, uranium or diamonds, but the raw materials are mostly exported unprocessed – so elites outside Africa profit. Almost 40 per cent of private African assets, i.e. tens of billions of pounds, are in foreign accounts. Probably no one can quantify exactly how many billions have disappeared into the pockets of corrupt regimes. Thousands of scientists, doctors and teachers leave the continent every year. These are the negative developments. But there are also some that spread confidence.

Almost 30 years after the genocide against the Tutsi, Rwanda is unrecognisable. One can get an idea of this in Kigali Heights, one of the business districts in the capital. Banks, start-ups and chic cafés have set up in glass office complexes, next to a luxury hotel and the congress centre completed in 2016. Rwanda, one of the most densely populated countries in Africa, has no sea access and hardly any raw materials. Therefore, the government wants to attract a lot of conferences and large events.

Rwanda is considered a model African state south of the Sahara, that is the narrative that is conveyed during my interviews, even in the spacious new building of the football association, not far from the congress centre. Jules Karangwa sits in one of the back offices on the first floor, he has a long list of tasks to complete. Karangwa was born the year before the genocide, his father was killed, but he managed to survive with his family in the west of the country. He studied history early on, read books, watched documentaries. Karangwa wanted to help rebuild the country; he studied law, worked for the university radio station, became a sports reporter. The salary was not that high, so he switched to the football association, where he works as a lawyer.

Jules Karangwa is symbolic of the growing middle class that wants to achieve a certain prosperity through education. From memory, he can recite some development data: 'In 1994, life expectancy in Rwanda was still 28 years, now it is almost 70.' More than 40 per cent of national spending goes on education and health. There are 2.5 murders per 100,000 people per year in Rwanda, compared to 13.6 in neighbouring Congo and 5.3 in the U.S. Rwanda ranks 48th in Transparency International's corruption index, while Italy ranks 53rd. Rwanda ranks 29th in the World Bank's index of business-friendly countries.

Football has always been an important sport in Rwanda, but it did not outshine everything like in Cameroon, Nigeria and Côte d'Ivoire. 'The collective trauma in our country runs deep,' says Karangwa. 'But the relaxed environment of sport helps us to start talking.' In 2004, ten years after the genocide, the national team qualified for the Africa Cup of Nations in Tunisia for the first, and so far only, time. They drew 1-1 with Guinea and beat the Democratic Republic of Congo 1-0. Millions of people sat in front of their televisions in Rwanda, but the team was unable to reach the quarter-finals.

Rwanda will not be a major power in football for the foreseeable future; its society has quite different problems, but sport can gradually convey the government's ambitions, writes author Brian Bertie in *Football Chronicle*. Rwanda is increasingly organising smaller regional and international tournaments, especially among young players. In 2011, the Under-17 squad qualified for the World Cup in Mexico, all the players having been born after the genocide. 'We always invite other national teams to our commemorative tournaments,' Karangwa tells us. 'We want to grow cautiously as an association, and more football pitches are being built for that. And maybe at some point we can host the big African championship.' In 2018, a FIFA Council meeting was held in Kigali. 'With each successive event, the world learns that we are optimistic about the future.'

The police are omnipresent

An important site for the past and future of Rwandan football is the Nyamirambo stadium in the west of Kigali, surrounded by dusty streets and low-rise buildings. Lively discussions take place in front of the barbershops and drinks shops, little boys in oversized football jerseys kick balls to each other. Behind the main stand rises a hill with dense rows of trees and family houses. During the genocide, hundreds of Tutsi were interned and murdered in stadiums like this one. In 1998, 20 perpetrators of the genocide were publicly executed in Nyamirambo. It was one of the last actions of this kind, and in 2007 the death penalty was abolished. Since then, Nyamirambo is supposed to have been a place of pleasure.

And you can feel that on a sunny afternoon during a home match of APR FC, Rwanda's most successful club. Almost 2,000 spectators spread out on the blue, yellow and green seats. Drummers and trumpeters have positioned themselves on the back straight, many faces are painted in the club colours of black and white, their non-stop music echoes far into the city. There is no stadium announcer, the screen is switched off, advertising banners and sponsors' logos can be counted on one hand, three vendors walk along the stands with their vendor's trays.

The club name APR stands for Armée Patriotique Rwandaise. Mubaraka Muganga, one of the club's vice-presidents, can explain what it means. The two-star general sits on a cushioned armchair in the VIP tribune, wearing a uniform, just like the rest of the board members of the club. 'Our club is closely linked to the freedom struggle,' says Muganga, looking proudly into the wide oval of the Nyamirambo. During the civil war in the early 1990s, fighters of the rebel army RPF often played football, giving rise to APR FC in 1993. 'This gave us different ideas and courage,' says Muganga, who was in his early 20s at the time. Sitting next to him in the stands is the club's honorary president, war veteran and former defence minister James Kabarebe. The military men keep to themselves during the game. 'We have already won the championship 17 times,' Muganga points out. 'No one will be able to do that any time soon.' What he doesn't mention is that APR receives more support from the state than any other team.

The mood at Nyamirambo is boisterous. On the sidelines, uniformed men with submachine guns survey the stands. It is an impression that is confirmed everywhere in Kigali: security forces are strongly present. People and luggage are checked at banks, hotels, supermarkets. For years, human rights organisations have been critical, saying the price of economic recovery is too high. 'The state spends a lot of money on its security apparatus,' says Gesine Ames of the Ecumenical Network Central Africa, a church network for human rights and development. 'In Rwanda, freedom of expression and freedom of the press have been severely restricted in recent years. The secret service is omnipresent, there are arbitrary arrests and deaths. People often say only what they want to be heard, and many critics have left the country.'

The state has been headed since 2000 by Paul Kagame, the former leader of the rebel army. The new constitution stipulated that a president could remain in office for a maximum of two terms. But this was changed after a referendum, and so Kagame was able to be elected a third time in 2017, with a suspicious 99 per cent of the vote. Kagame rejects international criticism of his concentration of power, saying he does not want to be 'lectured in a neo-colonial manner'. And certainly not by states that did not intervene in the genocide. Gesine Ames pleads for a differentiated view of Rwanda: 'We should not only look at the progress and the boom in the construction industry. Only a small elite benefit from this. We have to take a close look at the statistics: more than 40 per cent of the national budget is still based on foreign aid.' Although Rwanda has achieved a remarkable economic growth, more than a third of the population still lives in poverty.

Despite the authoritarian government, Rwanda is considered a reliable partner by many development ministries and aid organisations because they can be sure that the payments will reach the intended recipient. The long-time diplomat Volker Seitz, who worked for 17 years in various German embassies in Africa, paints a picture of questionable development aid elsewhere, the translated title of his book: *Africa is Being Poorly Governed or How to Really Help Africa*. According to Seitz, around £2 trillion in development aid has flowed from the global North to the South over the past six decades. Yet living conditions in many African countries have not improved significantly, Seitz writes, instead rulers have been allowed to omit important reforms: 'Development aid still has the character of indulgences for governments and many people in the North, where the main thing is to show altruism, compassion and generosity.' However, there are also many positive examples.

Espérance conveys confidence

In Kimisagara, a neighbourhood of Kigali with above-average unemployment, young people in colourful jerseys storm across a small artificial turf pitch bordered by blue boards with the FIFA logo and the words 'Football for Hope' on them. Behind the boards, players wait excitedly for their next assignment. Another group is working hard at the table tennis table, behind them a workshop on violence prevention is taking place in a low building. The name of the project is emblazoned above it: Espérance, hope.

Espérance was launched in 1996, two years after the genocide, at a time when many projects, churches and neighbourhood groups were committed to reconciliation. Espérance took up an idea that had already been implemented in other countries, for example in Medellín, Colombia: girls and boys from different backgrounds play football without referees, strengthening self-confidence, empathy and teamwork.

The head of Espérance, Victor Emmanuel Sewabana, sits in a small office with three large desks. He grew up in the neighbourhood and joined Espérance in its early days. 'There was a lot of mistrust then. We thought the killing might start again,' Sewabana says. 'Few young people dared to come to us. Parents everywhere warned against too much contact. Because it was often neighbours, teachers or coaches who took part in the genocide.' The government banned the ethnic division into Hutu and Tutsi, there was to be only one reference point: Rwanda. 'We focused on what we had in common. And football lends itself perfectly to that.'

How can reconciliation be shaped if biographical roots are not to be addressed? How can you involve children whose parents were among the perpetrators? After five or six years, Espérance had found a balance, with new partners: with FIFA, with the Streetfootballworld network. Espérance expanded its methods beyond football, introduced theatre, quizzes and music, with several coaches and volunteers. Representatives from the Rwandan Ministry of Sport, the United Nations and FIFA regularly drop by.

But does the international attention really help? The former German ambassador in Cameroon, Volker Seitz, says in his book: 'It is also true that countless development aid organisations profit from the fact that more and more money is being used for Africa. Because these funds are used to finance projects and personnel. In Africa, a kind of development aid industry has developed that has long since become self-perpetuating. None of these organisations can be expected to abolish themselves.' According to Seitz, there are sometimes 200 to 400 aid organisations in a country like Rwanda. Their staff need accommodation, office supplies and drivers. Foreign aid workers earn up to nine times more than their colleagues who come from the region, with the same qualifications.

Those who ask around among development aid workers often also encounter frustration and disillusionment: funding is usually limited in time, staff turnover is high, and measuring one's own effectiveness is complicated and expensive. 'In sport, too, development aid is increasingly becoming an industry,' says an expert who does not wish to be named. 'People are happy about every congress and every business trip. Discussions take place, brochures and nice image films are produced, but in the end little happens.'

Fred Coalter, a British expert on development aid in and through sport, mentions another point: 'Most projects are financed from the global North, thus local needs are often neglected.' Coalter is one of the few critical minds on the scene. He says that this also blocks access for him: 'Many donors want to have their worldview confirmed by uncritical experts.'

One who agrees in many aspects is Marc-André Buchwalder, CEO of the Scort Foundation, which is based in Switzerland and supported by patrons, i.e. independent of ministries and sports federations. 'Ten years ago we were still very naive,' says Buchwalder, referring to the environment of the 2010 World Cup in South Africa. 'Everyone believed that Africa could be put on the right track with a World Cup, it almost had religious overtones.' Countless projects came into being, such as the 20 'Football for Hope' centres across the African continent. Buchwalder says: 'When money is available, the impulse is often: we build something! But the staff and the embedding in the social environment are also important. Often people are left alone after a construction and the facilities rot.' In sport, too, there is a lack of a central office that pools different interests and skills across states. The Special Adviser to the United Nations Secretary-General on Sport for Developments and Peace could have been such an interface, but after the departure of Bremen's Willi Lemke in 2016, the role was abolished. Many diplomats and politicians want nothing to do with football's billion-dollar event culture.

On Arsenal's sleeve

Industrialised countries demand more initiative from African governments, but they do not always like how this is then implemented. Before Covid, Rwanda took in £300m a year in tourism, and this figure was expected to double by 2024. To make the national parks with their lakes and mountain gorillas better known, the Rwandan Development Corporation expanded its marketing to include football. For an estimated £30m per year, Arsenal advertised 'Visit Rwanda' on its jersey sleeves. Arsenal is the favourite club of many Rwandans and also of Paul Kagame; time and again the president writes about the Londoners on Twitter. In Europe, on the other hand, many politicians saw this sponsorship deal as a mockery: how could a country that receives millions of pounds in development aid from the British budget spend half of it on an enormously rich football club? 'This is an own goal for development aid,' commented Conservative MP Andrew Bridgen.

Many Rwandans feel personally affected by such criticism; for example Richard Bishumba, sports editor of the *New Times*, the leading newspaper in Kigali, says: 'Some Europeans don't want to change their perception at all, for them Africa will always remain poor. But the publicity with Arsenal aims to have a long-term impact. And already more tourists and investors have become aware of Rwanda.' Rwanda is spending money instead of preserving it: Richard Bishumba would like to see more campaigns like this.

According to various projections, Africa's population will double to 2.5 billion by 2050. In Rwanda, the birth rate is below the continent's average. What will happen when Paul Kagame actually steps down as president in 2024? How will society be affected if many perpetrators of the genocide are released from prison in the coming years? Will the country remain stable or will old conflicts erupt?

Rwanda is surrounded by crisis-ridden countries. In the west, in the Democratic Republic of Congo, many Hutu extremists live in exile and hope to recapture Rwanda. Kagame has repeatedly sent troops and weapons to prevent the militias from growing stronger. The Congolese government, however, forbade Kagame's interference. This was only one episode in the conflict-ridden relations between the central and east African countries.

Football has shown what is possible. In 2016, Rwanda hosted the small African championship, in which national teams have to be made up of players from their domestic leagues. The final in Kigali was won by the Democratic Republic of Congo, beating Mali 3-0. The Congolese fans had been allowed to cross the border without any problems, and now they were singing their anthem and waving their national flag. A few weeks earlier, this had been unimaginable. Paul Kagame was also sitting in the stands. He congratulated the winners, whom he usually hates to see win.

Murder and Matches

The 1978 World Cup in Argentina took place under a military dictatorship that probably cost 30,000 people their lives. The uncritical football associations strengthened the self-confidence of the torture regime, but the international attention also enabled human rights activists to find new partners and donations. Now, Argentina has probably the most vibrant civil society in Latin America, but the former world champions hardly play a role in commemoration.

IT TAKES almost an hour to walk around the fence. The ESMA (the mechanics school of the navy) was situated on a busy arterial road in the north of Buenos Aires. A compound with 34 buildings, with residential houses, a casino and workshops, a sports field and a chapel. During the military dictatorship, the largest secret torture centre was also housed here. Prisoners were drugged and later dropped alive from planes over the Río de la Plata. According to human rights organisations, around 30,000 people fell victim to the dictatorship between 1976 and 1983, most of them considered '*desaparecidos*', disappeared.

The political scientist Luciana Bertoia can tell a sad story about many places within the grounds. Since 2004, the area has housed a cultural centre with museums, memorials and human rights offices. 'The testimonies of 950 witnesses help us to better understand the past,' Bertoia says. She works for the non-governmental organisation *Memoria Abierta*, the open memory. A total of 5,000 people were imprisoned in the ESMA. Many women were robbed of their babies, who then grew up with military families. A few years ago, one of the activists met her grandson; he had been born in the ESMA during the 1978 World Cup.

On the upper floor of the building marked number 17, Luciana Bertoia guides us through an exhibition about sport in the military dictatorship. Black, chunky pillars are set up between white, cracked walls, with small TV screens in between, timelines and cheering photos of football, also short biographies of 'disappeared' athletes. One cartoon shows 11 muscle-bound players wearing soldiers' helmets and gas masks. Another portrays football officials in dark suits covering their eyes with both hands.

The speech made by Jorge Rafael Videla, then general and chairman of the military junta, at the opening of the World Cup, sounds from the loudspeakers. Eloquent words, accompanied by applause and doves of peace. Luciana Bertoia and her colleagues have initiated research into football. She says that sport does not play a major role in the culture of remembrance. *Memoria Abierta* wants to change that with documents and stories. 'Football can create an emotional connection with the subject among young people.'

The leader of the committee was shot

When Argentina became world champions on 25 June 1978, the regime firmly believed in its power. The Monumental Stadium, where the final was held, was a few hundred metres from the ESMA. Evidence of the torture centre had been removed. Tens of thousands of people celebrated in the streets. 'A guard was driving prisoners through the streets; he wanted to humiliate them,' Luciana Bertoia reports. 'Nobody dared to call for help. Probably nobody would have believed them anyway.' The activists want to convey such stories to the young generation, who grew up in democratic conditions; they want to approach schools and associations. 'They should know: the price for the World Cup triumph was high.'

There are few sporting events that have triggered such intense political debates as the 1978 World Cup. The tournament had been awarded to Argentina by FIFA 12 years earlier, in July 1966. Almost all political parties were happy about it, including left-wing and right-wing extremists, a rarity in Argentina.

A few days before the World Cup was awarded, the democratically elected president Arturo Illia had been forced to resign by armed police. Almost every democratic government in Argentina in the 20th century was forced to give way to a military regime. FIFA looked past these fragile conditions, even after the coup against President Isabel Perón in 1976, two years before the World Cup. The junta dissolved parliament, banned parties and trade unions, deposed the highest judges. Shortly afterwards, the World Cup organising committee resigned, and a few months later the new head was shot by left-wing extremists.

'It was a time of fear,' recalls Ezequiel Fernández Moores. 'We grew up thinking that conditions could quickly tip.' The renowned journalist writes for the daily *La Nación*, also for international papers like the *New York Times* and *El País*. In 1978, Ezequiel Fernández Moores was a young reporter in his early 20s. There was little talk of politics in his family, the domestic media were subject to censorship, and many journalists were close to the junta. During the World Cup, he met colleagues from Europe who had unvarnished information, including about human rights violations. 'From them I learned what was really going on in my country.'

Secret names for torture centres

Ezequiel Fernández Moores recounts his memories in an agency building in the centre of Buenos Aires. Most of the desks are empty, the economic crisis has weakened the editorial offices. He sits in a T-shirt and shorts in front of a pile of newspapers, files and notes. He is one of the few journalists in Argentina who has been reporting on politics and sport for decades. He has written a book about the 1978 World Cup and made several television documentaries, and so on: research, articles and interviews with contemporary witnesses.

A few years ago, he asked what was the most important sporting event in Argentina's history. Most of his interviewees named the 1978 World Cup, because the great football nation Argentina had finally earned its first title. Only after that did they name the 1986 triumph with Diego Maradona. It seems that 1978 still has a life of its own. 'We must not reduce the tournament to the sporting aspect. The political preparations started much earlier.'

The military had already built a shadow state before the 1976 coup. Its secret torture centres bore veiling names like Athletic Club, Olympus or Vesuvius. In 1976, according to documents and witness interviews, 3,525 people were abducted, in 1977 another 2,746. In the year of the World Cup, the junta had already eliminated most critics, but 797 people were still imprisoned, 63 during the tournament. The reason given was 'terrorism, corruption and criminality'.

Today, these crimes are well documented; in the bookshops of Buenos Aires, literature about the dictatorship fills metre-long shelves. 'But until 1978, Europe was not interested in Argentina,' says author Matías Bauso. 'Chile under Pinochet was considered the problem country of South America.' Bauso spent five years researching the political circumstances of the World Cup, and his 1,000-page book was published in Argentina in 2018. The title: *78. Historia oral del Mundial.*

There were protests against the World Cup, especially in France, Sweden and the Netherlands. At away matches, the Argentine team was greeted with critical banners. Amnesty International wrote a brochure, *Football yes – Torture no.* There was also talk of boycotts here and there. But this means of exerting pressure did not appear on the agenda until two years later, when 42 nations stayed away from the 1980 Summer Olympics in Moscow in protest against the Soviet invasion of Afghanistan.

The regime feared the loss of power

On one side of the Plaza de Mayo, the central square in Buenos Aires, is the Casa Rosada, the pink presidential palace. Between business people pressed for time and tourists with cameras, activists set up a small stage, in front of it two loudspeakers and folding tables with brochures. Slowly, the square fills up with people of different ages. They carry banners with peace messages, hand out leaflets and brochures. And they cheer as a minibus turns into the square, carrying women in white headscarves, aged between 80 and 90.

The *Madres de Plaza de Mayo*, one of the best-known human rights organisations in Latin America, still meet every Thursday. The applause and chants of their supporters drown out the noise of the rattling buses. In the spring of 1977, the *madres* (mothers) had publicly demanded information about the whereabouts of their children for the first time. Many of them had no political background. Since standing protests were forbidden, they walked around the square a few times. This was also the case on 1 June 1978, when world champions West Germany opened the World Cup against Poland in Buenos Aires.

The author Matías Bauso reconstructed that day in his book: the city seemed deserted, everyone was sitting in front of the television. But on the Plaza de Mayo, 20 women met, with the photos of their abducted sons. A Dutch camera team was there, filming a critical television report. Word spread and a week later many of the major European TV stations sent camera teams to the Plaza de Mayo. 'But this time no women came to the square,' Bauso describes. 'They were stopped by the police beforehand.'

The 1978 World Cup gave rise to myths. European players are also said to have been at the Plaza de Mayo out of solidarity, but Bauso has found no evidence of this. Argentina's decisive intermediate round match against Peru is particularly controversial. Argentina beat Peru 6-0 and millions of Argentines celebrated in the streets, even in the south of the country where temperatures approach freezing in the winter month of June. 'There had never been anything like it,' says Bauso. 'When some members of the junta saw these unrestrained crowds, their fears of losing power grew, but that turned out to be unfounded.'

General Jorge Videla had never shown any interest in football until 1978. For the World Cup, colour television was introduced in Argentina. Videla watched all Argentina's matches from the VIP box. Whether military or civilian, torturers or tortured – they cheered throughout the 3-1 win (after extra time) in the final against the Netherlands, according to the chronicles. In addition to Generals Videla, Emilio Massera and Orlando Agosti, FIFA President João Havelange descended from the stands to the players. Videla handed the trophy to captain Daniel Passarella, coupled with the words, 'You made us suffer, captain. But now we are champions.'

Even many of the 500,000 Argentine exiles in Paris, London and Mexico held back on criticism at that time. Experts like Matías Bauso speculate that Videla could have won a free presidential election the day after the final. Which leads to an important question that extends to the present:

do sporting events have the long-term propaganda effect that autocrats and dictators hope for?

The world champions do not want to look back

On 7 September 1979, an Argentina team, including Diego Maradona, won the Junior World Cup in Japan. At the same time, an international commission met victims of the dictatorship in Buenos Aires. On the radio, a well-known sports journalist called on celebrating fans to denounce the 'disappeared'. Matías Bauso, however, found little evidence that football strengthened nationalism: 'The propaganda didn't work for long domestically. The World Cup was a celebration for many, but no more. In terms of foreign policy, the junta's attempts at deception did nothing.' The *Madres de Plaza de Maya* were on the front pages in Europe. They received many donations, founded their own newspaper, built an academy.

The World Cup lasted 24 days, but to this day it doesn't seem to have really ended. New commentaries, photos, documents put some games and gestures in a different light. One example is the decisive intermediate round match: were the Peruvians influenced by General Videla in the dressing room? Perhaps even by his guest of honour Henry Kissinger, the former US Secretary of State? There are clues, but no hard evidence.

Journalist Ezequiel Fernández Moores has conducted long interviews with Argentina's world champions. He says of coach César Luis Menotti: 'I was critical of his attitude for a long time and wondered, should he perhaps have criticised the junta more clearly? But over time I have become more understanding. In recent years, his attitude seems a bit more negative to me. Most of the players also don't want to talk about the dictatorship any more. They say they had to do their job – and they didn't know about the torture centres.'

Menotti was a supporter of the Communist Party in 1978, a maverick of less than 40 years. He signed appeals in newspapers asking about the fate of the disappeared. He stressed at the World Cup, 'we play for the people'. He never said, 'we play for the military'. After the final, Menotti allegedly refused to shake hands with dictator Videla. Other observers say that the crowd on the pitch made this impossible. Final opponents, the Netherlands, stayed away from the celebratory banquet, allegedly in protest. Or was it because the bus got stuck in traffic?

Other reports add to the glorification, such as a 2016 article in a British newspaper that suggested black paint on the goalposts was a protest against the junta. But that, says human rights activist Luciana Bertoia, is nonsense. Interpretations are complex, sometimes contradictory, emphasises Thomas Fischer, professor of Latin American history at the Catholic University of Eichstätt-Ingolstadt in southern Germany. And he directs attention to appearance: the military around Videla wore side partings or crew cuts, even the taxi drivers were supposed to have their hair cut short. Most of Argentina's players had long hair, some beards. 'On a symbolic level, we can interpret this as demarcation,' says Fischer. 'And if the population cheered at the end, that doesn't mean they also said "we support the regime".'

Economic crises and social tensions had favoured the rise of some military regimes in Latin America from the 1960s onwards, in Bolivia, Peru, Ecuador and Uruguay. How much did personalities fight back? In Chile, the striker Carlos Caszely demanded the withdrawal of the dictator Augusto Pinochet. Some of his relatives had been tortured and harassed. Then, at the beginning of the new millennium, Caszely gave public support to the socialist president Michelle Bachelet. 'It's not that teams used to revolt in unison,' says Thomas Fischer. 'That was far too dangerous for most.'

Argentina's military regime was unable to maintain its power after losing the 1982 war over the Falkland Islands to Britain. The freely elected president Raúl Alfonsín started the legal processing of the crimes from the days of the dictatorship. But as early as 1986, the parliament passed the 'Final Act', which ruled out further prosecutions. Alfonsín's successor, Carlos Menem, pardoned convicted junta members. He made a pact with the strengthening military, fearing a sixth coup since 1930. In the 1980s, little was said publicly about the 1978 World Cup. And when it was, Menotti's tactics were compared with those of his successor Carlos Bilardo. The 1986 World Cup generation around Diego Maradona was seen as a distraction from the economic crisis. Some called it: anaesthesia.

A goalkeeper was kidnapped and tortured

With more than 30 years of distance, Daniel Eduardo Rafecas looks with unease at the late 1980s. 'During the years of impunity, members of the junta were able to continue their careers: as policemen, teachers or lawyers,' says the federal criminal judge in Buenos Aires. His court office near the main railway station is filled with books, files pile up on his desk. 'We had to wait a generation to be able to look honestly into the past.'

Under the left-wing president Néstor Kirchner, from 2003 onwards, criminal prosecution was pushed forward again and pardons were revoked. Legal impulses also came from abroad, through tribunals on Yugoslavia and Rwanda. As a young judge, Rafecas took over the coordination of about 120 criminal trials in Argentina in 2004. In the beginning, he was also threatened, once opening a package at home containing a dummy bomb. But the work of his 12-member team had an effect. 'The judiciary and human rights activists worked very well together, for example in obtaining documents. For the first time ever in Argentina's long history, society has faced one of its darkest chapters so critically and patiently.'

Commemorative work is subject to fluctuations and linked to political developments. Meanwhile, Argentina has arguably the most vibrant civil society in Latin America. When politicians demand a reduction in sentences for junta members, NGOs can quickly mobilise tens of thousands of demonstrators.

And what role does football play in commemoration? Argentinos Juniors, for example, Maradona's youth club, dedicated a mural in the stadium to murdered fans. In 2009, River Plate fans in Buenos Aires marched with banners from their stadium to the ESMA. In the Kirchner era, former player Claudio Morresi pushed projects as sports minister; his brother had been murdered after the coup at the age of 17. And in Ciudadela Norte, a small club in the west of Buenos Aires, Claudio Tamburrini organised a 'game for life'. The former goalkeeper had been kidnapped in 1977 and held under torture for four months.

But only a few of the 1978 world champions took part in commemorative actions: Osvaldo Ardiles and Leopoldo Luque met with Plaza de Mayo mothers at the beginning of the millennium. Ricardo Villa told in detail how he initially believed the junta's slogans, including the demonisation of the 'communist foreign country'. That he and his colleagues were surrounded by armed security during the World Cup seemed appropriate to the importance of the event. Only after his transfer to Tottenham Hotspur in 1978 did Villa receive full information, and later he became involved with Amnesty International.

Meanwhile, leading players such as the then-captain Daniel Passarella and top scorer Mario Kempes do not want to comment in detail on politics. Says author Matías Bauso: 'Football dominates our everyday culture, but it's not used as a medium of youth education; it's different in Germany or Britain.' FIFA and the Argentine Football Association (AFA) never seriously addressed the 1978 World Cup, when their leaderships collaborated with the junta. The big clubs also do not sufficiently address their involvement. 'It would be good if the world champions commemorated the victims of torture at some point in the ESMA,' says Bauso. 'But I think that's out of the question. Most footballers don't want to recognise their social role.'

When a jersey becomes a political symbol

Can history repeat itself in South America? In December 2018, Palmeiras São Paulo celebrated its tenth championship title in Brazil. On the pitch, the president-elect embraced the cheering players: Jair Bolsonaro wore a Palmeiras jersey, number 10 on the back. He kissed the crest, made triumphant gestures to the fans, raised the trophy in the air. The far-right Bolsonaro feels at home in football, says Antônio Leal, founder of the Brazilian football film festival Cinefoot: 'Most players in Brazil only think about themselves. They don't earn as much money as in Europe. They hold back on making political statements because they don't want to have problems.' The players of the southern Brazilian club Atlético Paranaense had even worn T-shirts for Bolsonaro during the 2018 election campaign.

Jair Bolsonaro is not a military dictator like Jorge Videla; he is the president of one of the world's most populous democracies. Yet the former paratrooper has frequently attracted attention with racist, homophobic and misogynistic statements. He also won the run-off election in October 2018 with promises to crack down on corruption and crime. Among his prominent supporters, several professional footballers stood out. Sport was an important communication channel for him.

Bolsonaro presents himself as macho, as a nationalist. His polarising statements seem to go down well in football, where provocation plays an important role, as do patriotism and masculinity. Palmeiras player Felipe Melo started the campaign by supporting Bolsonaro well before the first ballot. More than two dozen professionals followed, including former national players like Rivaldo, Cafu and Carlos Alberto, also volleyball players and the two-time Formula 1 world champion Emerson Fittipaldi. Probably his best-known supporter is Ronaldinho, football world champion in 2002. 'He joined Bolsonaro's party early on,' says journalist and cultural manager Fátima Lacerda from Berlin. FC Barcelona distanced itself from its former player and long-time ambassador Ronaldinho. Many of Jair Bolsonaro's supporters wear the canary yellow jersey of the Brazilian national football team at rallies, also as a distinction from the red of former president Lula's Workers' Party.

But there have also been players in Brazilian history who have spoken out against those in power: during the military dictatorship at the beginning of the 1980s, Sócrates had shaped a system of self-government at his club Corinthians São Paulo. Whether players, groundsmen or officials: everyone could get involved. The players of this *Democracia Corinthiana* campaigned for free elections. Instead of sponsors' logos, they wore election slogans on their jerseys. 'My friends and I were in our early 20s at the time; Sócrates gave us courage,' says cultural worker Antônio Leal. Sócrates died in 2011. 'I'm sure he would be campaigning against Bolsonaro today.'

A source of national pride

But it can also be done differently. Football often stands up to state power, for example in Colombia in 2021. In the port city of Barranquilla, the match between hosts América de Cali and the Brazilian club Atlético Mineiro had to be interrupted several times. Stun grenades exploded in the surrounding streets, police sirens blared and demonstrators shouted their frustration. The players retreated to their dressing rooms for a few minutes until the tear gas had dispersed. The match in the South American Copa Libertadores competition was played to a close, but almost no one was interested.

Colombia was experiencing a national crisis – again. Since the end of April 2021, tens of thousands had been protesting against inequality, police violence and corruption. More than 60 people are reported to have died, several hundred have been injured. 'The social disparity is particularly great in Colombia. Education, medicine, the tax system: people with low incomes are disadvantaged everywhere,' says Colombian footballer and activist Juliana Lozana. 'People want a life of dignity, but they are brutally beaten down by the police. Nobody thinks about football there.' The Copa América, the most important tournament in Latin America, had to be moved from Colombia to Brazil at short notice.

'Football is a source of national pride in Colombia,' says British Latin America researcher Peter Watson. 'The national team jersey is one of the few symbols that can temporarily transcend social divisions.' Time and again, Colombians rallied behind their national team. They were looking for a sense of community and wanted to separate themselves from criminal currents, from drug cartels or from the leftist underground movement FARC. Like other governments before him, President Iván Duque wanted to incorporate a tournament like the Copa América into the national narrative in 2021. But football could now deepen the political rifts.

Where this can lead is foreshadowed by the past. Colombian media currently recall previous hosting roles that became emblematic of crises. In 1986, the World Cup was to be held in Colombia, but the government returned the tournament in 1982 because of financial problems, and Mexico stepped in. In 2001, Colombia wanted to leave this trauma behind and host the Copa América for the first time.

At the turn of the millennium, Colombia was considered a leading nation – at least in football. The national team had qualified for the World Cups in 1990, 1994 and 1998. However, major clubs were infiltrated by drug cartels. After his own goal in the 1994 World Cup against the USA, the Colombian player Andrés Escobar was shot dead. Four years later, international Antony de Ávila dedicated a goal to two imprisoned drug lords who had financed his club América de Cali. 'The cartels wanted to influence the national coach's line-up of players,' recalls Jürgen Griesbeck, who organised football projects in Colombia in the nineties. 'Death threats and violence were part of everyday life.'

The FARC also endangered the Copa América in 2001. At that time, the self-proclaimed 'Revolutionary Armed Forces' had been fighting the Colombian state for almost 40 years. Attacks and assassinations, tens of thousands dead, hundreds of thousands of refugees. Shortly before the 2001 tournament, the FARC set off bombs and kidnapped Hernán Mejía, the vice-president of the Colombian Football Federation. The South American federation CONMEBOL wanted to cancel the tournament, but the Colombian government and its sponsors were against it. After terror threats, the teams from Argentina and Canada withdrew. But the Copa América took place and Colombia won the title.

The president of the country at the time, Andrés Pastrana, spoke of a 'cup of peace'. It was the basis for a narrative that the government under Juan Manuel Santos in particular wanted to continue writing from 2010 onwards. 'Santos "footballised" the political debate,' says Colombia expert Peter Watson. 'In many speeches and tweets he described the national players as ambassadors for unity, discipline and effort.' In the peace negotiations with the FARC from 2012, Santos used football for meetings and reconciliation. The Colombian national team qualified for the 2014 World Cup, and the Ministry of

Defence showed short films of signed footballs being dropped over FARC areas in the jungle, accompanied by the message: 'Guerrillas, don't miss the World Cup, demobilise, I'm saving a place for you.' FARC negotiators also wore the national jersey at the peace talks. Friendly matches between long-time enemies have been taking place since the 2016 ceasefire. NGOs use football to mediate conflicts.

But the peace remains fragile. Time and again, long-time FARC members criticise the Colombian government and call for the rebels to be rearmed. The 2021 protests against social inequality could further destabilise the situation. 'Politicians can use football to invoke national unity,' says Colombian activist Juliana Lozana. 'But they can also use it to manipulate the population.'

'We were robbed of the stadium'

Back to Argentina. On Avenida La Plata, the vibrant Buenos Aires gradually transitions into quieter housing estates in the south. In a narrow, terraced house, Club Athlético San Lorenzo de Almagro has one of its bases, with a pub, ticket office and gym, almost everything in the colours red and blue. A father looks at old photos and trophies with his children, two older men passionately discuss the previous match day. The fans Carlos Balboa and Eduardo Otero also feel at home here, but their mood can quickly change.

One of the city's largest supermarkets stretches over three blocks. The Gasómetro, San Lorenzo's stadium, stood on this site until 1982. The scene of championships, international matches and concerts with guitarist Carlos Santana or tango composer Osvaldo Pugliese. The graphic artist Carlos Balboa has not experienced the Gasómetro, he is too young for that, in his early 40s, and yet it is a place of longing for him. 'San Lorenzo was badly hit by the dictatorship,' he says. 'We were robbed of the stadium.' The club received the equivalent of

$1 million as compensation. Supposedly, social housing and roads were to be built on the site. Instead, the land was sold to a French supermarket chain for nine times the price. For 14 years San Lorenzo had to play in different stadiums and pay rent. 'We lost our identity.'

Founded in 1908, San Lorenzo won the championship 12 times. The club was long considered politically left-wing, with workers, artists and free spirits living in its home district of Boedo. That was enough to create distrust among the junta. The generals prevented the Gasómetro from hosting World Cup matches in 1978. After the demolition, San Lorenzo lost 15,000 members. But even after relegation to the second division, the club at times had the highest average attendance in Argentina, with 80,000 people coming to some matches. 'At that time, many fans of other clubs made fun of us. But they couldn't yet know why the stadium was expropriated from us,' says Carlos Balboa. 'During the dictatorship, people were afraid to speak their minds. San Lorenzo was not a club that rebelled against the junta either. But it brought people together. And there were chants now and then for the mothers of the Plaza de Mayo.'

Fans of San Lorenzo, Pope Francis' favourite club, raised money for the 'New Gasómetro'. It opened in 1993, near a high-crime neighbourhood. A decade later, in the awakening period under President Néstor Kirchner, more and more supporters joined forces for social engagement. They distributed flyers, launched internet campaigns, dreamed of a return to the old property. In 2011, the city parliament discussed how to compensate San Lorenzo for the expropriation. During each debate, fans demonstrated in front of the building. At the beginning it was a small group, but it grew bigger. In 2012, 100,000 people came to the Plaza de Mayo. 'Not all of them were fans of San Lorenzo, but they showed solidarity,' says lawyer Eduardo Otero. 'Otherwise, only trade unions can mobilise so many people.'

Behind the huge supermarket, San Lorenzo houses a sports centre with a volleyball hall, judo mats and physiotherapy. Young people in red and blue tracksuits go in and out. For them, the era of coups and torture centres is far away. But development in Argentina is not linear. Under conservative President Mauricio Macri, elected in 2015, reactionary politicians and literary figures have come forward again, casting doubt on the number of 'disappeared'. Macri, a millionaire entrepreneur and once president of the Boca Juniors football club, wanted to reform the economy by opening it up to international investors. Instead, inflation continued to rise and the domestic currency, the peso, lost half its value. In 2019, Macri was voted out of office. The Coronavirus pandemic hit Argentina particularly hard.

Argentines once again want a new dawn. Their football federation wants to host the 2030 World Cup, together with Chile, Paraguay and Uruguay. It would be a chance to take a critical look at their own history in football as well.

Conclusion

QATAR HAS probably invested around £2bn in European football clubs. Compared to its total investments, this is a manageable sum. The state-owned Qatar Investment Authority is said to have invested more than £300bn in dozens of countries. A good quarter is in Great Britain, the USA and France. Qatar invested in capital markets like the London Stock Exchange and in banks like Barclays and Credit Suisse. There are economic and political ties that were established long before the World Cup was awarded in 2010 and will survive 2022.

In Norway, football fans and players have been discussing a boycott of the World Cup in Qatar particularly intensively. What few of them probably know is that there is a free trade agreement between Norway and Qatar. Norwegian companies have invested almost £7.5bn in Qatar, including in agriculture and marine technology. These companies hardly play a role in the debate about human rights in Qatar.

In Germany, the criticism focuses on FC Bayern. The record-breaking champions are said to receive around £15m annually from the state-owned airline Qatar Airways. But even beyond that, the Qatari sovereign wealth fund is one of the largest foreign investors in Germany, with a volume of around £20bn. Qatar holds shares in Volkswagen, the sponsor of VfL Wolfsburg and in Deutsche Bank, the sponsor of the Frankfurt football stadium. German companies are also involved in major projects in Qatar: Deutsche Bahn and Siemens in the development of local transport structures, SAP in digitalisation.

In globalised football, everything is connected to everything else. It is therefore not surprising that protests come mainly from NGOs and fans, but not from the business community. The list of beneficiaries of a World Cup is long, even in Western Europe: sporting goods manufacturers enjoy better sales, television broadcasters get higher ratings. And industry also wants to sell more cars, planes and machinery to the Gulf. For years, German exports to Qatar have been around £1.3bn annually. In 2018, then Chancellor Merkel received the Qatari Emir al-Thani for an economic summit in Berlin. Both governments maintain a joint economic commission. The meeting was hardly discussed in the German media.

At the beginning of 2022, the Emir was again received by several Western heads of state, including US President Joe Biden and the new German Chancellor Olaf Scholz. The reason: After Russia's war of aggression on Ukraine, several states in Europe are courting on natural gas from Qatar. Criticism of human rights now hardly played a role anymore.

The United Nations or the Organisation for Economic Co-operation and Development (OECD) detailed the responsibility of companies for human rights at home and abroad years ago. These are questions that are comparatively new for football. How could European top clubs use their soft power to constructively influence the human rights situation in Qatar without foregoing the emirate's money?

As a basis, the clubs first need a serious human rights concept. Measured against the UN Guiding Principles, this would mean: a basic commitment to protect human rights, for example in association statutes; a debate with all employees; a critical inventory of all business relationships, including with sponsors, media partners and hosts of training camps; a self-critical documentation of grievances, early cooperation with external groups, with human rights organisations, trade unions or social institutions.

Overall, the aim is to reduce the risk of being involved in human rights violations. Implementing such a concept requires expertise and human resources. But most clubs and associations have followed a more traditional path in recent years. FC Bayern supported struggling clubs in dozens of charity matches. In 2005, the Munich-based club founded FC Bayern Hilfe e.V., a non-profit association which collects and distributes donations.

However, social policy must go further. It is not about how companies pass on part of their profits to charitable projects. It is about how exactly they generate those profits. On the one hand, all clubs support educational initiatives for disadvantaged children. On the other hand, they depend on sporting goods manufacturers who exploit young seamstresses in low-wage countries. On the one hand, many clubs have solar panels installed on their stadium roofs. On the other hand, they install environmentally harmful heating systems so that their grass grows even in winter.

The clubs that regularly play in the Champions League usually have more than 1,000 employees. Many of them are involved in marketing and expansion, especially for the Asian and American markets. The annual turnover of Real Madrid, Manchester City and FC Bayern exceeds £0.5bn each. Many of these clubs have set up charitable foundations for social projects, but these are mostly external organisations with no significant influence on the core of the football industry. Instead, clubs should set up their own sustainability department, for human rights issues, but also for climate protection, diversity and health promotion.

Given the large sums of money circulating in football, these departments could have a budget of £20m or £30m, for material resources, employees, human rights experts, social workers and cultural workers. They could have direct links to the board, interlocked with all other departments. Then the clubs could document and accompany their partnership with Qatar Airways, Emirates or Etihad in more detail, for example with a differentiated exchange with migrant workers or women's rights activists. Social policy and commerce do not have to be contradictory. With the right concepts, you can even win new fans and sponsors.

Russia, Qatar, soon the even stricter China – football has big tasks ahead of it. The European leagues could make human rights concepts a condition for a licence. But other interest groups can be active as well: club members can submit applications, establish supra-regional networks or reflect on their own behaviour, such as away trips to non-democratic states, the purchase of jerseys from low-wage countries or the use of multinational betting providers and pay-TV stations. Fans could approach sponsors or bring the issue to the attention of their constituency MPs. There is an opportunity in the World Cup in Qatar to do more than cultivate a moral conscience.

Bibliography

Baron, Stefan; Yin-Baron Guangyan, *Die Chinesen: Psychogram einer Weltmacht* (Berlin: Econ, 2018)

Bauso, Matías, *78. Historia oral del Mundial* (Buenos Aires: Sudamericana, 2018)

Beichelt, Timm, *Ersatzspielfelder: Zum Verhältnis von Fußball und Macht* (Berlin: Suhrkamp, 2018)

Blincoe, Nicholas, *More Noble Than War: The Story of Football in Israel and Palestine* (London: Constable, 2019)

Calic, Marie-Janine, *Geschichte Jugoslawiens* (München: C.H. Beck, 2018)

Chehabi, Houchang, *A Political History of Football in Iran* (In Iranian Studies, 4/2002: 371-402)

Davidson, Christopher, *Dubai: The Vulnerability of Success* (Oxford: Oxford University Press, 2009)

Dorsey, James M., *The Turbulent World of Middle East Soccer* (New York: Oxford University Press, 2016)

Downie, Andrew, *Doctor Socrates: Footballer, Philosopher, Legend* (London: Simon & Schuster UK, 2018)

Faqiryar, Mansur, *Heimat Fußball: Mein Leben zwischen Bremen und Kabul* (München: Knaus, 2018)

Felsberg, Stephan; Köhler, Tim; Brand, Martin, *Russkij Futbol* (Göttingen: Verlag Die Werkstatt 2018)

Freeman, Simon, *Baghdad FC: Iraq's Football Story: A Hidden History of Sport and Tyranny* (London: John Murray, 2005)

Gündoğan, Ilker; Sonntag, Albrecht, *Chinese Football in the Era of Xi Jinping: What do Supporters Think?* (In Journal of Current Chinese Affairs, 47: 103-141, 2018)

Kamrava, Mehran, *Qatar: Small State, Big Politics* (London: Cornell University, 2013)

Keddie, Patrick, *The Passion: Football and the Story of Modern Turkey* (London: I. B. Tauris, 2018)

Khalidi, Issam, *One Hundred Years of Football in Palestine* (Amman: Dar Al-Shorouk, 2013)

Korić, Ivan, *Fußball in Bosnien und Herzegowina als Opfer der Politik* (In Ost-West Europäische Perspektiven, 4/2013, 292-299)

Krais, Jakob, *Spielball der Scheichs: Der arabische Fußball und die WM in Katar* (Bielefeld: Verlag die Werkstatt, 2021)

Krug, Matthias, *Journeys on a Football Carpet* (Doha: Hamad Bin Khalifa University Press, 2019)

Lämmer, Manfred, *Deutsch-israelische Fußballfreundschaft* (Göttingen: Verlag Die Werkstatt, 2018)

Lowe, Sid, *Fear and Loathing in La Liga: Barcelona vs Real Madrid* (London: Yellow Press, 2014)

Malzahn, Philip, *Fußball in Ägypten – Sport und Ultras im sozialpolitischen Kontext* (Universität Leipzig, 2017)

McGeehan, Nicholas, *The Dark Side of Blue* (In 11 Freunde, 2/2018: 92-97)

McManus, John, *Welcome to Hell? In Search of the Real Turkish Football* (London: W&N, 2018)

Mennicke, Alexander, *Jedna si Jedina?! Nationale Identität und bosnischer Vereinsfußball. Empirische Untersuchung anhand des Todes von Vedran* Puljić (Universität Leipzig, 2015)

Mills, Richard, *The Politics of Football in Yugoslavia: Sport, Nationalism and the State* (London: I. B. Tauris, 2019)

Montague, James, *When Friday Comes: Football, War and Revolution in the Middle East* (London: De Coubertin, 2013)

Nusseibeh, Sari, *Es war einmal ein Land. Ein Leben in Palästina* (Berlin: Suhrkamp, 2009)

Raschke, Holger, *Football with a lot of Politics*. In: *Endemann, Martin; Claus, Robert; Dembowski, Gerd; Gabler, Jonas (Hrsg.): Zurück am Tatort Stadion. Diskriminierung und Antidiskriminierung im Fußball* (Göttingen: Verlag Die Werkstatt, S. 286-304, 2015)

Reiche, Danyel; Sorek, Tamir, *Sport, Politics and Society in the Middle East* (London: C. Hurst & Co, 2019)

Schweizer, Gerhard, *Iran verstehen: Geschichte, Gesellschaft, Religion* (Stuttgart: Klett-Cotta, 2017)

Seitz, Volker, *Afrika wird armregiert oder Wie man Afrika wirklich helfen kann* (München: dtv, 2018)

Springborg, Robert, *Egypt* (Cambridge Polity Press 2018)

Streppelhoff, Robin, *Gelungener Brückenschlag: Sport in den deutsch-israelischen Beziehungen* (Baden-Baden: Academia Richarz, 2012)

Strittmatter, Kai, *Die Neuerfindung der Diktatur: Wie China den digitalen Überwachungsstaat aufbaut und uns damit herausfordert* (München: Piper, 2018)

Sullivan, Jonathan, *China's Football Dream* (Nottingham: Asia Research Institute E-Book 2018)

Ulrichsen, Kristian, *Qatar and the Gulf Crisis* (London: C. Hurst & Co, 2020)

Zavarsky, Clemens, *Fußball im Krieg: Irak, Syrien und der IS* (In Ballesterer, Juni/Juli 2017: 16-31, 2017)

Author

Ronny Blaschke was born in 1981 in Rostock and studied sports and political science in his home city. The German journalist and author writes about political issues in sport, mainly for the media in Germany, Austria and Switzerland. He incorporates his research into political education, lectures and workshops with young people. Blaschke has received several awards for his work.